# MARGINAL PRYNNE

## 1600–1669

by
WILLIAM M. LAMONT

LONDON: Routledge & Kegan Paul
TORONTO: University of Toronto Press
1963

First published 1963
in Great Britain by
Routledge & Kegan Paul Ltd
and in Canada by
University of Toronto Press

Printed in Great Britain by
Western Printing Services Ltd

# EDITOR'S NOTE

UNLIKE so many history series this one will not attempt a complete coverage of a specific span of time, with a division of labour for the contributors based on a neat parcelling out of centuries. Nor will it, in the main, be a collection of political monographs. Rather, the aim is to bring out books based on new, or thoroughly reinterpreted material ranging over quite a wide field of chronology and geography. Some will be more general than others, as is to be expected when biography is included alongside of detailed treatment of some comparatively short period of crisis like the appeasement of the Axis Powers. Nevertheless, whatever mode of presentation may have been appropriate, each work should provide an exposition of its subject in context and thus enable the reader to acquire new knowledge amidst things he knows, or could have known.

MICHAEL HURST

*St. John's College,*
*Oxford*

# CONTENTS

ACKNOWLEDGEMENTS                                    *page* ix

INTRODUCTION                                              1

I     THE ATTACK ON LAUD                                11

II    LAUD'S REVENGE                                    28

III   PRYNNE JOINS THE RADICALS                         49

IV    THE TESTAMENT OF A RADICAL                        65

V     THE CIVIL WAR                                     85

VI    THE POPISH PLOT                                  119

VII   THE ERASTIAN TRIUMPH                             149

VIII  THE INTERREGNUM                                  175

IX    THE RESTORATION AND AFTER                        205

      APPENDIX A                                       232

      APPENDIX B                                       235

      BIBLIOGRAPHY                                     239

      INDEX                                            247

# PLATES

*Between pages 118 and 119*

1. 'The more I am beat down, the more I am lift up.' Prynne wore his hair long after 1637 to conceal his disfigurement. (*By courtesy of the Courtauld Institute of Art.*)

2. Prynne pays homage to Charles II, the Christian Emperor, at the Restoration. How insecure the Pope's Crown is in comparison. (*By courtesy of the Trustees of the British Museum.*)

3. Laud on trial with Prynne as prosecutor. (*By courtesy of the Trustees of The British Museum.*)

4. 'O Mr Burton, I am sick at heart': a Puritan caricature of Laud nauseated by his own misdeeds. (*By courtesy of the Trustees of the British Museum.*)

# ACKNOWLEDGEMENTS

I HAVE received help from many sources. The Central Research Fund of the University of London provided a grant which enabled me to research in Bath. The following Libraries offered kind assistance: the Victoria Art Gallery and Municipal Library, Bath; the Bodleian Library, Oxford University; the British Museum; the Public Record Office; the House of Lords' Record Office; Queen's College, Oxford University. Mr. Arthur Halfpenny, Mr. Philip Whitting, and Dr. Robert Leslie have been stimulating teachers and valued friends. My debt is overwhelming to Professor S. T. Bindoff, who first encouraged me to research, and to Mr. R. C. Latham, who first suggested the subject and who supervised my researches. My mother typed the first draft, and my wife and my father aided me in the correction of proofs and in the compilation of an Index. I should like to thank *History Today* for their help in providing photographs. During the last three years at Hackney Downs Grammar School, William Prynne was dragged into many lessons—though never by the ears. This book is offered as an act of contrition.

W. M. L.

Doctor Johnson to Boswell on a mutual friend:

'To be sure, he is a tree that cannot produce true fruit. He only bears crabs. But, Sir, a tree that produces a great many crabs is better than one which produces only a few crabs.'

*Boswell's London Journal*, ed. F. A. Pottle, (London, 1958), p. 226.

# INTRODUCTION

WILLIAM PRYNNE was the most prolific writer of the seventeenth century. He wrote more than two hundred pamphlets, many of inordinate length. His custom was to wear a long quilt cap, two or three inches over his eyes, protecting them from the light. A servant would bring him in a roll and a pot of ale every three hours to revive his spirits, and he would study and drink into the early hours.[1] A contemporary thought that Prynne's writing was as necessary to him as meat and drink: 'a thing without which he cannot live'.[2] Yet it was not inevitable that his writing should have concentrated on politics. He might simply have been the fussy dry-as-dust, pleased that a young scholar like Anthony Wood 'should have inclination towards venerable antiquity'. Or he might simply have been the conscientious local administrator, thanked by Bath Council for his 'readiness to promote the advantages of this Citty' as Recorder.[3] But fear of a Popish Plot drove him into national politics.

It is interesting that a contemporary should describe him as having 'the Countenance of a Witch' and that another should speak of his 'long meager face . . . eares cropt close to his head, which is stuft with Plots'. Prynne was obsessed with fears of Jesuit plots. The Jesuits were everywhere and could 'metamorphose themselves into any shape'. A weary public servant

---

[1] John Aubrey, *Brief Lives* . . . ed. O. L. Dick (London, 1950), p. 250.

[2] (Anon.), *A Word to Mr. Wil Pryn* (London, 1649), pp. 5–6.

[3] Anthony Wood, *Life and Times* . . . ed. A. Clark (Oxford, 1891), ii, pp. 110–11; Bath, Victoria Art Gallery and Municipal Library: Council Minutes, Numb. 2, f. 89.

complained to another of receiving a letter from one William Prynne, 'a stranger to him, speaking of fears and jealousies, of plots and designs of Jesuits and Romanists against the Church and Religion'. He was afraid that it would 'stir up hornets'.[1] Through his pamphlets, Prynne did stir up hornets; he lost his ears in the reign of Charles I, was honoured by Parliament in the Civil War, was imprisoned by Cromwell in the Interregnum and was in turn revered and reviled in the reign of Charles II.

The negative aim of his pamphlets was to check the growth of Popery. Their positive aim was to raise the moral standards of the country. He wanted England to be a community where men were abstemious, serious-minded, short-haired and shunned plays. This was a Puritan programme, yet Prynne did not want England to become another Geneva. This was a programme to be carried out by Christian Emperors, as it had been in the past to the annoyance of Papists. England needed another Emperor Constantine, not another John Calvin. Prynne believed that the historical significance of the English Reformation lay in the restoration of the powers of the Christian Emperor. He admired Tudor Archbishops like Cranmer and Whitgift because they had respected the Royal Supremacy. So closely did Prynne identify moral reform with the Royal Supremacy that he acclaimed Whitgift—the opponent of the Presbyterian, Cartwright, in Elizabeth's reign—as 'an arrant Puritane'.[2]

Yet when Prynne wrote his first pamphlet in 1626 he knew that England's moral standards had declined. Englishmen now cared more for the curl in their locks than the squint in their souls; their barber had become their chaplain; they would rather read Shakespeare than the Bible; they profaned the Sabbath with sports; they questioned the Calvinist doctrine of Predestination. The diagnosis was Puritan, but the remedy was Anglican. Prynne was not asking for a Presbyterian discipline, only for the Christian Emperor to use his strength. Why did Charles I fail to behave like a Constantine—or even like an Elizabeth? Not, thought Prynne, because of personal

[1] Aubrey, op. cit., p. 250; (Anon.), *A Speedy Hue and Crie* . . . (London, 1647), p. 6; William Prynne, *The Substance of a Speech* . . . (London, 1649), p. 107; *Calendar State Papers Domestic, Charles II, 1666–1667*, p. 318.
[2] Prynne, *A Breviate of the Prelates Intollerable Usurpations* . . . (London, 1637), p. 123.

weakness. He could only attribute this failure to the influence of the ubiquitous Jesuits. When Prynne began writing in 1626 the nominal head of the Church of England was Archbishop Abbott. He was no moral crusader, but not even Prynne could read in this easy-going courtier the malevolent genius of Jesuitry. But Prynne did suspect one man who was becoming increasingly powerful: William Laud.

Laud, in 1626, was only Bishop of Bath and Wells and did not become Archbishop of Canterbury until 1633. Yet early on in Charles's reign he acquired the substance of power. He was no Roman Catholic, but he did seek consciously to reverse certain tendencies in the teachings of his Tudor predecessors. He thought that they had become too austere in their services, too rigidly Calvinist in dogma, too dependent on the Crown. There was nothing original in these criticisms: Andrewes, Mountague, Bilson and Bancroft had voiced them before him. But, to Prynne, they underlined the Jesuit threat, and most emphatically in the assault on the Royal Supremacy. Laud had no quarrel with the Crown—the more conventional criticism of him was that he was, if anything, too servile to it—but he did think that his Tudor predecessors had placed too much emphasis upon the powers which they derived from the Crown, *iure humano*, and not enough upon those which they derived from God, *iure divino*. To Prynne, the *iure divino* claim betrayed the Papist design. He gave an analogy, which he drew from a sermon by Bishop Jewel. One Pompeius had built a theatre contrary to the magistrate's orders, but he set a place of religion over it, and called it the Temple of Venus:

> . . . Whereby hee provided that if any would overthrow it because it was a Theatre, they might yet spare it for the Temples sake; for to pull down a Temple was sacriledge. . .[1]

The bishops were building on the Royal Supremacy and were using the *iure divino* claim to avoid retribution. *Iure divino* was their Temple of Venus.

Prynne cruelly parodied the aspirations of Laud. Clarendon had seen that it was the indolence of Abbott, not the intemperance of Laud, that had undermined the Church. Laud wished to use the independent power of the Church to correct

[1] Ibid., p. 137.

the moral failings of the age. One of Prynne's greatest blunders was to publish Laud's diary in the Civil War in order to destroy him. It had the opposite effect: Puritans like Walwyn and Robinson were surprised to find how much common ground they shared with him. When Laud, for instance, confessed that he had dreamed of taking the Duke of Buckingham to bed with him, he seemed to Prynne at his most contemptible, whereas to less coarse-grained Puritans, who knew what it was to confide to diaries their temptations to sin, he seemed at his most touchingly vulnerable.

Prynne's injustice to Laud was complemented by Laud's injustice to Prynne. Laud saw Prynne as another Martin Marprelate—one of these Genevan extremists who threatened the unity of the Church and the safety of the State. He never understood Prynne's abhorrence of Elizabethan separatism as something akin to Popery in its threat to the Royal Supremacy. Laud was as incapable of recognizing Prynne's conservatism as Prynne was incapable of recognizing Laud's Puritanism.

Prynne was as popular as he was prolific: a Royalist opponent in the Civil War said that his books were more prevalent than ministers' sermons. He won over contemporaries by the weight, rather than the depth, of his writings. A critic once laughed at him for trying to prove the sovereignty of Parliament by 'morall sentences out of Seneca'; that was his strength.[1] In an age that revered precedents none ranged so far as Prynne for authorities to support his statements. Professor Haller has pointed out that few of his readers could have followed him with understanding, but 'many an earnest if simple mind must have been persuaded that truth must surely lie where, in so good a cause, appeared so much zeal and learning'.[2] Why then was Prynne neglected by contemporary biographers? He was acclaimed as a martyr when his ears were cut off, yet, despite the Puritan genius for biography, there is no contemporary Life of Prynne. Perhaps what chilled his contemporaries was his assurance. There was, in Prynne, a fatal lack of introspective curiosity; there was none of that painful exploration of personal inade-

[1] (Anon.), *The Fallacies of Mr. William Prynne* (Oxford, 1644), p. 1; (Anon.), *A Serious Epistle to Mr. William Prynne* (London, 1649), p. 9.

[2] William Haller, *Tracts on Liberty in the Puritan Revolution, 1638–47* (New York, 1934), i, p. 25.

quacies which, to Puritans, vindicated Baxter and almost extenuated Laud. This does not explain Prynne's maltreatment by later generations.

When R. E. M. Peach, a local Somerset antiquarian, delivered a paper on Prynne in 1890, he made two important judgments. First, he claimed that no further biography of Prynne was likely:

> The 'Fragmentary Biography' of Prynne, by the late John Bruce, published by the Camden Society, contains as much of the personal history of that remarkable man as is likely to be written in a biographical form.

Second, he pointed to the need for a wider study based on a close analysis of his writings:

> . . . to trace the history of Prynne; to analyse his public character in its relation to the times in which he lived, and the influence he exercised over events out of which grew such immense results . . .[1]

Peach's conclusions were based on sound reasoning: on a recognition both of the paucity of material relating to Prynne's personal life and of the profusion of material relating to his public writings. Later events have falsified Peach's conclusions, not his reasoning. For, although an American scholar, Mrs. Kirby, produced a biography of Prynne in 1931, it was not based on new unprinted sources relating to his private life; instead, it projected Bruce's unfinished account beyond the sixteen-thirties, where he had left the narrative of Prynne's career, by the intelligent correlation of information from Prynne's published works to the known narrative of public events in which he played a part. This was not, however, the detailed analysis of his writings which had seemed the more important task to Peach in 1890, and which still seemed so to Professor Haller in 1938.[2]

To one contemporary critic of Prynne's writings, the neglect by future generations of his pamphleteering would have seemed

---

[1] R. E. M. Peach, *History of Swainswick* (Bath, 1890), p. 46. The work to which he refers is a biographical fragment by J. Bruce in *Documents Relating to Proceedings Against William Prynne*, ed. S. R. Gardiner (Camden Society, New Series, xviii).

[2] E. W. Kirby, *William Prynne* (Camb., Mass., 1931); W. Haller, *The Rise of Puritanism* (New York, 1938), p. 393.

as healthy a development as it was an inevitable one. He wrote, in an address to Prynne, with prescient asperity, that 'to me you have writ a very few things, they being such as no man will enquire after, but such as delight in Things obsolete and antique'. The profuse citations of ill-digested authorities, which won him the nickname of 'Marginal Prynne,' were no substitute for reasoned analysis. The writer thought it a pity that Prynne was not born of German parents, suggesting that he then 'might have outdon the reputation of the greatest of their Authors, who are commonly valued at the rate of their boldnesse and prolixity'.[1]

This patronizing dismissal of Prynne set the tone for much of his contemporaries' criticism. His opponents, at varying levels of humour, satirized his literary defects. Milton warned Prynne that he would expect 'other arguments to be perswaded the good health of a sound answer, than the gout and dropsy of a big margent, litter'd and overlaid with crude and huddl'd quotations'. Samuel Butler thought that Prynne's unique crime was to cast holy things, not unto dogs, but into doggerel. Clarendon derived masochistic pleasure in exile from reading 'ill books'; Prynne was a great favourite with him. Sir Richard Baker thought that Prynne understood little of what he wrote:

> . . . he delivers the words as a Parrat, that pronounceth the Syllables, but not as a man that understands the meaning . . .

Baker believed that 'the man had an itch to be writing a Book'. An amusing satire on Prynne in 1659 also made the point that he had 'arrived at such an Atheletick Habit in the career of writing, that if he may not scribble and print too, he cannot live, and if he live, he must write, and if he write, it must be against Governments'. The writer concluded with the hope:

> . . . that William may have liberty to write against Prynne, Prynne against the Esquier, the Esquier against the Utter Barrister, the Utter Barrister against the Bencher of Licolnes Inn, and to retrograde, till he himself (when he shall become himself) thinks fit to have leasure to desist and to be quiet.[2]

---

[1] (Anon.), *A Serious Epistle to Mr. William Prynne* . . . (London, 1649), pp. 6–7.

[2] John Milton, *Colasterion* . . . (London, 1645), p. 2; Samuel Butler, *Posthumous Works* . . . (London, 1732), p. 84; *Calendar of the Clarendon State*

Prynne had his admirers as well as his critics but even they tended to concentrate on the magnitude of his sufferings and heroic defiance of tyranny rather than on the more debatable ground of his literary powers.[1]

Yet Peach's belief that Prynne's writings deserved a close critical analysis, was in essence, correct. The value which the Royalists placed on his contribution to the Restoration was as much a recognition of his polemical cogency as of his personal valour. Thus a Royalist reported in 1659 that Prynne 'hath made full satisfaction to the presse for former erratas', and even claimed:

> . . . His quill doth the best present right to . . . our Egle and, tho' his eares are lost, he heares now very well and speaks more loyalty to a generall reception then any other.[2]

Moreover, criticism of Prynne reached its height in the period between 1658 and 1659: there was an hysterical stridency about the campaign which was, in itself, an oblique tribute to his power.[3] The form which the criticism took was instructive: a claim that Prynne was contemptible by civilized standards, but with an undue influence over the lower orders. Marchamont Needham, perhaps himself the foremost journalist of his day, thought that this was Prynne's conscious aim:

> . . . feeding the Phantasie with such Feares and Jealousies, as the weaker sort of men (fruitfull enough in these times) create

[1] (Anon.), *Canterburies Pilgramage* (London, 1641), no pagination; (Anon.), *The Armies Remembrancer* (London, 1649), p. 31; *The Faithfull Scout*, Numb. 6 (May 27–June 3, 1659).

[2] *The Nicholas Papers* (Camden Society, Third Series, xxxi,), iv, p. 157. Similar appreciations are recorded in *The Letter Book of John Viscount Mordaunt, 1658–60* (Camden Society, Third Series, lxix), p. 126; *Calendar of the Clarendon State Papers*, ed. F. Routledge (Oxford, 1832), iv, pp. 592, 603, 606, 615; Roger L'Estrange, *L'Estrange, His Apology* (London, 1660), p. 81; Peter Heylyn, *Cyprianus Anglicus* (London, 1668), p. 156.

[3] Henry Stubbe, *The Common-Wealth of Israel* (London, 1659), p. 6; Edmund Ludlow, *Memoirs . . .*, ed. C. Firth (Oxford, 1894), ii, p. 272; (Anon.), *The Character or Ear-Mark of Mr. William Prinne* (London, 1659), p. 2; (Anon.), *Mr. Pryns Good Old Cause Stated and Stunted* (London, 1659), passim; (Anon.), *A Reply to Mr. William Prinne* (London, 1659), p. 2.

*Papers*, i, ed. Ogle and Bliss (Oxford, 1872), p. 372; Sir Richard Baker, *Theatrum Triumphans . . .* (London, 1670), pp. 91, 37; (Anon.), *To The Supream Authority of England, Scotland and Ireland* (London, 1659), single sheet.

unto themselves out of what they read rather than any Satisfaction to the more solid part of the world.

An Independent opponent similarly complained that Prynne was:

> . . . a man of such Renowne and name, (and for high Desert I heartily acknowledge) That his name onely has rendered his subitane Apprehensions, in deed and truth such, to seem good and solid Reasons; and so to passe through the City, as having Truth and Reason in them . . . the weakest and sleightest as ever came from so solid a man . . .yet they take with the people.[1]

Parliament did not authorize Prynne, at the height of the Civil War, to write a defence of its sovereignty and to prosecute Laud, without a similar belief that his words would 'take with the people'.

On literary grounds it is easy to explain the neglect of Prynne. A wearisome prolixity, a humourless scurrility, a complete lack of depth: these qualities are commonly, and rightly, associated with his pamphleteering. But it is illogical to discount Prynne's historical importance on literary grounds: the lack of interest shown in a successful, if crude, controversialist becomes less easy to explain. Neglect of him then becomes defensible only on the ground that he is irrelevant as well as unsubtle: that he stands for an iconoclasm so crude and unenlightened that enhanced understanding of his position would still not mean a corresponding gain in the understanding of problems of the period. Contemporaries, naturally enough, were swift to make this point in controversy. To them he was a paranoid personality: 'a constant opponent of all governments'; 'the Spirit of Contradiction'; one 'who should the Apostles come from Heaven, sent thence to institute a Government . . . would dissent from, and wrangle with them'.[2]

Professor Haller was not blind to Prynne's shortcomings, but rightly saw that this did not lessen the need for an analysis of his writings:

[1] Marchamont Needham, *The Lawyer of Lincolnes-Inne Reformed* (London, 1647), p. 1; Hezekiah Woodward, *Inquiries into the Cause of our Miseries* (London, 1644), p. 11.

[2] *Mercurius Democritus*, Numb. 5 (May 31–June 7, 1659); (Anon.), *Democritus Turned Statesman* (London, 1659), p. 6; (Anon.), *A Word To Mr. Wil Pryn* (London, 1649), p. 5.

Prynne is another figure of the Puritan Revolution who deserves closer critical study than he has so far received.

Yet his own assessment of Prynne's contribution before the Civil War varied little from the conventional criticisms:

> . . . just the kind of person to turn the doctrines of the preachers into reckless assault upon the existing order . . . His avowed aim could be construed only as the overthrow of everything established in the church.

It is this presupposition which is at the root of the slighting treatment given to Prynne in the valuable analyses of constitutional and ecclesiastical ideas of the period by Professor Judson, Dr. Jordan and Professor Haller himself.[1]

This study of Prynne's controversial writings is offered as a corrective to these interpretations: its starting-point is a testing of Professor Haller's judgment on the young Prynne. It is true that more respectful views of the older Prynne have begun to appear: Dr. Pocock has emphasized his part in the revaluation of historical concepts of the constitution; Mr. Hill has scrutinized closely his attitude to tithes; Mr. Woolrych and Professor Davies have praised his contribution to the Restoration.[2] Thus study aims at an over-all reassessment of Prynne, which will set in perspective, not only these, but other subtleties of development and inconsistencies of thought which do not support Professor Haller's picture of the crude iconoclast. This study is both more, and less, than a biography. It is more, because the attempt is continually made to relate Prynne's ideas carefully to contemporary controversies. It is less, not simply because it begins with his writings and not with his birth and early career, but because it does not consider his University connections, his legal work, his service on the Committee

[1] W. Haller, *The Rise of Puritanism* (New York, 1938), pp. 393, 219; M. A. Judson, *The Crisis of the Constitution* . . . (New Brunswick, 1949), omits Prynne; W. K. Jordan, *The Development of Religious Toleration in England* (London, 1938), iii, p. 277, discounts Prynne.

[2] J. G. A. Pocock, *The Ancient Constitution and The Feudal Law* (Cambridge, 1957); C. Hill, *Economic Problems of the Church from Archbishop Whitgift to the Long Parliament* (Oxford, 1956); A. H. Woolrych, 'The Good Old Cause and the Fall of the Protectorate', *Cambridge Historical Journal*, xii, 2, 1957, pp. 133–61; Godfrey Davies, *The Restoration of Charles II* (Oxford, 1955), p. 96, criticises a nineteenth-century dismissal of Prynne as a 'rhinocerous in blinkers'.

of Accounts during the Civil War, or his valuable antiquarian studies. New material has been used, not to supplement biography, but to throw light on developments in his thought. Prynne's pamphlets provide the basis of this study, together with the vast literature which surrounds them.

In an unusually self-deprecating mood in 1649, Prynne stressed his limitations:

> . . . I do not professe my self to be any great Statesman, as exactly to know, what ever is secretly transacted among us . . .

This modest disclaimer did not prevent him from devoting the rest of his life to the pursuit of such knowledge. He went on to name one advantage which he did possess. This was the advantage which justified, as nothing else did, the attempt at a critical study of his writings:

> I have for many years last past been as curious an observer of all the great transactions of Affairs in Church or State, and of the instruments and means by which they have been covertly contrived and carried on, as any man in this House or Kingdome . . .[1]

[1] Prynne. *The Substance of a Speech* . . . (London, 1649), pp. 107–8.

# I

# THE ATTACK ON LAUD

IN 1637 William Prynne, Henry Burton and John Bastwick were sentenced to the loss of their ears for their writings against Archbishop Laud. Burton embraced Bastwick twice before the sentence was carried out and was 'heartily sorry he missed Mr. Prynne'.[1] The phrase underlines the irony of Prynne's career: everyone was heartily sorry, but everyone missed Mr. Prynne. Everyone admired his integrity, but nobody wrote his biography.

The Puritan hero of 1637, who lifted his eyes to Heaven as the executioner hacked at his ear, was the same man who embarrassed Pepys in 1662 by pulling out of his pocket, records of the immoral lives of nuns, at a public dinner.[2] An indifference to the reaction of other men lay at the root of both excesses —heroic in the pillory, boorish at the table. Both responses would have seemed natural to Prynne. When he urged his countrymen in 1628 to give up the custom of drinking healths, he warned them that 'they must not so much regard what others doe, as what themselves are commanded, and injoyned for to doe: the Word of God must be their Rule, and Square, not the Lives and Actions of other men'.[3] Few Calvinists would have quarrelled with the sentiment; Prynne was unique in taking it seriously. If other Calvinists had followed his example, our literature would have been the poorer. True Calvinism is the enemy of biography: the lives and actions of other men are

---

[1] William Prynne, *A New Discovery of the Prelates Tyranny* . . . (London, 1641), p. 48.

[2] Samuel Pepys, *Diary* . . ., ed. H. B. Wheatley (London, 1904), ii, p. 229.

[3] Prynne, *Healthes Sicknesse* . . . (London, 1628), p. 60.

not relevant to men who reject personal merit as the passport to salvation. Yet most Calvinists found their burden of guilt insupportable without some reassurance that they would be saved. Might not reassurance come from that very consciousness of guilt which indicated a superior insight to that of their fellow men? So the Calvinist looked inward, and examined his soul in diaries and journals: Richard Baxter could deplore his addiction to 'the excessive gluttonous eating of apples and pears'.[1] And when the Calvinist looked outward, he examined with equal intensity the lives of holy men who had inspired him: Burton praised Perkins, Bastwick praised Rogers.[2] The dogmatic truants were revealing writers.

Prynne stands apart from his fellow Puritans by his lack of introspective curiosity. Less is known about Prynne's personal life than almost any other public figure of the time: he wrote few letters, he named few influences, he inspired few anecdotes. Prynne effaced himself in public controversy.

Prynne had a comfortable background. He was born in Swainswick, near Bath, in 1600. His father, Thomas Prynne, was a farmer, and his mother, Marie Sherston, was the daughter of an Elizabethan Mayor of Bath. He went to Bath Grammar School until 1616; he graduated at Oriel College, Oxford in 1621; he went to Lincoln's Inn in the same year. The terms of his father's will of 1620 indicate that there was no fear of poverty: William obtained the lease of the Swainswick farm and was instructed to pay his brother Thomas and his sisters Katherine and Bridget £200 each.[3] He was later to be chided in pamphlets for his snobbery. Sir Richard Baker, for instance, suggested that Prynne was excessively critical of comedies because they were 'but the Commonalty of Plays', whereas he spared tragedies— the Gentry of Plays—'for their Gentry's sake'. Another critic, in 1656, thought that Prynne opposed the admission of the Jews for fear that 'his chambers in Lincolnes-Inn should have been

[1] Richard Baxter, *Autobiography* (Everyman's Library), p. 5.
[2] Henry Burton, *A Narration* . . . (London, 1643), p. 1; John Bastwick, *The Second Part of that Book* . . . (London, 1645), preface.
[3] Detailed biographical information on Prynne is available in: R. Warner, *The History of Bath* (Bath, 1801), pp. 204-7; R. E. M. Peach, *History of Swainswick* (Bath, 1890), pp. 58-61; *Documents Relating to Proceedings Against William Prynne*, ed. S. R. Gardiner (Camden Society, New Series, xviii), passim.

for their habitation, or else his Mannour of Swainscomb, or Swainswick, of which he writes himself Esquire'. These critics came nearer to understanding Prynne than did a critic of 1713, who thought that he had aimed at 'the exaltation of Sovereign Mob' and 'selling the Gentry for Slaves'.[1]

Prynne was no more a religious radical than he was a social radical. Two opponents, Peter Heylyn and Anthony Wood, claimed that Prynne learnt his religious radicalism from John Preston, the lecturer at Lincoln's Inn.[2] But they could not draw any examples of this radicalism from his personal life: they were defeated by his reticence. His attitude to apples and pears was to remain a mystery for ever. They could only argue that his attitude to bishops was clearly expressed in his pamphlets. They were typical of all critics of Prynne's radicalism in basing their judgment upon his writings. And their judgment was wrong.

In the period between 1626 and 1640 Prynne was a moderate. Against the excesses of a minority of Anglicans he appealed to the moderation of the majority, and to the sure traditions of the Church of England, represented in its purest form in Queen Elizabeth's time. His language was violent but was limited in its application to the small group around Archbishop Laud. He felt that they were subverting the Church of England by their failure to attack social evils, such as stage plays, drinking of healths and long hair. With relish he attacked Caroline Teddy Boys who would 'rather have the Commonwealth disturbed, than their Haire disordered'.[3] They were introducing dangerous innovations in church ceremony, such as bowing at the name of Jesus and moving the Communion Table from the centre of the church. They were questioning the Calvinist dogma of Predestination: to Prynne, this was analogous to questioning that the Sun went round the Earth 'because one

[1] Sir Richard Baker, *Theatrum Triumphans* (London, 1670), p. 25; D. L., *Israel's Condition and Cause Pleaded* (London, 1656), p. 70; Nestor Ironside, *A Second Whig-Letter* . . . (London, 1713), p. 18.

[2] Peter Heylyn, *Cyprianus Anglicus* (London, 1668), p. 156; Anthony Wood, *Athenae Oxonienses*, ed. W. A. Bliss (Oxford, 1817), iii, p. 184. Irvonmy Morgan, *Prince Charles' Puritan Chaplain* (London, 1957), repeats this charge, but without substantiating it from documented evidence.

[3] Prynne, *The Unlovelinesse of Love-Lockes* (London, 1628), dedicatory epistle.

13

brainesicke Copernicus out of the Sublimitie of his quintessen-
tial, transcendentall speculations, hath more senselessly than
metaphysically, more ridiculously, than singularly averred it'.
Prynne was not above a little chauvinism to dismiss these
followers of Arminius. Thompson was a 'dissolute, ebrious,
prophane, luxurious English-Dutchman', and of Baro—the
'exotique Frenchman'—he said:

> This branded illegall witnesse then being at the very best a
> Forraigner, doth only marre, not help their cause.[1]

Against all these excesses, Prynne described the virtues of the
Elizabethan Church: rigidly Calvinistic in dogma, austere in its
services, loyal to the Crown. The contrast was facile, but it was
not necessarily insincere. Laud's opponents in Parliament
similarly argued that they were defending the Elizabethan
Settlement from doctrinal and ceremonial innovations. But
they did not say that they were also defending the Royal
Supremacy from constitutional innovations. Prynne did, and
this makes him unique among the critics of Laud.

The Parliamentary opposition professed loyalty to the Crown,
but could not ignore the absolutist doctrines proclaimed in sermons by Anglican court divines, such as Mainwaring, Dickinson and Sibthorpe.[2] By their servility to the Crown the Anglicans
weakened the concept of a 'balanced polity'. Laud's opponents
would have preferred to attack the court divines for seeking to
overthrow monarchs, as the Jesuits were, with their 'deposition'
theories. But how could a Mainwaring be called a regicide?
Instead, Laud's opponents were driven to deny that Geneva
and Rome thought alike about resistance. Necessarily their
attack had to be indirect: Popery and tyranny were twins;
Anglicans, who encouraged the Crown towards tyranny and
away from the balanced polity, were playing the Papist game
and were undermining the legal basis of monarchy. Yet they
could still only argue that, in ultimate effect, Jesuit and
Anglican views of monarchy were similar: they were forced to
concede that, in immediate intention, they were strikingly

[1] Prynne, *Anti-Arminianisme* . . . (London, 1630), pp. 268-70.
[2] Roger Mainwaring, *Religion and Alegiance* (London, 1627); William
Dickinson, *The King's Right* (London, 1619); Robert Sibthorpe, *Apostolike
Obedience* (London, 1627).

THE ATTACK ON LAUD

dissimilar. Selden expressed the difference pithily: 'The Catholicks in England goe one way and the Cort Clergie the other.'[1] The indirect attack upon the bishops for anti-royalism —which ultimately was expressed in the Grand Remonstrance —was clumsy, but providential: it lacked the cogency of a direct attack, but it united splendidly Puritan and Parliamentarian. The King had been led astray by the advice of evil counsellors into absolutist ways: in defence of the balanced polity, Parliament must provide good advice to the King, while those clergymen who had given bad advice should make way for those with a greater reverence for Parliament and Common Law. Sibthorpe's comment on the situation is interesting, since it recognizes the contribution which court divines like himself had made to the alliance between Puritanism and the Common Law:

> The Catholicks make the Church above the King; the Puritans, on the other hand, make the Law above the King.[2]

Religious and constitutional objections could fuse against a clerical régime which enjoined 'Apostolike Obedience' to the imposers of Ship Money.

Prynne's writings, in the period between 1626 and 1640, fascinate by their neglect of the orthodox constitutional points. Prynne did not worry because the bishops praised the Crown too much: in 1637 he wrote *A Breviate Of The Prelates Intollerable Usurpations Upon The Kings Prerogative*. Henry Parker complained that the Clergy 'wed the King to their quarrell'; Prynne complained of 'the antipathie of the English lordly prelacie' to 'regall monarchy'.[3] Prynne's case was simple: the Laudian bishops were not content to derive their authority from the Crown, *iure humano*; instead, they claimed an independent right for the office, *iure divino*. He argued that the Elizabethan bishops had been content with the *iure humano* claim; the *iure divino* claim challenged the Royal Supremacy.

To question the sincerity of his position is to underrate the

---

[1] John Selden, *Table Talk*, ed. F. Pollock (London, 1927), p. 29.

[2] Sibthorpe, op. cit., p. 20.

[3] Henry Parker, *The Case of Shipmony Briefly Discussed* (London, 1640), p. 33. The quoted reference is to the title of a Prynne pamphlet: *The Antipathie of the English Lordly Prelacie Both to Regall Monarchy and Civill Unity . . .* (London, 1641).

formative influence exercised on him by the great Tudor apologists of Protestantism, Foxe and Jewel. Foxe's *Acts and Monuments* and Jewel's *The Defence of the Apology of the Church of England* were often chained in churches, together with the Bible and Erasmus's *Paraphrases*.[1] This alone gave their work a stature denied to more ephemeral writing. One pamphlet by Prynne in 1637 cited Foxe and Jewel no fewer than sixty-seven times in over three hundred pages.[2] This was not exceptional: similar surveys of other pamphlets would yield similar results. Neither such statistical evidence, nor the unvarying reverence with which Prynne speaks of them, can do full justice to the extent of their influence. With pride Prynne presented volumes of Foxe's work to his native parish church at Swainswick.[3] It is not too much to say that Prynne's early works are one sustained, enthusiastic commentary on Foxe. From Foxe he borrows his historical interpretations: sympathy for the maligned King John (a victim of monkish prejudices); reverence for the Protestant martyrs; admiration for Tudor Protestant divines; exaltation of Queen Elizabeth as another Constantine. From Foxe and Jewel, above all else, Prynne derived the concept of 'empire': of history seen as the projection of the conflict of Pope and Emperor throughout the centuries. It was this imperial tradition that sustained Prynne in his awe of magistracy and his abhorrence of Papist clericalism: the two constant themes in all Prynne's writings.

The opening passage of the Act in Restraint of Appeals of 1533 was the basis of the works of Foxe, Jewel, Tyndale and other Tudor divines:

> Where by divers sundry old authentic histories and chronicles it is manifestly declared and expressed that this realm of England is an empire, and so hath been accepted in the world, governed by one Supreme Head and King having the dignity and royal estate of the imperial crown . . .[4]

[1] H. J. Cowell, *The Four Chained Books* (London, 1938). F. A. Yates, 'Queen Elizabeth as Astraea', *Journal of the Warburg and Courtauld Institutes*, x, 1947, stresses the decisive influence of Foxe and Jewel on their contemporaries and the important part they played in reviving an imperial cult around the person of Queen Elizabeth.

[2] Prynne, *A Quench-Coale* . . . (London, 1637).

[3] (Bodleian Library) Tanner MSS. 69, f. 1.

[4] J. R. Tanner, *Tudor Constitutional Documents* (Cambridge, 1951), p. 41.

THE ATTACK ON LAUD

Foxe's history, for all its harrowing details, was an exercise in optimism. It set out to show that the martyrs had not died in vain; that their sufferings had been part of a divine pattern. There were five periods of Church history foreshadowed by St. John in the Book of Revelations. They were realized in: persecution under heathen Emperors; glory under the first Christian Emperor, Constantine; decline under the Roman Church; Antichristian enormities under the Hildebrandine Papacy. Foxe was writing at the time of the fifth period: the struggle between Christ and Antichrist. The Reformation in England marked the triumphant return of the Christian Emperor. The Marian interlude was the retort of Antichrist, but when things were at their lowest the second Constantine, Elizabeth, had come in answer to Latimer's prayers:

> . . . for whom this grey-headed father so earnestly prayed in his imprisonment; Through whose true, natural and imperial crowne, the brightnesse of Gods word was set up again to confound the dark and false-vizored Kingdom of Antichrist.[1]

Because Prynne accepted Foxe, he accepted Anglicanism. Defects within the Church were not pointers to fundamental weaknesses in the Church; they reflected, rather, the tremendous conflict between the forces of Christ and Antichrist in the Church's crucial fifth period. A temporary victory by the agents of Antichrist was not a total one. Foxe's moral was clear to Prynne: a steadfast refusal to deviate from Elizabethan traditions would secure victory for Christ. Prynne warned the Laudians that the *iure divino* claim for episcopacy meant 'setting up a Papall and Episcopall exploded usurped Jurisdiction, Independent on, and underived from the Imperiall Crowne'.[2]

Had Prynne's fears any substance? If Mainwaring's were the authentic voice of Anglicanism, Prynne had purchased his royalism at the price of relevance. But Laud and his followers —Heylyn, Boughen, Hoard, Pocklington and Cosin—clearly did support the *iure divino* claim for episcopacy. Laud recognized also the need to emancipate the Church from dependence upon Foxe and Jewel:

[1] John Foxe, *Acts and Monuments* (London, 1837), vii, p. 466.
[2] (British Museum). Additional MSS. 37682, f. 73–73v.

though these two were very worthy men in their time, yet every thing which they say is not by and by 'the doctrine of the Church of England.'[1]

Cosin's was a celebrated case. He denied that he had ever said that the King had no more power of excommunication than the man that rubbed his horse's heels; what is not often realized is that the denial itself contains quite a powerful defence of clerical superiority. Only exceptional circumstances, such as the proceedings against Cosin, brought these sentiments to light.[2] Nor was there any cause for them to come to light, when a King reigned who looked upon *iure divino* claims for episcopacy as a mark of Anglican strength. Charles I caused tongues to wag at Court in 1637 with the rumour that he had denied that he was head of the Church.[3] The Laudians did not need to emphasize clerical superiority with such a King on the throne. They did not surrender the vital thesis that episcopacy rested on divine right, not royal grace. From this position of strength, they could pay effusive compliments to a delightful nursing-father. But an ungodly ruler would provoke a different response. As the Puritan, Stephen Marshall, pointed out in 1643, then 'the world would hear another Divinity' from High Church Anglicans. And the world did. When there were fears that Charles I would desert episcopacy in 1648, it was two Laudian divines, Heylyn and Boughen, who stressed that the *iure divino* status of episcopacy protected it from royal caprice. And when his son took the Covenant in 1650, Anglicans were not as disturbed as they would have been in the time of Cranmer.[4]

Laud was only following Jacobean divines, such as Carleton,

[1] William Laud, *Works* . . . (Oxford, 1847–60), iv, p. 226; Peter Heylyn, *Cyprianus Anglicus* . . . (London, 1668), p. 301; Edward Boughen, *A Sermon Concerning Decencie and Order in the Church* (London, 1638), pp. 17–23; Samuel Hoard, *The Churches Authority Asserted* (London, 1637), p. 62; John Pockling-ton, *Altare Christianum* (London, 1637), pp. 33–4; (B.M.) Harleian MSS. 750, f. 290.

[2] John Cosin, *Correspondence* . . . (Surtees Society, lii), pp. 147–50.

[3] G. Albion, *Charles I and the Court of Rome* (London, 1935), pp. 402–5.

[4] Stephen Marshall, *A Copy of a Letter* (London, 1643), p. 12; Heylyn, *Extraneus Vapulans* (London, 1656), p. 168; Boughen, *Mr. Gerees Case of Conscience Sifted* (London, 1648), p. 20. Boughen's pamphlet was a reply to: John Geree, *The Sifters Sieve Broken* (London, 1648). In his pamphlet, Geree argued—like Prynne—from Tudor Anglican writings that the King could determine the religion of the State.

Bancroft, Bilson, Downame, Sparke and Barlow, in his emphasis upon the *iure divino* claim for episcopacy. They had consciously used the claim to break away from the imperial tradition of Foxe and Jewel. A growing confidence in the intrinsic values of Anglicanism; a supicion of the theology of Elizabeth's successor; a sensitivity to taunts from a radical wing, led by Cartwright, about the inadequacy of *iure humano* claims: all contributed to the movement.[1] The opponents of these bishops saw the importance of this development and attacked it as an assault upon the Royal Supremacy: 'they have fancied to themselves another sort of Bishops'. A generation earlier than Prynne, men like Bolton, Reynolds, Baynes and Bradshaw, were appealing to Tudor Anglican traditions against *iure divino* novelties.[2]

Prynne was a Jacobean nonconformist, not least in his exaltation of Elizabeth. When Anthony Wood came to London in 1667 to study records in the Tower of London, he described how 'Mr. Prynne received him with old fasion complements, such as were used in the raigne of King James I'.[3] It might appear from Prynne's writings against the Laudians that he had been guilty of a similar anachronistic slip—a failure to project himself beyond the time of James I to the changed atmosphere later. His point of view might seem irrelevant to 1641, when the stock complaint against bishops was not their challenge to monarchy, but their exaltation of it. This is not entirely

[1] George Carleton, *Jurisdiction, Regall, Episcopall, Papall* (London, 1610); Richard Bancroft, *A Sermon Preached at Paules Crosse* (London, 1588); Thomas Bilson, *The Perpetual Government of Christes Church* . . . (London, 1593); George Downame, *An Extract of a Sermon* . . . (London, 1608); Thomas Sparke, *A Brotherly Persuasion to Unitie and Uniformitie* . . . (London, 1607); William Barlow, *Concerning the Antiquitie and Superioritie of Bishops* (London, 1606). E. T. Davies, *Episcopacy and the Royal Supremacy* (Oxford, 1950), contains a good summary of this development. M. A. Judson, *The Crisis of the Constitution* . . . (New Brunswick, 1949), although making excellent points about Anglican sycophancy, does not perhaps emphasise enough this other tendency within Anglicanism.

[2] Robert Bolton, *Two Sermons* (London, 1635); John Reynolds, *A Replye Answering a Defence of the Sermon* (London, 1613); Paul Baynes, *The Diocesans Tryall* (London, 1621); William Bradshaw, *English Puritanisme* (London, 1605).

[3] *The Life and Times of Anthony Wood*, ed. A. Clark (Oxford, 1891), ii, pp. 110–11. Cf. J. G. A. Pocock, *The Ancient Constitution and the Feudal Law* (Cambridge, 1951), p. 167, on Prynne: 'in essentials a survivor from the age of Coke.'

true. Not only Prynne, but Bastwick, Burton, and Bagshaw—whose tutor at Brasenose College, Oxford, had been Bolton, a leading Jacobean imperial nonconformist—had suffered for their hostility to *iure divino* claims. Jacobean writings of Baynes and Reynolds against the *iure divino* claims were reprinted in 1641. D'Ewes, in the Commons in 1641, was as impressed as Prynne had been in 1637 by the evidence from the trial of Bastwick that Laud, Neale, White and Juxon supported the *iure divino* claims. These claims were not ignored in the Civil War pamphlet controversies. If this attack was emphasized less in the Grand Remonstrance than the orthodox constitutional case, it was more because it was impolitic than because it was irrelevant. Laud shrewdly noted that although he had been accused of undermining the Royal Supremacy in the original charges against him, this was withdrawn in the later charges. He rightly saw that he could hardly be accused, at one and the same time, of undermining the royal prerogative and of advancing it above the law.[1] Another reason for not emphasizing Prynne's point was that, by 1641, the ecclesiastical radicals were as anxious to discredit Foxe and Jewel as Laud had been: 'root and branch' was incompatible with episcopacy, whether *iure humano* or *iure divino*.[2]

When Prynne defended the Crown against the bishops, he was less perverse than might at first have appeared. His perversity was more apparent in wrenching the Laudians out of their historical context, and in treating them as an isolated phenomenon. But unless Prynne isolated the disease, the demand for a total cure would have seemed irresistible. Prynne knew that the Laudians were not the first Anglicans to put for-

---

[1] Simonds D'Ewes, *Journal* . . . ed. W. A. Notestein (London, 1923), p. 241; Laud, *Works* . . . iv, pp. 150–1.

[2] Some Scottish clericalists were genuinely misled by a pamphlet of a Scottish Anglican: John Wemys, *De Regis Primatu* (Edinburgh, 1623). They thought that it spoke for Laud's views on Church and State: Robert Baillie, *The Life of William now Lord Arch-Bishop of Canterbury Examined* (London, 1643), pp. 124–5; George Gillespie, *Aarons Rod Blossoming* (London, 1646). p. 163. In reality it exalts Crown above Church in a way which would have shocked Laud. It belongs to the imperial tradition of Tudor Anglicanism—even frequently quoting Marsilio of Padua (cf. Yates, loc. cit., pp. 43–4, for an appreciation of Marsilio's importance in imperial propaganda).

ward the *iure divino* claim: Laud and Heylyn both acknowledged
their debt to men like Bilson and Bancroft.[1] Yet Prynne did not
attack the Jacobean High Churchmen, although he attacked by
name their successors and appealed to their predecessors. Had
he made such an attack, his moderate case would have been
destroyed. Its strength depended upon the antithesis which he
could draw between the whole weight of previous Church
tradition and the novel dabblings of a few benighted persons.
The crime of men such as Laud, Cosin, Mountague, Wren and
Heylyn was their apostasy from the recognized Anglican traditions. No other interpretation was compatible with Foxe.
And until 1641—when Prynne joined the radicals—he refused
to expose the High Church tendencies of men whom he admired
for their Calvinism. He wished to show that deviations from
Calvinist doctrine and simplicity in ceremony necessarily
accompanied deviations from loyalty to the Crown. 'Arminianism' was a term which was rarely used in England in the
period before the Civil War to stand simply for acceptance of
Arminius's doctrinal views: it was often used to indicate the
philosophy of Laud's group in a generalized way. When
Prynne called Laud an 'Arminian' the term had some validity:
Laud had a coherent attitude on doctrinal, ceremonial and
constitutional controversies along the lines which Prynne
indicated. Prynne's analysis broke down when he sought to
isolate these tendencies in one group, clearly marked off from
their contemporaries. The great Jacobean anti-Arminians in
doctrine, Carleton and Downame, were also powerful champions of the *iure divino* claim for episcopacy. Had Prynne been
determined to discredit episcopacy, he could have pointed to the
suspect tenets of even its more enlightened advocates. The opposite was true: Prynne tried to conceal the phenomenon of High
Church Calvinism. His moderate thesis was too dependent upon
faith in good bishops to allow that faith to be undermined. By
good bishops, he meant men who were clearly distinct from
Laud's group, and who followed the traditions of Foxe and
Jewel. Among contemporary anti-Laudians he praised Hall,
Davenant, Morton, Williams, Usher: these were the bishops
who were fighting for the Church of England in her crucial

[1] Laud, *Works* . . ., iv, pp. 310–11; Heylyn, *A Briefe and Moderate Answer*
(London, 1637), p. 64.

fifth stage of history. It was important to isolate them from the Laudians.

Yet who were the Laudians? To imply, as Prynne did, that they were a coherent group working to one sinister end—the subversion of the Church to their principles—was false. Sir John Lamb justly reproached Laud in 1641 for his failure to be a good party man:

> You would be ruled by nobody, nor communicate yourself to any that I know, nor make yourself any party at Court, but stood upon yourself: it may be that was your fault . . .[1]

Prynne refused to recognize that there were many points on which his admired bishops agreed with the 'Laudians'. Mountague, in an interesting letter to Cosin in 1625, acknowledged that Hall, Morton and Usher had attracted much popular support based upon a misconception of the extent of their disagreement with Laud. This misconception had been fed by some of Laud's sympathisers: Mountague himself, on other occasions, had dismissed Hall, Davenant and Morton as Puritans, and had even called for an 'Inquisition' half-seriously to combat the influence of Hall.[2] Yet he was right to stress the limits of their disagreement with Laud. Williams's biographer, Hacket, conceded the differences in ceremony and personality between Williams and Laud, but denied Prynne's accuracy in extending them to doctrinal and constitutional controversies. Similarly, Heylyn conceded the differences in doctrine between Morton and Laud, but denied Prynne's accuracy in extending them to ceremony. With some embarrassment, Prynne acknowledged that the second edition of Morton's *Institution of The Sacrament* . . . of 1635 supported Heylyn's point. But he refused to recognize that such a position could be maintained sincerely by a bishop like Morton:

> This I can hardly believe, that that addition to the second is Bishop Mortons owne, but a trick of legerdemaine thrust in by some other, without his privity with purpose to blemish this incomparable peece of his, to draw a scandall upon him.[3]

[1] *Cal. S.P. Dom., Charles I, 1640–41*, p. 131.
[2] Cosin, *Correspondence* . . ., pp. 80, 32.
[3] John Hacket, *Scrinia Reserata* (London, 1692), p. 87; Heylyn, *Cyprianus Anglicus* . . ., p. 293; Prynne, *A Quench-Coale* . . ., p. 289.

Prynne's faith in the moderate bishops was touching, but dangerously vulnerable: it is against this background that his peculiar venom against moderate bishops in 1641, such as Williams, Morton, Usher and Hall, becomes credible— especially against Hall, the staunch Calvinist who produced the classic defence of episcopacy by divine right in 1640.

If Prynne had developed his defence of the Royal Supremacy as one argument with which to beat the Laudians, he would merely have been restating a Jacobean principle with unusual emphasis. But Prynne did more: he developed this argument with such obsessive intensity that he completely neglected the orthodox constitutional objections to the increased powers of the Crown. Two Anglicans had been singled out for special hostility by Parliament: Mainwaring, for his extravagant praise of the Crown; Mountague, for his doctrinal deviations from Calvinism. Prynne criticized only Mountague. His solitary reference to Mainwaring was as late as 1656 in a pamphlet warning preachers to avoid excessive praise of Cromwell. And, since Prynne objected more to the legality of Cromwell's authority than to the extent of his power, his hostility then to 'Parasites' cannot be given a wider reading. It is true that Prynne mentioned Sibthorpe's sermon as a point against Laud in his prosecution of the Archbishop, yet this was not for absolutist doctrines but for the anti-Papal passages allegedly expunged from the sermon by Laud's agents.[1]

Prynne wrote only one pamphlet on constitutional controversies before the Civil War. His protest against Ship Money was written anonymously in 1637 but was not published until 1641—the year, it will be argued, when Prynne's attitude changed. For by 1641 Prynne was a radical and was respectably orthodox in his criticisms of Laud: to antedate this development is to diminish the cataclysmic significance of that year; to assume its inevitability is to diminish the interest of Prynne. Only in attacking Ship Money did he attack the menace of tyranny. He reminded Charles I of the words of his father:

> . . . a King Governing in a settled Kingdome leaves to be a King and degenerates into a Tyrant as soone as he leaves to rule by his Lawes . . . they that persuade them to the contrary are

[1] Prynne, *A Summary Collection* (London, 1656), p. 25; Prynne, *Canterburies Doome* . . . (London, 1646), p. 246.

Projectors, Vipers and Pests, both against them and the Common-wealth.

Prynne added in the margin:

Note well the fitting Epithets.[1]

This was as near as Prynne came to criticizing the Crown until 1641; although he tactfully cloaked his rebuke behind praise of James I, he was notably less 'royal' when he discussed con-stitutional, rather than ecclesiastical, issues. And so, with this exception, he refused to discuss constitutional issues at all. This was not because he thought them uninteresting: after 1641 he wrote more pamphlets on State than on Church, and his argu-ments against Ship Money showed a sure constitutional grasp. When Prynne delivered a lecture to law students on the Peti-tion of Right at the Restoration, he became inspired:

the most benefitiall, necessary . . . and universall Law of all others . . . a rehearsall and ratification of the highest nature of all those antient fundamental Lawes contrived for by the wisdome of all former Parliaments, and so earnestly contested for in all ages when infringed . . .[2]

In the sixties he preserved his royalism by attacking the Inde-pendents under Cromwell, 'who at first pretended to rescue and defend it from former encroachments'; in the thirties he preserved his royalism by ignoring the 'encroachments'. In no pamphlet before 1641 did Prynne defend the Petition of Right against the extension of the powers of the Crown. Prynne's fundamental lack of sympathy for the constitutional case of the Parliamentary opposition comes out most strikingly in a pamphlet which he wrote in 1629. This evidence is most im-pressive because it comes out incidentally, in the form of an analogy, in a pamphlet on doctrine. In showing God's omni-potence, Prynne compares God's liberty with a King's. Both have a complete free will in selection:

We see that earthly Monarchs doe oft dispence and, cast their honours, favours, and disfavours upon men, advancing this man, and displacing that; Upon no other grounds at all, but that it is their pleasure; yet, who may say unto them, what doest thou?

[1] Prynne, *An Humble Remonstrance Against the Tax of Ship-Money* . . . London, 1641), p. 39.
[2] (B.M.) Stowe MSS. 302, f. 48-9.

God's sovereignty is like a King's: 'an absolute, a free, a just prerogative . . . he wrongeth none in pardoning some, or damning others'. No analogy could have been less welcome to the Parliamentary opposition. Court divines had compared Kings to Gods in their arbitrariness: Prynne reversed the figures, but the equation was the same.[1]

Mrs. Kirby, in her biography of Prynne, did mention that he seemed oddly uncritical of the King's foreign policy and his attempts to limit the powers of the Commons. She does not pursue the question further, nor does it affect her final judgment that 'Prynne, as the mouthpiece of Parliament, must be regarded as chief of the pamphleteers of the years before and during the Civil War'.[2] But the effect of the evidence is to destroy this judgment: Prynne, the mouthpiece during the Civil War of the Commons, was not before then its most strident apologist. Prynne wanted to rescue the King from the encroachment upon his powers by bishops, not to rescue the Common Law and Parliament from the encroachment of the King, misled by the advice of bishops.

Henry Parker was one of the toughest minds on the Parliamentary side during the Civil War. He sympathized with much that Prynne wrote against Laud. He too resented the *iure divino* claim for episcopacy as a constitutional challenge to the Royal Supremacy, and praised the Elizabethan Settlement as its antithesis. Such was his Erastianism that he felt that even the Elizabethan Anglicans should have given more power in ecclesiastical matters to the Crown. But Parker could not rest content with Prynne's straightforward defence of the Crown against episcopal encroachments. Parker could not ignore the fact that, in constitutional matters, the royal prerogative was being extended, not diminished, and that this process, so dangerous to Parliament and the Common Law, was being exploited, if not created, by Anglican divines. He pointed out that 'Mainwaring's Doctrine is common at Court', and that bishops meddled in legal matters 'for Pulpits were not Publike enough to preach an unlimitable prerogative in'. He linked antipathy to Laud with sympathy to Parliament by advising Charles I to listen to his critics in the Commons rather than to

[1] Prynne, *God No Impostor Nor Deluder* . . . (London, 1629), pp. 28–32.
[2] E. W. Kirby, *William Prynne* (Camb., Mass., 1931), pp. 16, 185.

his flatterers in the pulpit. Parker, of course, like all the orthodox critics of the bishops, argued that ultimately 'Mainwaring's
Doctrine' would destroy the Crown. John Milton, similarly
argued that the Laudians had a double plan: 'to thrust the
Laitie under the despoticall rule of the Monarch, that they
themselves might confine the Monarch to a kind of pupillage
under their Hierarchy'. Neither Milton nor Parker forgot that
their main clerical enemy was the sycophant. As anxious as
Prynne to defend the Royal Supremacy against the bishops
in ecclesiastical matters, Parker could not extend this royalism
into constitutional matters. Prynne's royalism survived even
this test.[1]

Prynne described, in one pamphlet before the Civil War,
how many men swore that they had seen two suns and an enormous inverted rainbow on the morning of 23 February 1637.
Prynne interpreted this as an indication that God was preparing
to bend His bow in anger at those who had scorned a Covenant
with Him. He noted that Foxe had recorded the same pheno-
mena in London on 15 February 1555, presaging the slaughter
of the martyrs. Even the superstitious Prynne did not believe
that history would repeat itself—not even for his beloved Foxe.
The contrast between the piety of Charles I and the impiety of
Mary satisfied Prynne that the analogy was false.[2] This was not
humbug. Prynne was no lackey: his subsequent career and
suffering testify to that. His admiration of Charles I was intellectual rather than politic—inextricably bound up with his
acceptance of Foxe and Jewel. Prynne was a very straight
person in his dealings with others, but with an unlimited capacity for self-deception. He wished to believe that Charles was
a Constantine, and so he believed that Charles was a Constantine. His faith in Charles, like his faith in the moderate
bishops, was facile, intense and sincere. The group around Laud,
stung by his criticisms, wished to destroy Prynne as the enemy
of both Crown and Church. As early as August 1626, Mountague was falsely ascribing a seditious pamphlet to Prynne,
and in an undated letter, probably about the same time, he
said that 'prejudicate opinion transposeth the most without

[1] Henry Parker, *A Discourse Concerning Puritans* (London, 1641), pp. 50–2;
John Milton, *Of Reformation* . . . (London, 1641), p. 67.
[2] Prynne, *A Quench-Coale* . . ., p. 316.

knowledge, as it doth the laweyers of Lincoln's Inn'. By June, 1628, Cosin was appealing to Laud for royal action against Prynne and Burton:

> It is his gracious defence against the overgrowing faction, more than any private revenge, that I seek against these two barking libellers.

Yet how could Prynne, most royal of pamphleteers, be shown to be against the Crown? Strafford's growl that 'these men do but begin with the Church that they might after have freer Access to the State' was one thing; documented evidence of sedition was another.[1]

Much as Elizabeth—according to Foxe—answered Latimer's prayers, so Prynne answered those of the Laudians. In the early thirties, he wrote a treatise against stage plays called *Histrio-mastix*: by 1634 he faced a charge of treason.

[1] Cosin, *Correspondence* . . ., pp. 102, 86, 139; Strafford, *Letters and Dispatches* . . ., ed. W. Knowler (London, 1739), ii, p. 101.

# II

# LAUD'S REVENGE

'THEY went through the world, like Sir Artegal's iron man Talus with his flail, crushing and trampling down oppressors, mingling with human beings, but having neither part nor lot in human infirmities, insensible to fatigue, to pleasure, and to pain, not to be pierced by any weapon, not to be withstood by any barrier.'[1]

Macaulay believed that the strength of the Puritans lay in their isolation—in their refusal to conform to the standards of their fellows. Thomas Wilson, an influential 'root and branch' minister in the Civil War, expressed the Puritan creed in 1641: 'till a man seems odde to the world, he is never right in religion and righteousnesse.'[2] Prynne's test came, first in 1634 and then —most cruelly—in 1637. He withstood both barriers, and became, to Puritans, the Cranmer of his generation. One of the first actions of the Long Parliament was to release him from exile in the Channel Islands.

Prynne became a symbol of opposition to the Crown—but haltingly and accidentally. This was not his intention: his attack on Laud had been a defence of the Crown. But to many people it seemed that an attack on Laud was an attack on the Crown: Prynne's prosecution in Star Chamber in 1634 was intended to convert this vague sentiment into a legal principle.

The pretext for the prosecution was that in his pamphlet, *Histriomastix*, Prynne had attacked female actors at the same time as the Queen was taking part in Montague's *The Shepherd's*

[1] Lord Macaulay, *Critical and Historical Essays* (London, 1898), i, pp. 52-3.
[2] Thomas Wilson, *Davids Zeale for Zion . . .* (London, 1641), p. 17.

28

*Pastoral*. Prynne pointed out in defence that his *Histriomastix* had been long in preparation, and that the date of its complete publication was still a month earlier than the Queen's performance. This was a plausible defence, and one which convinced even some of his critics. Thus Joseph Mede, writing to Sir Justinian Isham in January 1634, could say—'And see the luck of it: it must be published even just the next day after the Qu(een)'s Pastorall.'[1] Yet Prynne's case was less strong than might appear. For he had inserted additional criticisms in an Index, and his objections cannot remove the suspicion that he had in mind the rehearsals of the Masque which took place at the time that the Index was passing through the press.

The prosecution, in any case, had more to offer against Prynne than circumstantial evidence. The Laudians had long been incensed by his criticisms, and were intent upon his public humiliation. They wanted to tear aside his protestations of loyalty to the Crown, and show the seditious implications of his arguments. Peter Heylyn, Laud's devoted follower, was entrusted with the task of drawing up the detailed charges against Prynne. Gussoni, the Venetian Ambassador, recorded his impression that *Histriomastix* contained 'scandalous and biting remarks, about the civil and ecclesiastical government of his kingdom'. Pagitt wrote from the Middle Temple to Harrington that Prynne's work was 'extraordinarily stufft with quotacons of old Authors work wch . . . are his only arguments', but added:

. . . But I do not conceive this to be the cause why he is called in question, but some exorbitant passages concerning ecclesiastical governments . . .

Now these were precisely the reactions which were sought for by the prosecution: both comments were made in early

---

[1] *The Correspondence of Bishop Brian Duppa and Sir Justinian Isham 1650–60*, ed. Sir J. Isham (Publications of the Northamptonshire Record Society, xvii, 1950–1), p. xxxv. A full list of the charges against Prynne is contained in (Public Record Office) S.P. 16/534; the fullest account of the trial is contained in (B.M.) Add. MSS. 11764, which is reproduced by S. R. Gardiner in: *Documents Relating to Proceedings Against William Prynne* (Camden Society, New Series, xviii); although less full (Bodl. Lib.) Douce MSS. 173 contains some interesting additional material about the trial. Gardiner does not refer to the latter source.

1634 by observers who had no first-hand knowledge of the work.[1]

Prynne was, in many ways, the first modern historian: solemn, prolix, and packed with footnotes. This attack upon stage plays revealed him at his worst. But it was not enough for the prosecution to demonstrate his bigotry. They also wished to show that underlying the bigotry was a subversive craving for novelty, which threatened the State. Cottingham put the case for the prosecution:

> The truth is, Mr. Pryn would have a newe churche, newe govern-ment, a newe kinge, for hee would make the people altogether offended with all thinges att the present.[2]

Too often this caricature—put out by his opponents—has been accepted as a faithful picture of Prynne. His *Histriomastix* was actually as conservative as his other writings before 1641. Nowhere did he express more eloquently his love of the past than in a pamphlet of 1628:

> Strange it is to see, and lamentable to consider, how farre our Nation is of late degenerated from what it was in former Ages: how farre their Lives, and their Professions differ.

His subject was: *The Unlovelinesse of Love-Lockes*. Prynne made it clear at the beginning of *Histriomastix* that it should be linked with his other ethical writings, against health-drinking and long hair. *Histriomastix* was not simply an attack upon plays, but upon all other 'universall overspreading still-increasing evills'. Prynne turned for support to Hall, Reynolds and John White. He followed White in extolling Constantine for his suppression of plays, in linking Constantine with 'our famous Queen Elizabeth', and in comparing the depravities of the time with those that faced Constantine when he began his reform. Prynne thus could claim to be echoing a great and revered Anglican divine in stressing the hope of moral reform through the agency of the godly magistrate.[3] The unfortunate

---

[1] *Calendar State Papers Venetian Charles I*, xxiii, p. 196; (B.M.) Harleian MSS. 1026, f. 44v.

[2] *Documents Relating to Proceedings Against William Prynne . . .*, p. 16.

[3] Prynne, *The Unlovelinesse of Love-Lockes . . .* (London, 1628), dedicatory epistle; Prynne, *Histriomastix . . .* (London, 1633), pp. 123–6, 467, 715; John White, *Two Sermons* (London, 1615), pp. 16–17, 36, 37, 22.

converse to this was, however, that Prynne drew attention to the judgments of God upon magistrates who had failed to implement a godly discipline. This was consistent with the devotional spirit within Puritanism which found expression in the careful record of evils committed and of divine retribution —Prynne had contributed a preface to a pamphlet by Burton which had traced God's judgment upon Sabbath-breakers. The classic exposition of this theme was Thomas Beard's *The Theatre of Gods Judgements*. In 1631 the third edition of this work had been published, and Prynne quoted from it extensively in *Histriomastix*. Beard must be counted alongside Foxe and Jewel as a formative influence on Prynne. In the preface to his work, Beard explained that the value of history lay in its rescue from oblivion of examples of divine retribution. From Beard, Prynne borrowed exhaustive citations of God's judgments upon sinners and detailed criticism of dancing, plays and other moral abuses.[1]

Ostensibly the most damaging evidence against Prynne was his attack on female actors; in reality, he was most vulnerable in his Beard-like didacticism. From his exhaustive record of actions against ungodly magistrates, the prosecution could infer Prynne's approval of—even incitement to imitate—such actions. Heath pointed out at Prynne's trial that he thus made Emperors responsible for their deaths:

> . . . for to taxe the person of a Kinge to bee infamous for dauncing, or seeinge a maske or playe, and then by examples to give intimacion of the lawfullnes of murthering for the same, a cryme of the highest nature . . .

Now Prynne's only defence could be that he saw Charles I as another Constantine, not as another Nero. This was true—it was evident in his other writings—but it was an empirical, and therefore unconvincing reply. Thus *Histriomastix* could be described in his formal expulsion from Lincoln's Inn as containing 'divers incitements of his people to sedition'; Laud

---

[1] Thomas Beard, *The Theatre of Gods Judgments* (London, 1631), pp. 43–6 and preface. Beard had justified the use of profane writers in so pious a search: a point frequently made against Prynne at his trial (*Documents. . . .*, p. 12). Beard's work is among the list of books presented by Prynne to the Abbey Library, Bath; see the original catalogue of benefactors in Victoria Art Gallery and Municipal Libraries, Bath.

could compare Prynne with Ponet; Heath could say that 'it would have been noe streyne of lawe to have him arraigned for high treason'.[1]

But there was nothing in the arguments put forward at his trial to show that he was engaged in a destructive campaign against ecclesiastical government. His opponents recognized his conservatism, and even turned it against him: Laud invoked Prynne's revered Foxe against him; Noy noted Prynne's praise of Henry VIII's reign; even Prynne's panegyrics on Elizabeth were interpreted as a sneer against the present reign.[2] In the detailed list of charges drawn up against Prynne, there are many examples of wilful wresting of his text: his statement that plays were insufferable in a well-ordered state produced the comment—'Ergo our state not civill ordered'; his statement that the prodigal expense of plays made them intolerable in a Christian, frugal state produced the comment—'Ergo our state not frugall or not Xtian'; his statement that there were more playhouses now than in the time of Nero or Caligula produced the comment—'. . . our King, more vitious than Nero: or the most vitious Catigula'. Although the list is headed—'The Passages against the King and State in *Histriomastix*. Such also as occurre against the Church and Clergie in the same Author'—no attempt is made at all to substantiate the second charge. Even the 'exorbitant passage concerning ecclesiastical government', to which Pagitt referred, is seen later to be innocent of so weighty an inference:

> . . . for I heare he compares the playing on the organs twixt the first and second lesson to Enterludes in Stage-playes . . .[3]

Prynne's references to the Church in *Histriomastix* reveal, once more, the moderate. He cited Hooker and Hall against the Brownists' arguments that episcopacy was wholly corrupt. He pointed out that although 'we all condemne them' for their

[1] *Documents* . . ., pp. 18–19; *The Records of the Honorable Society of Lincoln's Inn. The Black Books* (London, 1898), p. 317.
[2] (Bodl. Lib.) Douce MSS. 173, f. 6v; (P.R.O.) S.P. 16/534, f. 152. Prynne, *Histriomastix* . . ., p. 834, exempted Foxe—along with Chaucer, Bale, Skelton and a few others—from his strictures against the writers of plays, 'their subjects being al serious, sacred, divine'.
[3] (P.R.O.) S.P. 16/534, f. 147–f. 150v; (B.M.) Harleian MSS. 1026, f. 44v.

radicalism, those who argue that plays should be totally abolished cannot be similarly condemned. Unlike episcopacy, stage plays were wholly vicious and could not have their abuses regulated and reformed within the existing structure.[1]

S. R. Gardiner pointed out that:

> Prynne had made no attack upon the constitution in Church or State. He had merely spoken in rude and intemperate language of amusements patronised by the King.[2]

The rude and intemperate language was insisted upon repeatedly as a major charge against Prynne at his trial, but one critic had the wit to see that soured misanthropy on so generalized a scale robbed the attack of particular application:

> . . . it was fitter to be called *Anthropomastix*; then *Histriomastix*, the scourge of mankind rather than the Kings sacred person . . .[3]

An inelegant style and a jaundiced view of humanity were not, in themselves, direct criticisms of episcopacy.

Laud had his revenge: Prynne was imprisoned for life, fined £5,000, and lost both his ears in the pillory. On 11 June 1634, Prynne sent a protest to Laud against this sentence. On 16 June, Laud sent the letter to the Attorney-General. On 17 June, the Attorney-General challenged Prynne with this document. According to the Attorney-General, Prynne said that he could not tell if it were his unless he read it. Once he had obtained possession of the document, he tore it into small pieces and threw it out of the window. This was one writing of his which —as he himself said—'should never rise in judgment against hime'.[4]

But there were other writings to rise in judgment against him. Although he was imprisoned in the Tower of London, he continued to smuggle out pamphlets. Laud became convinced that Prynne was engaged in an active intrigue with two fellow Puritans, John Bastwick and Henry Burton.

Their backgrounds had little in common. Bastwick, a nomadic and peripheral figure, had studied at Emmanuel College, Cambridge, without taking a degree; served as a soldier in the

---

[1] Prynne, *Histriomastix* . . ., pp. 38–9.
[2] S. R. Gardiner, *History of the Great Civil War* (London, 1901), vii, p. 333.
[3] (Bodl. Lib.) Douce MSS. 173, f. 14.     [4] *Documents* . . ., p. 57.

Dutch Army; studied medicine at Padua; and had begun his most serious controversies against the Laudians only four years before his trial in 1637. Burton, on the other hand, had graduated from St. John's College, Cambridge; had been Clerk of the Closet to Prince Charles; had lost that appointment in 1625; had resisted Laudian encroachments from that date onwards; and had met with governmental disapproval on two occasions before 1637. Their contemporaries' readiness to see in the three figures, the personification of Law, Medicine and Gospel, was as much a pointer to their disparate backgrounds as to the catholicity of the opposition to Laud.[1]

Burton was as ready as Prynne to attack the doctrinal innovations of a Mountague and the ceremonial innovations of a Cosin. In some respects, however, he went further than Prynne: he attacked Mainwaring and the court divines; he was sceptical of Hall and the worth of moderate bishops in general; he came near to resistance theories, as Heylyn noted. Both attacked the *iure divino* claim, but to Burton the evil actions of bishops mattered more than the title under which they did them; to Prynne, the evil actions were the necessary consequence of the false constitutional principles. Thus Burton, in 1636, could deny, like Prynne had done, that the King was implicated in the bishops' guilt, but could take the argument one step further than Prynne. He considered what would happen if the King were implicated in their guilt:

> . . . For the Power that is in the King is given unto him by God, and confirmed by the Lawes of the Kingdome. Now neither God in his Law, nor the Lawes of the land, doe allow the King a power to alter the State of Religion, or to oppresse and Suppresse the faithfull Ministers of the Gospell, against both Law and Conscience . . .[2]

This came as close as any statement in 1636 to an apology for resistance. Although hypothetical, it represented an advance upon anything which Prynne contributed to the subject. Another mark of Burton's bolder approach was his willingness, even in the thirties, to emphasize the shortcomings of the

---

[1] John Bastwick, *The Confession of the Faithfull Witnesse of Christ* . . . (London, 1641); Henry Burton, *A Narration* . . . (London, 1643); D. Lloyd, *Memoires* . . . (London, 1668), p. 137.

[2] Burton, *An Apology of an Appeale* . . . (London, 1636), p. 72.

martyr-bishops, such as Cranmer and Ridley. To Prynne, on the other hand, they were irreproachable: they had fired his imagination first in the pages of Foxe and could never be quite human again.

Burton was never really close to Prynne. During the Civil War they quarrelled, and Burton tried to appease Prynne with memories of former friendship. Even so he was forced to admit that they had met rarely: 'more frequent had it been, had your occasions, and sometimes mine own, permitted.'[1] A barrier to intimacy lay in their attitude to bishops: although Burton did not openly express Independent views until 1641 he had clearly gone much further than Prynne in his criticism of episcopacy.

Prynne had a Corvo-like appetite for quarrels. Bastwick was one of the few persons with whom he did not quarrel—despite a profound disagreement in 1645. When Bastwick died in 1654, Prynne honoured his memory by making public a protest against the imposition of an excise on hops: his appeal to the spirit of 'my dearly-beloved Christian Brother, and fellow sufferer, for Religion and Liberties' is one of the finest passages that Prynne ever wrote.[2] Bastwick was the most attractive figure of the triumvirate that opposed Laud: Prynne was too solemn, Burton was too pliant. Bastwick, on the other hand, had an indomitable sense of fun. When he explained in 1645 how he had come to write tracts against Laud, he said that an old man had asked him to write for the people. Bastwick said that he was hard put to it to think of a theme. Write against bishops, the old man counselled, for he could not endure them. Bastwick thought it over for a while, bearing in mind that the old man was a cheerful, pleasant soul. Eventually he produced his *Letany*, which when the old man heard it, 'made him laugh as if hee had been tickled, so that I never saw a man more pleasant'.[3] The raconteur's frivolity was as alien to the high-mindedness of Tew as it was to the fanaticism of Prynne. Clarendon saw Prynne as a man to be taken seriously. With some insight, he described a nature which has been distorted by too uncritical a zeal for reading and by too susceptible an

---

[1] Burton, *A Vindication of Churches Commonly Called Independent* . . . (London, 1644), p. 44.

[2] Prynne, *A Declaration and Protestation* . . . (London, 1654), p. 28.

[3] Bastwick, *A Just Defence* . . . (London, 1645), p. 11.

association with divines. Prynne's gravity took some of the edge from his fanaticism for Clarendon; Bastwick's flippancy was a more serious barrier to a sympathetic understanding, and Clarendon dismissed him as a 'half-witted, crack-brained fellow . . . with some wit and much malice'.[1] But Clarendon was wrong to dismiss Bastwick as a lightweight, because his tone was light; in principle, though not in temperament, Bastwick was at one with Prynne in the period before the Civil War.

Bastwick concentrated his attack, like Prynne, upon the *iure divino* claims of the Laudians. Like Prynne, he professed reverence for the 'Kings Bishops', who remained content with the Tudor imperial claims. In 1645 he claimed that his advocacy of Presbyterianism was 'no new opinion of mine, but that which I have once and again suffered for'. Bastwick believed that a study of his earlier writings would reveal that 'the cause of all my sufferings was this, and this only, That I maintained that all Churches were to be governed by an Aristocraticall and Presbyterian government'.[2] His earlier writings do not support this claim. He was not a radical in the Burton sense: he continually championed *iure humano* episcopacy; he praised the moderate bishops; he shared Prynne's interest in the Laudians' legal excesses. On the other hand, he was not so convincing a moderate as Prynne. He made a sentimental reference to 'the old Puritans of England', but there was not the same dependence upon the moderate nonconformist traditions of Foxe and Reynolds as could be detected in Prynne's writings. Instead, when he named a formative influence upon his thought he spoke of Richard Rogers: an intimate of Cartwright, who had signed the Book of Discipline, and who had been an enthusiast for the classical organization. Moreover, Leighton—who was one of the few 'root and branch' advocates among English Puritans before the Civil War—also named 'that Honourable Protomartyr Mr. Rogers' as a decisive influence on his advocacy of a total reformation.[3] Bastwick saw the martyrs' warts with a

---

[1] Clarendon, *The History of the Rebellion* . . ., ed. W. Macray, (Oxford, 1888), i, pp. 265–6.

[2] Bastwick, *Independency Not Gods Ordinance* . . . (London, 1645), p. 6.

[3] Bastwick, *The Second Part of That Book* . . . (London, 1645), preface; Alexander Leighton, *An Appeal to the Parliament* . . . (London, 1628), p. 158.

clarity which was denied to Prynne. He had served in the Dutch Army, and Thomas Raymond emphasized the impetus which his writings had given to ecclesiastical radicalism in Amsterdam, when he condemned 'that filthy, dirty, rayling piece of Bastwicks'. The prosecution in 1637 alleged, against Bastwick but not against Burton and Prynne, seditious activity in Scotland and the encouragement of Presbyterianism there.[1] Therefore Bastwick's claim that Presbyterianism was his real aim, may be true, even though his claim, that this is clearly expressed in his early pamphlets, is not. At least it makes possible the view that, in his concern for the rights of the civil magistrate and his faith in a moderate episcopacy, Bastwick may have been disingenuous in a way which Prynne was not.

Burton asked in 1645 how it had come about that 'my two fellow-sufferers and myselfe, should fall at this odds'.[2] Yet later differences were discernible even in the thirties. All three professed moderation: Prynne meant it, Bastwick may have meant it, Burton did not mean it—and confessed so later. Laud did not discriminate between them. In a letter to Hall, on 11 November 1639, he spoke of 'the furious Aerian heretics, out of which are now raised Prynne, Bastwick and our Scottish masters'. In the framing of the charges against them in 1637 collusion was assumed with little factual basis. At their trial, Anthony Marshall alleged that Burton had often been admitted to the Tower of London to talk with Prynne, and that Bastwick 'often had consultation with Burton at his house in Friday Street' about the printing of *Newes from Ipswich*.[3] But direct evidence of collaboration was not forthcoming, although Prynne contributed prefaces to works by Bastwick and Burton.[4] On the joint authorship of *Newes from Ipswich*, Clarendon said that the three 'found some means in prison of correspondence which was not before known to be between them', but cited no evidence to support his claim. In their later controversial conflicts, nostalgic reference was made by all three to the time of their

---

[1] *The Autobiography of Thomas Raymond* . . . (Camden Society, iii, xxviii), pp. 32–3; (P.R.O.) S.P. 16/538, f. 99; (B.M.) Add. MSS. 11308, f. 100.

[2] Burton, *Vindiciae Veritatis* . . . (London, 1645), p. 2.

[3] *Cal. S.P. Dom. Charles I, 1639–40*, pp. 87–8; H.M.C., *4th. Report*, p. 233.

[4] John Bastwick, *Flagellum Pontificis* . . . (London, 1635); Henry Burton, *A Divine Tragedie* . . . (London, 1636).

common antipathies and sufferings—'a threefold concord, not easily broken'—but not to active collaboration. In the absence of more direct evidence, Laud was reduced to collecting extracts from Burton's sermons with legal touches which seemed to indicate the hand of Prynne.[1]

Prynne's second trial in 1637 produced no further evidence that he was dedicated to the overthrow of episcopacy. There was so little direct evidence offered against him, that he could say with justice that 'there is no booke layd to my charge'.[2] Apart from the vague charges of collusion, the most serious accusation that Prynne faced was the authorship of the pamphlet, *Newes from Ipswich*.[3] It is still not clear whether he did write it. The subject-matter revealed the same concern for conditions in East Anglia under Wren's episcopate which Burton was expressing in sermons at this time—Heylyn noted this point— but the language and marginal references smack of Prynne.[4] On the other hand, the pamphlet has a wit and brevity more characteristic of Bastwick. The external evidence is equally unsatisfactory: at the trial, Bastwick strongly denied authorship; so did Burton in 1644—when nothing was at stake; Prynne did not cite it in a long list of his ecclesiastical writings in 1643.[5] Sir John Bramston attributed it to Prynne; Heylyn and Dow, to Burton.[6] It is possible that the work may not represent the sole effort of any one of the three, but may be the

[1] Clarendon, op. cit., i, p. 267; *Cal. S.P. Dom. Charles I, 1637*, p. 48.

[2] Prynne, *A New Discovery of the Prelates Tyranny* (London, 1641), p. 15.

[3] For the collective guilt charged by the Attorney-General in his information at the trial, see (P.R.O.) S.P. 16/534, f. 392v; for his reiteration of points brought previously against Prynne from *Histriomastix . . .*, see (B.M.) Add. MSS. 11308, f. 102.

[4] Benjamin Hanbury, *Historical Memorials* (London, 1839), i, pp. 554–5; Heylyn, *Cyprianus Anglicus . . .* (London, 1668), p. 309.

[5] Prynne, *A New Discovery . . . .*, pp. 18–19; Burton, *A Vindication . . .* (London, 1644), pp. 71–2; Prynne, *The Popish Royall Favourite . . .* (London, 1643), pp. 35–6. The pamphlet is not included in the first catalogue of his works drawn up by Prynne's publisher, though it appears in the second catalogue. See: *A Catalogue of Printed Books* (London, 1643); *An Exact Catalogue . . .* (London, 1660), p. 2.

[6] *The Autobiography of Sir John Bramston* (Camden Society, First Series, xxxii), p. 69; Heylyn, *A Briefe and Moderate Answer* (London, 1637), p. 15; Christopher Dow, *Innovations Unjustly Charged Upon the Present Church and State* (London, 1637), pp. 12, 13.

product of collusion between them, or even the work of a fourth person, either acting upon their instructions or, more indirectly, inspired by their writings.

The Laudians were determined to destroy the Puritans: all three were sentenced to the loss of their ears in 1637. An additional refinement of cruelty for Prynne was the carving of the initials 'S.L.' across his cheeks. To Laud, they stood for 'Seditious Libeller'; to Prynne, 'Stigma of Laud'—the most pardonable pun in English history. Legends proliferated about Prynne's ears. To the Puritans, a miracle had taken place: his ears had been cut off in 1634, but God had made them grow again. The Laudians were more prosaic in their explanation: the ears had been lightly cropped the first time, but this time there was to be no opportunity for miracles. One writer, Rossingham, believed that Prynne had offered the hangman five shillings 'to use him kindly the time before', and that Prynne had not kept his bond. Afterwards he had given the hangman only five sixpences. If this is true, it is an unusual illustration of the correlation between Calvinism and the acquisitive instinct—and one with disastrous consequences for Prynne. As Rossingham remarked, after the second execution: 'nowe the hangman was quitt with him'.[1]

These stories illustrate the powerful hold which the executions had upon the minds of ordinary people. They inflamed indignation in a way which previous cruelties had not—including Prynne's recent punishment, and Leighton's only a few years further back. The humiliation of Law, Gospel and Medicine served as a paradigm of the isolation of the Laudian régime. Prynne wrote a full account of his sufferings which, when published in 1641, intensified the agitation against Laud. Prynne described how the executioner heated his iron very hot, and burnt one of his cheeks twice. After this, he cut one of his ears so close that he cut off a piece of Prynne's cheek too, and cut him deep in the neck, near the jugular vein. Then, hacking the other ear until it was almost off, he kept it hanging and went down from the scaffold. He was called back by the surgeon, who made him perform a complete amputation. Prynne described his response:

---

[1] *Documents* . . ., p. 87.

At which exquisit torture he never moved with his body, or so much as changed his countenance, but still lookt up as well as he could towards Heaven, with a smiling countenance, even to the astonishment of all the beholders. And uttered (as soon as the Executioners had done) this heavenly sentence: 'The more I am beat down, the more am I lift up.'[1]

Such language could find ready response in men who had been reared on Foxe. Rossingham wrote that 'at the cutting of each eare there was such a roaringe as if every one of them had at the same instant lost an eare'.

On 27 July 1637, Sir Kenelm Digby complained that fewer people would come to see the King and Queen then than those who had flocked a week earlier to see the three victims of Laud. Nor, he wrote, would there be 'such venerations as the Puritans keep the bloody sponges and handkerchiefs that did the hangman service in the cutting off their ears'. As a good Catholic, he added: 'You may see how Nature leads men to respect relics of martyrs.' And when Prynne was banished to seclusion in the Channel Islands from 1637 to 1640, his journey from London became, to Laud's chagrin, something of a triumphal march. Contemporary literature abounds in references to the sufferings: evidence of the powerful emotional response which they had excited. The woman who named her cats, Prynne, Burton and Bastwick, and then cut off their ears was certainly crazed, but in another sense symbolized only in an extreme form the interest aroused by the sufferings. Poor Nehemiah Wallingford shows how the knowledge of these sufferings could stiffen the resolve of a timorous nature. He was in trouble with the authorities for having had in his possession one of the seditious pamphlets. His was a minor offence—and the punishment would not be severe—but this was no consolation to Nehemiah. Yet whenever he felt broken, he remembered the ordeals of Prynne, Burton and Bastwick:

It made me rejoice that I was partakers of Saints Sufferings, it made me to pray more often and more fervently.[2]

---

[1] Prynne, *A New Discovery* . . . no pagination.
[2] *Documents* . . ., p. 87; *Cal, S.P. Dom, Charles I, 1637*, p. 332; (Guildhall Library) MSS. 204, Nehemiah Wallingford, *Mercies of God* . . ., f. 270 et seq.

Prynne became the symbol of radical aspirations almost by accident: his writings remained resolutely moderate. Even if he wrote *Newes from Ipswich*, he was still no radical. Anthony Wood was alienated by some of the epithets used against bishops in that pamphlet, but even he recognized that it was limited in its application to the clique around Bishop Wren.[1] In other words, the pamphlet would still have been compatible with his general attitude, best epitomized in the concluding words of another pamphlet, which called for 'the extirpation of that generation of vipers, which hath long been gnawing out their owne mothers bowels'.[2] In his fight against vipers, whom he had identified more consistently than any other pamphleteer as the direct enemies of Church and Crown, Prynne could claim to be both a staunch Royalist and a loyal Anglican; never more so than when he was abusing the vipers.

That Laud and his sympathizers should fail to see Prynne as a moderate conservative is hardly surprising. Magnanimity could hardly stretch to an understanding of their opponent's identification of themselves as 'vipers'. Yet the cause of misunderstanding lay at an even deeper level. Laud had genuine reason to doubt professions of loyalty to the established church by opponents. In the pamphleteering against Laud at this period, only rarely—in a writer such as Leighton—is a direct attack made upon episcopacy. In part this is to be explained by the survival of old traditions of moderate nonconformity into the thirties, but this is only one half of the explanation, and not necessarily the more important half. There was a genuine radical feeling which was never fully expressed in the pamphlets, but which cloaked itself in an attack upon abuses within the Church. The politic need for moderation was well expressed by some ministers in 1642 when they published posthumously the earlier sermons of John Ball. They acknowledged that his nonconformity seemed to be directed far more against separatists than against Anglicans, but pointed out that 'the state of the times wherein this piece was penned would not brooke more plainnesse'.[3] Prynne and Burton both claimed to

---

[1] Anthony Wood, *Athenae Oxonienses* . . ., iii, p. 847; H.M.C. *4th. Report*, p. 292.    [2] Prynne, *A Quench-Coale* . . ., p. 320.

[3] John Ball, *An Answer to Two Treatises of Mr. John Can* (London, 1642), preface.

41

be fighting in the thirties against the bishops' excesses, not against their office, but their difference in motive emerged in 1644. Prynne then claimed that:

> . . . none of us suffered for opposing, writing or speaking against the Bishops legall authority . . . but only against their pretended divine right to their Episcopall Lordly power.[1]

Burton, in his reply, could have taken refuge in the traditional Independent apology for earlier backsliding of a 'progressive comprehension'.[2] Instead, to his credit, he acknowledged that only politic considerations had restrained him from the real attack upon episcopacy itself, not merely its abuses.[3] Moderation was, for Burton, a pose; for Prynne, a principle. Criticism of Prynne's position from 1641 to 1644 can focus upon his failure to sustain that principle, but not upon a discrepancy then between his words and his deeds. That Laud should regard the moderate professions of each as equally meaningless was understandable, but erroneous.

Prynne attacked cant whenever he came across it: one reason for his hatred of plays was that acting required men 'to seeme that in outward which they are not in truthe'.[4] When searching through Laud's papers during the Civil War, Prynne found two letters from John Durie in 1634 pleading for reordination at the hands of an Anglican bishop. Prynne published the letters in 1650 to denote his contempt for a 'conscience . . . tender, yet stretching, and mutable with times and preferment'. Samuel Hartlib's defence of Durie—'the difference of times, and what a change all things have been under since the year 1634'—was directed along lines singularly abhorrent to Prynne.[5] Similarly, Prynne found among Laud's papers Hugh Peter's submission of 17 August 1627. Peter's recent biographer, R. P. Stearns, acknowledged that it was a 'weasel-worded document', but defended this Independent trait:

[1] Prynne, *A Full Reply* . . . (London, 1644), p. 7.
[2] For an explanation of the significance of this term, see: A. S. P. Woodhouse, *Puritanism and Liberty* (London, 1950), p. (45), n. 1.
[3] Burton, *A Vindication* . . . (London, 1644), p. 72.
[4] Prynne, *Histriomastix* . . ., p. 159.
[5] Prynne, *The Time-Serving Proteus and Ambidexter Divine* (London, 1650), p. 2; John Durie, *The Unchanged, Constant and Single-Hearted Peacemaker* (London, 1650), Introduction.

It was the price they paid out of their consciences for the opportunity to reform the English Church in their own fashion.

To Prynne, the price would have been too high in terms of personal integrity and he published the recantation in full, with the comment:

> If Master Peter be now of another Judgement, it manifests either his grosse ignorance or temporizing then, or his levity now, and that he is as unsteady in his opinion, as in excentric motion from place to place.[1]

Prynne attacked the Independent notion of the 'new light' as a justification for change in policy. Ironically, those were the terms in which the bogus retraction of his *Histriomastix*, published in 1649, defended his supposed change of attitude:

> ... it was when I had not so clear a light as now I have; and it is no disparagement for any man to alter his judgment upon better information ...[2]

In fact, Prynne's Calvinistic regard for constancy as a divine attribute and a worthy human aspiration led him into a retrospective attempt to impose upon his earlier actions a logic and consistency which were not always there. This was as much self-deception as deception of others. But his hatred of hypocrisy was deep-rooted enough to protect him from the profession of the politic falsehood. It was an opponent who said of him:

> I am confident that whatsoever Mr. P. writeth (though I approve not all that is set out in his name) he writeth with a very upright and sincere heart ...[3]

Prynne's belief in a moderate episcopacy was sincere, rooted as it was in a philosophical acceptance of Foxe and Jewel and in a sentimental acceptance of the value of ancient traditions. Milton had said of Camden that he loved bishops as he loved old coins—for antiquity's sake.[4] The same was true at this period of Prynne.

[1] R. P. Stearns, *The Strenuous Puritan: Hugh Peter, 1598–1660* (Urbana, 1954), p. 43; Prynne, *A Fresh Discovery* ... (London, 1645), p. 33.
[2] (Anon.), *Mr. William Prynne his Defence of Stage-Plays* ... (London, 1649), p. 5.
[3] John Ley, *The New Querie* (London, 1645), p. 46.
[4] Milton, *Of Reformation* ..., p. 17.

Towards the end of Elizabeth's reign Cartwright, in the course of polemical exchanges with Archbishop Whitgift, had moved to a more radical position which had greater affinity with clerical Scottish Presbyterianism than with the traditions of English nonconformity. The Laudians, in attacking Prynne as the spiritual descendant of Cartwright, betrayed their misunderstanding of him. Giles Widdowes acknowledged that 'Puritan' was a generic and misleading term, but went on to attack Prynne through an attack upon Cartwright's theocratic views. Peter Heylyn directly linked Prynne, the admirer of the Elizabethan Church, with its radical critics, who 'had as evil will to the church as he, and spread abroad amongst that party in Queene Elizabeths time'.[1] Yet, in the controversy between Whitgift and Cartwright, Prynne's sympathies were wholly with the Anglican who defended the rights of the civil magistrate, and who pleaded against clericalism for episcopacy *iure humano*. Prynne defined Puritans as those who 'maintaine the Kings Ecclesiasticall Prerogative', and claimed Whitgift as 'in this very point ane arrant Puritane'.[2] When Prynne argued that Scripture laid down no immutable form of church government, John Goodwin pointed out that he was in the Anglican tradition and quite distinct from Cartwright. Prynne directly referred to Cartwright in a discussion on excommunication as an 'Opposite', which drew an eloquent rebuke from the Presbyterian, George Gillespie:

> . . . And are the old non-Conformists of blessed memory, now Opposites? Where are we? I confess as he now stands-affected, he is opposite to the old non-Conformists, and they to him.

But Richard Baxter agreed with Prynne in repudiating the ancestry of Cartwright for English nonconformity. When Prynne attacked Cosin's ceremonial innovations, he pointed to the encouragement which they gave to those critics of the Church who dismissed her as degenerate. He named the critics —'Papists, Brownists, Anabaptists, Separatists, and Nonconformists'—and said that such excesses

---

[1] Giles Widdowes, *The Schismatical Puritane* (Oxford, 1631), preface; Peter Heylyn, *A Briefe and Moderate Answer . . .*, p. 12.

[2] Prynne, *A Breviate of the Prelates Intollerable Usurpations . . .* (London, 1637), pp. 122–4.

. . . hath caused many, both now and heretofore [a marginal note refers the reader to 'Master Cartwright against Whitgift'] to disaffect the Discipline, and Government of our Church: and to condemne not only the persons, vices . . . but even the very calling of our Bishops (which is in it selfe Honourable, Lawfull, Good and usefull in the Church; especially, if it be rightly managed:) as Antichristian, and repugnant to the word of God, both to their own, and our shame and scandall . .[1]

Laudianism explained but did not excuse separatism.

Alexander Leighton was the outstanding exception to the moderation—real or assumed—of Laud's opponents. Almost alone among them, he sustained the Cartwright tradition in an attack upon episcopacy itself. Inevitably, Prynne's name was bracketed with his. In 1637 the Reverend George Garrard referred to 'the cropt libellers' and then wrote of 'Dr. Leighton who is *homo eiusdem farinae*'; in 1640 Sir William Calley wrote of 'their cases being not much unlike'; Heylyn drove home the identification closer still:

. . . how have both Church and State been exercised by those factious Spirits, Layton, and Prynne, and Bastwick, with H. Burton the Dictator.[2]

In reality, Leighton stood for everything to which Prynne was opposed—in the period before 1641. Leighton opposed episcopacy, whether the warrant was *iure divino* or *iure humano*; he defended Cartwright and attacked the moderate Anglicans, in whom Prynne had placed his trust, such as Whitgift, Downame and Morton; he attacked the authority of the martyr-bishops and the prestige of Constantine and Elizabeth as Christian Emperors.[3] No wonder a supporter of the Royal Supremacy in ecclesiastical matters welcomed the punishment of the theocratic Leighton as a demonstration of the power of

[1] John Goodwin, *A Moderate Answer* . . . (London, 1645), p. 5; Prynne, *A Vindication of Four Serious Questions* . . . (London, 1645), p. 7; George Gillespie, *Aarons Rod Blossoming* . . . (London, 1646), p. 585; (Doctor Williams's Library) Baxter MSS. 59.2, f. 218v–219; Prynne, *A Briefe Survey* . . . (London, 1628), p. 83.
[2] *Cal. S.P. Dom. Charles I, 1637*, p. 344; *Cal. S.P. Dom Charles I, 1640–1641*, p. 312; Heylyn, *A Briefe and Moderate Answer* . . ., p. 5.
[3] Alexander Leighton, *An Appeal to the Parliament* . . . (London, 1628), pp. 3, 8, 24, 28, 80, 88, 111, 72, 153.

the Crown! Similarly, Prynne was unsympathetic towards Leighton, despite their mutual sufferings, because he was aware of this distance between them. Thomas Fuller, an Anglican critic perspicacious enough to note the moderation of Prynne's early writings—'he began with the writing of some useful and orthodox books'—observed that Prynne's record of the trial of Laud ignored the Archbishop's severity against Leighton 'chiefly because . . . his faults were of so high a nature, none then or since dare appear in his defence'.[1] Prynne was equally reluctant to emphasize the Leighton case in his pamphlets against Laud. Yet Leighton's sufferings in 1630 were a dramatic prologue to his own in 1634 and 1637. Prynne only mentioned Leighton's punishment to throw into relief the much greater severity used upon the later victims. His lack of sympathy with Leighton was one more expression of his moderation.[2]

In the catalogue of Prynne's works, published at the Restoration, a Biblical text was appended:

Of making many Books there is no end, and much study, (or reading) is a werisomnesse to the flesh.

Across his copy Anthony Wood heartlessly added: 'And Ears.' An anonymous satirist suggested, in 1659, that a special place should be reserved in the Westminster Assembly for 'sacred Reliques of Well-affected Persons in the Commonwealth'; high among his list of suggestions were 'the flappets of Mr. William Prynn's Eares'.[3] It was only possible at a later date for both writers to discount Prynne's sufferings in this laconic manner. At both the actual time of execution, and for a considerable time afterwards, they were regarded as a vital impetus to radicalism. The return of Prynne and his colleagues from exile; the investigation of the Commons into the proceedings against them; Prynne's detailed account of their sufferings: all these had in 1641 a calculated inflammatory effect so that an opponent could rightly call them a 'prognosticall Prologue to

---

[1] (Bodl. Lib.) Selden MSS. Supra 108, f. 97; Thomas Fuller, *The Church History of Britain* . . ., ed. J. Brewer (Oxford, 1845), vi, pp. 112, 67.

[2] Prynne, *A New Discovery* . . ., pp. 186–90.

[3] (Bodl. Lib.) Wood MSS. D. 22, f. 2; (Anon.), *Eighteen New Court-Queries* (London, 1659), p. 5.

something like our Tragicall Warre'. A cavalier journal complained in 1648 that the Civil War might have been averted if the punishment of the three conspirators had not been so maladroitly handled. Another compared bitterly the apathy with which the injustices to the King had been received with the atmosphere when Prynne, Burton and Bastwick had been sent to prison—

the whole Kingdome was alarmed with cryes of Injustice.[1]

No analysis of Prynne's position can ignore his sufferings: the slicing of ears, at the very least, would seem a challenge to his hopes for moderation. It is important to realize that Prynne did not see his sufferings in that light: that, at least until 1641, his belief in moderation survived even the test of the executioner's knife. Although his sufferings, and his account of them, helped to strengthen radical ecclesiastical tendencies by giving them a powerful emotive focus, Prynne did not value his activities for that reason. True, he wished to inflame public anger against Laud and his associates, but it was still in service of the moderate episcopacy which he revered. The violence inflicted on him by the prelates may have intensified the rancour of his attack, but did not alter its nature; if he somewhat self-consciously saw in these sufferings a re-enactment of Foxe's history, he did not forget the philosophical framework in which Foxe's history was set. He did not broaden the range of his attack to embrace all bishops in his anger; instead, in the very speech which he made at the execution of his sentence, he went out of his way to emphasize the distinction between the Laudians and the moderate bishops:

And yet the next (for ought I know) that is to follow us and receive a Censure in Starre-Chamber, is like to be a Bishop.[2]

[1] (Anon.), *The Fallacies of Mr. William Prynne* . . . (Oxford, 1644), p. 33; *Mercurius Pragmaticus*, Numb. 18, January 11–18, 1648; *Mercurius Melancholicus*, Numb. 1, December 25, 1648–January 1, 1649.

[2] Prynne, *A New Discovery* . . ., pp. 43–4. This was not mere rhetoric: he probably had John Williams specifically in mind. Robert Woodford noted in his diary for 2nd September 1637 that 'I heare from London today that the Bishop of Lincoln is like to loose his head the next tearme; and its said Mr. Prinne is or shall be sent for the next tearme to dye': H.M.C., *9th. Report*, ii, p. 496. Cf. *Diary of John Rous*, ed. M. Green (Camden Society, 1855), p. 37, for Puritan gossip on this topic.

Henry Parker believed that in nothing were the Laudians more disingenuous than in their fear of Prynne as a dangerous revolutionary. He ridiculed their fear of 'paper machinations':

> ... the more few Puritans remayned, and the more moderately those few became inclined, the more furiously their enemies raged against them. Bastwick, Prin and Burton the onely men which Law can take hold of, are Names now as horrid in the world as Garnet, Faux, Ravilliack.[1]

[1] Henry Parker, *A Discourse Concerning Puritans* ... (London, 1641), p. 7.

# III

# PRYNNE JOINS THE RADICALS

In November, 1640, Prynne was recalled from exile. Robert Woodford described the fantastic scenes in London:

> Oh, blessed be the Lord for this day! This day those holy living Martyrs Mr. Burton and Mr. Prynne came to towne and the Lord's providence brought me out of the Temple to see them. My heart rejoiceth in the Lord for this day; its even like the returne of the captivity from Babilon. There went to meet them about 1500 or 2000 horsemen, and about 100 coaches, and the streets were all thronged with people, and there was very great rejoicing.[1]

Woodford's heart rejoiced in the Lord for this day of triumph, but not all his colleagues were equally pious or equally complacent. Laudianism had perished, but what was to take its place? Two men in particular were watching the movements of Prynne with interest: Robert Baillie and John Williams. Both had opposed Laud, but from different motives. Baillie was a Presbyterian zealot from Glasgow, who had been sent to London in 1640 to draw up accusations against Laud. He wanted to see a classical discipline on the Scottish model established in England. Williams, Bishop of Lincoln, had been opposed to Laud before 1640: he had been charged in Star Chamber in 1628 with betraying the secrets of the privy council and in 1635 with subornation of perjury; he had been suspended from the exercise of his function in 1637 and had been imprisoned in the Tower of London from 1637 to 1640. He became the focal point of compromise in 1640; he was the

[1] H.M.C., *9th Report*, ii, p. 499. Other excited comments are to be found in: (B.M.) Add. MSS. 38490, f. 10; H.M.C. *12th Report*, i. p. 10; *Cal. S.P. Dom., Charles I, 1637*, pp. 252, 287, 311; Strafford, op. cit., ii, pp. 99, 115, 119.

natural leader of all who wished to repudiate Laudianism, but not Anglicanism. Prynne had never shown sympathy for Scottish clericalism; in this he differed from Bastwick and Burton. But he was widely regarded as an apostle of violence, and he had suffered appallingly at the hands of Anglicans. Both Baillie and Williams were anxious to bind this popular martyr to their cause, and both had grounds for hope. One of Baillie's first instructions to his fellow-Presbyterian, Alexander Cunningham, in 1640, was to 'try the present estate' of Prynne and his colleagues; one of Prynne's first actions on his return from exile was to have consultation with Williams.[1]

The differences between the rival positions emerge clearly from the pamphlets and speeches of the period. First, there is a clear repudiation from the Anglicans of the Laudian *iure divino* claims for episcopacy. The repudiation was almost total; moderation had become respectable. Baillie commented with disgust on the changed temper of Anglican divines: 'who yesterday did rage like Lyons, today take upon them the skin of the meekest lambs.'[2] Only the luckless Joseph Hall was out of step: a lamb in the thirties—Mountague had called him a Puritan—he roared like a lion at a time when Laud was languishing in a cell. His claim that episcopacy existed by divine right was at variance with the Anglican efforts at compromise, expressed through plans associated with Nicholas, Usher and Williams' Committee.[3] Laud's faithful biographer, Peter Heylyn, tried to explain away Hall's lack of support in 1640:

> For whilest the humbly Reverend Remonstrant was pleased to vindicate as well his owne as the Churches honour, there was

[1] Robert Baillie, *Letters and Journals* . . . ., ed. D. Laing (Edinburgh, 1841), i, p. 226; Peter Heylyn, *Cyprianus Anglicus* (London, 1668), pp. 464–5.

[2] Robert Baillie, *The Unlawfulnesse and Danger of a Limited Episcopacie* . . . (London, 1641), p. 2.

[3] Hall defended the *iure divino* claim in three pamphlets: *Episcopacy by Divine Right* . . . (London, 1640); *An Humble Remonstrance* . . . (London, 1640); *A Defence of the Humble Remonstrance* . . . (London, 1641). The Anglican efforts at compromise are described respectively in: *Cal. S.P. Dom. Charles I, 1640–1641*, pp. 484–5; W. A. Shaw, *A History of the English Church, 1640–60* (London, 1900), i, pp. 70–3; Thomas Lathbury, *A History of the Convocation of the Church of England* (London, 1853), p. 261.

small cause, or rather none, that other men should interpose themselves at all, or robbe him of the glory of a sole encounter . . .[1]

According to Heylyn, only a keen sense of chivalry had silenced the supporters of Laud. His apology did not disarm the more sceptical critics, but it was important as testimony, from a sympathizer, of Hall's isolation.

The fiercest attacks on Hall came from Anglicans; the men who favoured 'root and branch' were ambivalent in their attitude to him.[2] The 'rooters' were anxious to condemn episcopacy but, with hopes of a *iure divino* Presbyterian discipline, were anxious to avoid condemnation of the *iure divino* claim itself. To turn from them to their Jacobean predecessors, who had attacked views similar to Hall's in bishops like Barlow and Downame, is to be made aware of the distance between the radicals of 1640–1 and the earlier nonconformists in their attitude to the civil magistrate. The sermons preached before the Commons between 1640 and 1642 by 'root and branch' ministers do not argue a different interpretation. Mrs. Kirby thought they did: that the ministers' professions of respect for the magistrate indicated that 'the tone of the sermons was then, Erastian'.[3] But the great Erastian, Thomas Coleman, was aware in 1646 of the fallacy of accepting these professions at their face value. He quoted extravagant assertions about the nature of magistracy from the sermons of ministers such as Hill, Wilson, Burges, Marshall, Spurstow and Palmer, culminating in a panegyric on monarchy from Thomas Case. Coleman noted that this was Erastianism, 'a step higher than

[1] Heylyn, *The Historie of Episcopacie* . . . (London, 1642), preface.

[2] For fierce Anglican attacks on Hall, see (Anon.), *An Anti-Remonstrance* . . . (London, 1640), pp. 3, 4, 7; George Morley, *A Modest Advertisement Concerning the Present Controversie About Church-Government*, (London, 1641), p. 19; Edward Dering, *Collection of Speeches* . . . (London, 1641), pp. 57, 111, 125. For ambivalent radical comments, see: Smectymnuus, *An Answer to a Booke entitled, An Humble Remonstrance* . . . (London, 1641), p. 63; Alexander Henderson, *The Unlawfulness and Danger of Limited Prelacie* . . . (London, 1641), pp. 1, 8; Henry Burton, *The Protestation Protested* . . . (London, 1641), no pagination; John Milton, *Of Reformation* . . . (London, 1641), p. 47.

[3] E. W. Kirby, 'Sermons before the Commons, 1640–2', *American Historical Review*, xliv, 1938–9, p. 546. Her thesis is criticized more fully by me in an article, 'Episcopacy and a "Godly Discipline", 1641–6', *Journal of Ecclesiastical History*, x, i, April, 1959, pp. 74–89.

ever I or Erastus himself went'. He was right to see, in the identification of Case as an Erastian, the *reductio ad absurdum* of such reasoning:

> . . . But Mr. Gillespy will say, it is well known these are not Erastians in their opinions. I grant it. But what are they in their words? And why is Mr. Gillespy offended at me alone? What? because I preach as I think? for our preachings are the same, but not our opinions.[1]

The preachings in the sermons—apart from what one minister called, with remarkable candour, these 'soft and silken phrases' in praise of the magistrate[2]—do reflect radical opinions at this period: impatience with compromise and stress upon zeal; contempt for the Elizabethan Church and the Emperor Constantine; pressure for a *iure divino* church government and the summoning of a synod of divines to implement God's Word, against the magistrate's wishes if necessary. The moderate Anglicans could, therefore, attack the *iure divino* claim, whether it was made on behalf of bishops or presbyters. Falkland, for instance, readily conceded that bishops did not exist by divine right, but denied that they should be rooted out altogether as diabolical. They existed by the magistrate's favour: their sanction was *iure humano*.[3] The pattern of controversy was clear: the Laudians were attacked by most fellow-Anglicans because they claimed that their office was divine, and by their opponents because it was not.

The second difference between the two groups is in their ascription of guilt. The moderates limited the attack to a small group around Laud and looked to 'good' bishops as a corrective; the radicals insisted that guilt was universal and clung to the office. As one anonymous satirist put it:

> The rest of his Feather that sang the same note
> Confesse they sayd not by heart but by rote . . .
> But now they all Cry and repeat the same thing,
> Good honest men they were mearely drawn in.

Many Anglicans pleaded for the 'good honest men'. In the

---

[1] Thomas Coleman, *Maledicis* . . . (London, 1646), pp. 36–9.
[2] Nathaniel Hardy, *The Arraignment of Licentious Libertie* . . . (London, 1647), dedicatory epistle.
[3] *Speech of Lord Falkland* . . . (London, 1641), p. 14.

debate on the Root and Branch Petition, Rudyerd defined his aim: to 'punish the present offenders and preserve the calling for better men hereafter'. The basis of his hope was the quality of the non-Laudians: 'We have some good bishops still, who doe preach every Lords Day.' In the same debate, Falkland enumerated the charges against the Laudians in the same violent terms as had the ministers in their sermons to the Commons, but with an important rider:

> I wish wee may distinguishe betweene those who have beene carried away with the streame, and those who have been the streame that cary'd them.

He pointed to the staunch Calvinism of many bishops in mitigation. When Morley also made the distinction between 'good' and 'bad' bishops, Baillie objected:

> Those of the Prelates who count themselves most orthodox and innocent, cannot be excused of these crimes, which by their connivence they did foster, and well neere as much promoove by their suffering, as the others who were esteemed more guiltee by their doing.

He asked why it was that they only ever had expressed dissatisfaction with the 'Canterburian Prelats' in private—a point which Henderson also made. When the Scottish Commissioners drew up their grievances against the bishops in 1640, they were at pains to emphasize that the guilt was functional, not personal, in nature.[1]

The third difference followed from this: the radicals could not concede the worth of any bishop; the moderates pointed to the 'good honest men' in the past. In particular, they praised the worth of the Marian martyrs. Lewis du Moulin thought that the attitude taken to the martyrs was the great dividing-line in 1640: that a crucial line of defence for episcopacy was that bishops 'have been godly Martyrs in Queene Maryes daies' and that the radical reply was that martyrdom 'argued the goodnes of theire consciences not of their Callings'. An

---

[1] (Anon.), *A Satyre Upon the State of Things this Parliament* . . . (London, 1641), no pagination; *Speeches of Sir Benjamin Rudyerd* . . . (London, 1641), p. 20; *Speech of Lord Falkland* . . ., p. 11; Morley, op. cit., p. 19; Baillie, *The Unlawfulnesse* . . ., p. 43; Henderson, op. cit., p. 15; Prynne, *Canterburies Doome* . . ., p. 37.

Anglican answered criticism of individual bishops with this pertinent rhyme:

> Are they Episcopal? grant it; what then?
> Cranmer and Ridley, were not they good men?

Sir John Wray made the same point in the Commons in December 1640, when he advocated a limited episcopacy. He said that he was completely opposed to the Beckets, Wolseys, Bonners and Lauds of episcopacy, but added:

> . . . if in the counter-ballance there may be found but one good Cranmer, or one good Latimer and Ridley, I would prise and esteem them . . .

When John Hacket looked back on the fallacies of 1641, he gave pride of place to the radicals' repudiation of the martyr-bishops. Fiennes argued in a speech to the Commons in February, 1641, that the martyrdom of the bishops was irrelevant to a discussion of the nature of their office:

> For the martyrs and reformers of the Church that were Bishops, I doe not understand that that was any part of their reformation, nor of their martyrdome.

William Thomas, speaking to the Commons in May 1641, catalogued the vices of the bishops throughout history and made no exception of the Tudor bishops:

> I will deliver their actions no less detestable, nay rather more heynous after the reformation than before.

He pointed out that even Cranmer and Ridley had supported the claim of Lady Jane Grey against that of the rightful successor, Mary. 'Smectymnuus' wrote of one 'great designe' of the prelates to hinder reformation: from Elizabeth's reign onwards there was an unbroken chain of 'lamentation, mourning and woe'. And when the pamphlet described Mary's reign it was not in the martyrs, but in the 'inhumane butcheries, blood-shedding and cruelties of Gardiner, Bonner and the rest of the bishops in Queen Maries dayes', that it traced the ancestry of the bishops.[1]

---

[1] (Bodl. Lib.) Engl. Hist. MSS. C. 303, f. 8; (Anon.), . . . *A Poeme* . . . (London, 1656), p. 19; *Speeches of Sir John Wray* . . . (London, 1641), p. 6; John Hacket, *Scrinia Reserata* . . . (London, 1692), p. 196; *Speech of Nathaniel Fiennes* . . . (London, 1641), p. 6; *Speech of William Thomas* . . . (London, 1641), p. 19; Smectymnuus, *An Answer to a Booke* . . ., p. 103.

The radicals were also anxious to debunk the Elizabethan Church, which one pamphleteer had called 'the happiest that ever England knew'.[1] The title of a radical pamphlet of 1641 betrayed their motive: *Queen Elizabeths Bishops: Or, A Briefe Declaration of the Wickednesse of the Generality of those Bishops . . . Writ of Purpose to keepe the Kings Good Subjects From Being Cheated.* The writer had been suspicious of Charles I's aims. Baillie had described how Charles had summoned both Houses to White-hall in January, 1641, and had encouraged their reforming efforts, but warned them:

> . . . about the notion of removing bishops, he told them expressly that he would never permit that State to be put down, or removed from the parliament. Abuses in the government; he would be content were rectified and reduced to the order in Queen Elizabeth's time.

Baillie commented on the reaction to this announcement that 'to this part of the speech was no hum, no applause, as to the rest'.[2]

Thus, even as early as 1640 and 1641, it was possible to detect a clear division between the moderate and radical opponents of Laud. Everything, which the moderate Anglicans stood for then, was what Prynne had suffered for in the thirties: the repudiation of the *iure divino* claim; the localized guilt of the Laudians; the worth of the martyrs; the recognition of the value of the Elizabethan Church by the civil magistrate. Moreover, Prynne had greatly admired John Williams in the thirties: Robert Woodford had thought that they might die together in 1637.[3] Williams had been anxious to dissociate himself from Prynne then for that very reason. George Thomascn, the bookseller, had smuggled a copy of Prynne's manuscript against Ship Money to Williams in the Tower. Williams decided to appease Laud by sacrificing Prynne, and on 3 August 1637, he informed Laud about what had taken place, with a thinly-veiled hint about the authorship of the pamphlet:

> . . . penned by some young Lawyer (without doubt) more melitiously then learnedly. I therefore conceived it my duty, to send both the Copy and Originall unto your Grace . . .

---

[1] (Anon.), *Prerogative Anatomised* . . . (London, 1644), p. 4.
[2] Baillie, *Letters and Journals* . . ., i, p. 292.
[3] H.M.C. *9th Report*, ii, p. 496.

The ensuing investigation involved, among others, Thomason and Williams himself. The commission which examined them, including Juxon and Windebank in its number, caught Williams out in contradictions and elicited from him one more innuendo:

> . . . and looking upon the writing he found it written in an ill hand, such as he could not well read whereupon he thought it was some Lawyers hand . . .

The commission were unsympathetic and Williams was frightened. He wrote abjectly to Laud on 26 August 1637, expressing the hope that 'neither my receiving of that discourse (from a common STATIONER and not any Autor or Abettor of the businesse) nor yeat my Carriage and demeanour in TRANSMITTING thereof hath given your Grace or his Majesty any offence'. But Williams had failed in his primary purpose: his perfidy had not convinced Laud of his loyalty.[1]

There is no evidence to suggest that Prynne was aware of Williams's attempted betrayal; indeed, shortly after his return from exile in November 1640, Heylyn recorded with dismay that Prynne was admitted to a private conference with Williams, which in his opinion 'boded no great good to the Church or State'.[2] The evidence is not lacking in contemporary comment for the view, nevertheless, that Prynne had joined the radicals; it is the quality of that evidence which is suspect. Both in his lifetime, and after, Prynne attracted the facile interpretation: few took the trouble to look further than his violent language to understand what he meant. Many identifications of Prynne as a radical in 1640 and 1641 were based on a misreading of his principles. When Godfrey Goodman, Bishop of Gloucester, attributed his sufferings to the malice of Prynne, it was at a time when Prynne was a fellow-victim. Thomas Barlow, Bishop of Lincoln, wrote in 1669 that Prynne's praise of the Royal Supremacy would have been more timely in 1641 than in 1660. He pointed out that Prynne had sided with the radicals in 1641. But his ignorance of the position at that time of Prynne (who was not a Member of Parliament until 1648), was shown when he said that the Royal Supremacy had been challenged then by the Commons, 'of which number Mr. Prynne was one and a

---

[1] (Bodl. Lib.) Cherry MSS. 2, f. 145–f. 163.
[2] Heylyn, *Cyprianus Anglicus* . . ., p. 465.

most zealous and furious abetter of their practices'. A satirical play of 1641 contained an easily recognizable character, 'Master Prinner', who headed a chorus of common people and was said to 'burne in zeale of heart, and contend for the reformation of religion'. Further comment, however, attributed to him anarchical notions about church government, egalitarian ideals for society, and a hatred of anything which was ancient: this was on a level of idiocy with the pamphlet of 1780 which hailed Prynne as an apostle of democracy.[1] A pamphlet commonly attributed to Prynne—*Lord Bishops None of the Lords Bishops*—would have established him as a zealous 'root and branch' advocate as early as November 1640; its author was, however, Henry Burton.[2] If all the evidence of Prynne's radicalism had been of this quality, there would have been no reason to suppose that Prynne had disowned earlier ideals. But there is one piece of evidence that is unanswerable, because it comes from his own pen. In July 1641, he had written a pamphlet entitled, *The Antipathie of the English Lordly Prelacie, Both to Regall Monarchy, and Civill Unity*. It clearly advocated 'root and branch' rejection of episcopacy and, equally clearly, repudiated Williams for 'his late extraordinary stickling (much spoken against) to maintaine the Lordly jurisdiction, and secular authority of our Prelates'.[3] Thus it is possible to place Prynne's change of attitude between November 1640 and July 1641; at some date in that period he became fully persuaded of the need for the radical solution. Why he did so emerges clearly from an analysis of his pamphlet—his most remarkable effort—which will be considered fully in the next chapter.

Prynne had joined the radical party in 1641. To use the term 'party' to connote a coherent organization, or even a specific ecclesiastical programme, would be misleading in the fluid situation of 1641. One cannot even say that Prynne had

[1] (B.M.) Egerton MSS. 2182, f. 8; Coll. Reg. Oxon. MSS. CCCXL, f. 93; (Anon.), *Mercuricus Britanicus, Or The English Intelligencer. A Tragic-Comedy at Paris* (London, 1641), no pagination; (Anon.), *Equitable Representation Necessary* . . . (London, 1780), p. 23.

[2] My reasons for making this ascription will be published in a forthcoming article, 'Prynne, Burton, and the Puritan Triumph', in the *Huntington Library Quarterly*.

[3] Prynne, *The Antipathie* . . . (London, 1641), i, p. 334.

necessarily been won over to an uncritical acceptance of Scottish Presbyterianism. But he did clearly desert the moderate traditions of nonconformity when he accepted the need to destroy episcopacy 'root and branch'. Cornelius Burges, one of the London preachers, wrote to Richard Baxter in 1659 to deny that English nonconformists had deviated in the early forties from their predecessors' faith in a reformed episcopacy. He claimed that there had been no commitment to Presbyterianism or Independency, and that clericalist tendencies only emerged in 1643 under the influence of the Scots.[1] Burges and Prynne both argued later, from their absence of a formal commitment to Presbyterianism, a positive distaste for it: no decisive break had taken place in 1641 in their attitude to episcopacy. Similarly, when Mrs. Kirby studied the ministers' sermons from 1640 to 1642, she believed that the distinction between radical and moderate was blurred in the unconstructive violence of antipathy to Laud. She post-dated radicalism to the time when Scottish influence was strongest; her search for radicalism became, in effect, a search for anticipations of such influence. She ignored major differences of emphasis in the sermons, for instance, of Burges and John Gauden, and saw Burges as a radical only in his demand for a covenant with God, which she saw as 'a prophecy of the Solemn League and Covenant'.[2] But Burges was no creature of the Scots. He made clear in his sermon that he was using the term only in a theological sense; Baillie's journal showed how the Scots mistrusted him; in 1643, unwillingness to surrender rights to the Scots made him refuse initially to take the Solemn League and Covenant.[3] If acceptance of Scottish Presbyterianism is made the criterion of English ecclesiastical radicalism in 1641, then Burges was not a radical. While a coherent attitude on the controversial issues of 1641 cannot denote party membership in a rigid sense, yet in a loose sense it can justify the description of Burges and Prynne as radicals. For to search for party divisions in 1641, only in the sense of allegiance to coherent ecclesiastical groupings, is to run the risk of assuming that English

[1] (D.W.L.) Baxter MSS. 59.3, f. 80.     [2] Kirby, loc. cit., p. 533.
[3] Cornelius Burges, *The First Sermon* . . . (London, 1641), p. 56; Baillie, *Letters and Journals* , . . . i, pp. 302–3; John Lightfoot, *Works* . . . (London, 1823), xiii, p. 11.

Puritanism had undergone no serious transformation in that year, and of post-dating the development to 1643 and beyond, when external pressure is named as the chief cause. J. H. Hexter saw that such reasoning was fallacious: although his researches had undermined the concept of clear-cut party divisions in the Commons, both under Pym's leadership and in 1648–9, he saw the value of separating a 'godly' party from the conservative opinions of Anglicans and old nonconformists in 1641:

> Regardless of how they might differ as to the ideal church of the future, they all agreed on the necessity of a drastic change in the church of the past.[1]

Symptomatic of this transformation was the radicals' willingness to turn for guidance from John Foxe to Thomas Brightman. Brightman, whose *A Revelation of the Revelation* had been published in 1615, acknowledged his debt to 'our John Foxe' for his pioneer labours in the field of apocalyptic interpretation, but emphasized Foxe's limitations:

> ... somewhat more general and more obscure, such as the condition of that time would suffer, but this is most full and copious, because there was nowe greater knowledge of matters attained, than ever before this ...

Foxe had brought his account of events up to the year 1560. Brightman argued the need to supplement this with the additional insight gained from knowledge of Elizabeth's achievements. Both Brightman and Foxe believed that Elizabeth's accession, in apocalyptic terms, signified the blast of the seventh trumpet. But Brightman warned of the inadequacy of achievement when set against the nature of expectation:

> ... blessed Queen Elizabeth, who happily begun and proceeded in the work of Reformation, according to the time and those days she lived in: the finishing whereof will be required of this Generation; otherwise expect God hath a sad Controversie with this Land ...

[1] J. H. Hexter, 'The Problem of the Presbyterian Independents', *American Historical Review*, xliv, 1938–9, pp. 29–49; J. H. Hexter, *The Reign of King Pym* (Harvard, 1941), p. 99. His distinction is accepted in: M. F. Keeler, *The Long Parliament, 1640–1* (Philadelphia, 1954), p. 12. Valuable light is thrown on this 'party' in : Valerie Pearl, *London and the Outbreak of the Puritan Revolution* (Oxford, 1961), pp. 160–76.

Brightman praised Elizabeth, but tempered it with incredulity that a graceless England should be so favoured by God. He showed how far removed from true ethical ideals was Elizabeth's church settlement, with its 'hotch potch lukewarmness', and stressed the 'neede of zeale to the intent wee may attayne to a full reformation'.

Brightman's major contribution to theological interpretation—which one pamphleteer in 1641 called 'Mr. Brightmans stupendious Revelations'—was the identification of the Genevan and Scottish Churches, the zealous, with Philadelphia, and of the Church of England, the lukewarm, with Laodicea:

> ... both they and their whole luke-warme Hierarchie should quite be overthrowne, and never recover their dignity again.

Foxe's regard for the Godly Prince was criticized by Brightman, no less than his regard for the Church of England as the Church of Christ:

> It is a matter, indeed to be admired with astonishment, that the Church should be so glorious in her sunnelike robes under the persecuting Emperours, and yet should be thus mournfully clad in this calme and suneshine weather that her Nursing Father brought unto her.

For Brightman believed that the decline of the Church dated from the reign of Constantine, the first Christian Emperor. He used this belief slyly to damn James I while seeming to praise him:

> But now is his Kingdome to be especially extolled with praises, when he doth make his Majesty to be visible after a sort in the Kings them selves ... And yet this is no strange thing neither. He raigned thus in auncient times by meanes of Constantine, and other Godly Emperours ...

In his devaluing of Constantine and Elizabeth, Brightman struck at the imperial myth. He deplored the lukewarmness which had frustrated the Elizabethan reformation and warned that God might turn to other nations who were zealous for a covenant with Him. Philadelphia, not Laodicea, was to be His Nation.[1]

---

[1] Thomas Brightman, *A Revelation of the Revelation* ... (Amsterdam, 1615), pp. 507, 397, 133, 128, 165, 364, 417, 314, 388, 390.

When Benjamin Hubbard expounded his concept of a progressive reformation in 1648 he referred to 'the Prophet of this Centurie, the bright burning light of our age Master Thomas Brightman'. This praise is hardly excessive to describe the extent to which the radicals of 1641 relied on Brightman as an answer to the moderate Anglicans' reliance on Foxe. The radicals' reliance on Brightman partly explains their uncompromising rejection of lukewarm episcopacy without a more specific commitment to an alternative programme than an honouring of zeal. Vines pointed out in 1656 that Brightman had rejected episcopacy as 'loathsome' without advocating separatism; Canne argued that the one must follow from the other, but Ball disagreed. This was Brightman's strength in 1641: he could attract separatist and non-separatist, John Goodwin and Thomas Edwards, in the rejection of a totally corrupt, lukewarm episcopacy. There were many enthusiastic references to Brightman from radicals: Case borrowed arguments from him when he urged the taking of the Covenant in 1643; Fuller noted his value for militants; Pocklington thought that he and Cartwright were the most influential English radicals; Symmons asked Parliamentary prisoners at Shrewsbury why they had taken up arms against their sovereign and was told: "tis prophesied in the Revelation, that the Whore of Babylon shall be destroyed with fire and sword, and what doe you know, but this is the time of her ruine, and that we are the men that must help to pull her downe.'[1] When the Puritan ministers had produced their classic apology for resistance, they had warned the Royalists to remember 'Mr. Brightmans Propheticall Interpretation of the spewing out of the Laodicean Angell'.[2] The ministers in 1641 were tireless in the task of propagating their warnings and prophecies. Sir Edward Dering

[1] Benjamin Hubbard, *Sermo Saecularis* ... (London, 1648), p. 28; Richard Vines, *A Treatise* ... (London, 1656), p. 242; John Canne, *A Necessitie of Separation* ... (London, 1654), pp. 18–21; John Ball, *An Answer* ... (London 1642), p. 33; Thomas Edwards, *Gan-graena* ... (London, 1646), iii, dedicatory epistle; Thomas Case, *The Quarrell of the Covenant* ... (London, 1643), p. 47; Thomas Fuller, *The Church History of Britain* (Oxford, 1845), v, p. 383; John Pocklington, *Altare Christianum* ... (London, 1637), p. 35; Edward Symmons, *Scripture Vindicated* ... (Oxford, 1645), preface.

[2] *Scripture and Reason Pleaded for Defensive Armes* ... *by divers Reverend and Learned Divines* ... (London, 1643), p. 66.

described their reaction to his proposal of a reformed episcopacy in June 1641:

> Art thou for us or for our adversaries? So said one of the usual blacke walkers in Westminster Hall. Another of our Parliament-pressing Ministers, after I had delivered my sense upon Episcopacy in the House came to me and told me plainely, That my conscience was not so good as in the beginning of the Parliament.

It is significant that one of the 'Rooters', whom Dering found annoying later, was a 'W.P.' who accused Dering of having a Pope in his belly: the language, as much as the initials, indicates Prynne.[1]

It was through the 'Parliament-pressing' ministers that Brightman's influence was distilled. In their sermons before the Commons between 1640 and 1642, both Holmes and Symonds directly quoted from Brightman, and Holmes' description of the 'New Jerusalem' was almost completely lifted from Brightman. Yet, indirectly, almost all the sermons show a similar debt to Brightman: the stress on zeal; the devaluing of Elizabeth and Constantine; the total repudiation of episcopacy; the ethical craving for reform, if necessary against the magistrate's wishes, expressed by Case in the words:

> Oh, if it might be reported in London that England is reformed —that such a drunkard, such a swearer, such a covetous man . . . is become a new man.[2]

This ethical craving is the dominant quality of Prynne's pamphlet of 1641. It comes out strongly, too, in his address to the Roundheads in 1643:

> . . . I shall in my daily Prayers recommend your Honours, Person, Forces, and Military proceedings, till through his blessings on them, the house of the Lord shall be established in the top of the mountain, and exalted above the hills . . .

In a preface to Fairfax in a pamphlet of 1645, he called the

[1] Dering, *Collection of Speeches* . . . (London, 1641), pp. 3, 162. Cf. Samuel Butler, *Posthumous Works* . . . (London, 1732), p. 99. When parodying Prynne, Butler dismissed an opponent in the words: 'By all which it appears that ye have a Turk, as well as a Pope, in your Bellies.'

[2] Nathaniel Holmes, *The New World* . . . (London, 1641), p. 72; Joseph Symonds, *A Sermon* . . . (London, 1641), no pagination; Thomas Case, *The Second Sermon* . . . (London, 1641), p. 47.

settlement of church discipline 'according to Gods Word, and the Purest times' as 'one principle end of Your and Our taking Defensive Armes'.[1] It seems fair to assume that Prynne's ethical concern was, in part, a reflection of the influence exercised on him by the London ministers of that period, because of knowledge both of the type of pressure which they exercised, and of Prynne's links with them and approval of their aims.[2] Moreover, curious supporting evidence is provided by Prynne's revulsion against radicalism in 1645. In that year he attacked too much devolution of power into the hands of the ministers, because he had become sceptical of their power to implement ethical reforms. He made clear his admiration for the London ministers, who, he noted, were constant advocates of a 'thorough and compleat Reformation' in their sermons and had warned their congregations persistently that 'lesse will not be accepted of God or good men', but by 1645 he recognized that their zeal was atypical. One London minister, Herbert Palmer, rebuked him for his pusillanimity; he significantly accused Prynne of desertion of party by desertion of Brightman:

> Mr. Brightman (whose interpretation of Revel. 3 concerning Sardis and Laodicea, have been to admiration, and neare to Propheticall) makes England, as you know, the Anti-type of the latter: surely whoever thinks he is at all in the right therein, and withall have seene that lukewarme Angell so strangely spawned out . . . ought to take speciall heed, that they themselves degenerate not into like lukewarmnesse . . .[3]

It was the ministers' triumph to persuade a moderate nonconformist like Prynne, in 1641, that only a total rejection of episcopacy could save England from profanity. The explanation of Prynne's change of front does not lie in deception: a process foreign to his nature. But neither does it lie in self-deception: Robinson, in 1645, stressed the implausibility of Prynne's being

[1] Prynne, *The Popish Royall Favourite* . . . (London, 1643), dedicatory epistle; Prynne, *A Vindication of Four Serious Questions* . . . (London, 1645), dedicatory epistle.

[2] H.M.C. *9th Report*, ii, p. 499; William Walwyn, *A Helpe to the Right Understanding of a Discourse Concerning Independency* (London, 1645), pp. 5–6; Prynne, *A True and Perfect Narrative* . . . (London, 1659), p. 46; Prynne, *A Seasonable Vindication* . . . (London, 1660), p. 89.

[3] Prynne, *A Vindication of Four Serious Questions* . . ., p. 54; Herbert Palmer *A Full Answer to a Printed Paper* . . . (London, 1645), p. 25.

unaware until that date of the concessions to clericalism involved in an advocacy of a total reformation, even if it fell short of a direct commitment to Scottish Presbyterianism.[1] Acceptance of Brightman's interpretation of Scripture, pointing to the rejection of episcopacy and the need for zealous reform, created an atmosphere favourable to the advancement of radicalism in 1641, and was welcomed as such by Baillie. This was not the same as an unequivocal acceptance of the Scottish model, and Baillie could deplore in 1645 the extent to which apocalyptic interpretations continued to influence 'the most of the chiefe divines here, not only Independents, but others, such as Twis, Marshall, Palmer, and many more'.[2] But in 1641 there is no reason to suppose that Baillie's hopes were based on an illusory calculation of the strength of sentiment in favour of Scottish Presbyterianism in England; rather, they were founded on a realistic recognition that radical apocalpytic interpretations had created a psychological climate favourable to the advance of Baillie's hopes, even without commitment to a specific programme. This is certainly true as an explanation for Prynne's volte-face in 1641: the constitutional objections to a possibly clericalist solution weighed less with him at that time than its ethical advantages. It is necessary to turn to his pamphlet of 1641 to understand what he thought were the ethical advantages, and how far he had considered the constitutional objections.

[1] Henry Robinson, *The Falsehood of Mr. William Pryn's Truth Triumphing* (London, 1645), p. 7.
[2] Baillie, *Letters and Journals* . . ., ii, p. 313.

# IV

# THE TESTAMENT OF
# A RADICAL

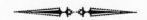

PRYNNE renounced Foxe in 1641. In 1630 he had asked:

> Shall we thus repay our blessed Martyrs for all their glorious
> sufferings, as now for to dis-martyr, yea, uncrowne, and, to tread
> them under foot . . .[1]

To understand why the rhetorical question of 1630 should have
become the aim of 1641, it is necessary to understand the
significance of the martyr-cult in controversies of the time. Foxe
and Jewel spoke for the moderate. The zealots on either side
found their prestige a source of embarrassment. This explains
what otherwise is a paradox in Anglican apologetics: the
Laudians, resting their case ultimately on tradition, were
forced through the immediate need to discredit their predecessors to exalt reason and to decry tradition in the manner
of the Tew Circle. Downame anticipated Laud in his disregard
for the traditions which had gathered about the martyrs and
the names of Jewel and Foxe:

> . . . if it were true that the Bishops having better informed them-
> selves Concerning their functions . . . would it follow that their
> late thoughts which commonly are the wiser were false and
> worthie to be confuted?

Similarly, Hall argued against reliance upon such authorities:

> . . . we cannot prescribe to other mens thoughts; where all is

[1] Prynne, *Anti-Arminianisme* . . . (London, 1630), dedicatory epistle.

said men will take liberty (and who can hinder it?) to abound in their own sense . . .[1]

It was not from their doctrinal beliefs that either Downame or Hall derived this faith in individual reason: both were staunch anti-Arminians. It was the logic of controversy that drove them inexorably to empiricism; the *iure divino* claim for episcopacy ran counter to the whole weight of previous Anglican tradition.

Prynne was aware of the need for the High Church Anglicans to decry the traditions of the martyrs, and played on this in the speech he made before the sentence was carried out on him in 1637:

> Gentlemen, look to your selves; you know not whose turne may be next: If the Martyrs that suffered in Queen Maries days are accounted and called Schismaticall Hereticks, Factious Fellows; Traytors and Rebels, condemned by Holy Church: What shall we look for?[2]

Ironically, it was to be from Prynne and his fellow-radicals that the assault on the cult of the martyrs was to come in 1641; by that year, the martyrs had become the rallying-point for moderate Anglicans.

Professor Haller has stressed Foxe's formative influence on Puritan thought in the seventeenth century;[3] what he has failed to show is the extent to which Foxe's influence could retard the Puritan Revolution. Thus Professor Haller regards Milton's *Of Reformation* as a continuation of the Foxe tradition, when its real significance is to repudiate that tradition. Prynne and Milton complement Brightman; they attack Foxe's history, and he attacked Foxe's theology. Both Prynne's *The Antipathie* and Milton's *Of Reformation* contain expressions of scepticism about history. Prynne warns at the beginning of his work of the pitfalls of history: that for much of our earlier history we are dependent on the testimony of monkish historians, who naturally seek to extenuate and, if necessary, to conceal clerical

---

[1] George Downame, *A Defence of the Sermon* . . . (London, 1611), i, p. 6; Joseph Hall, *An Humble Remonstrance* . . . (London, 1640), p. 26; Laud, *Works* . . ., iv, p. 226.

[2] Prynne, *A New Discovery* . . . (London, 1641), p. 44.

[3] W. Haller, 'John Foxe and the Puritan Revolution', *The Seventeenth Century*, ed. R. F. Jones (Stanford, 1951), pp. 209–24.

frailties. Thus, Prynne can look with sympathy on the maligned figure of King John:

> see now to what extremities this poore King was brought by these rebellious and traytorly Prelates . . .

It follows that Prynne, despite his wearisome citation of precedents from history, did not have an uncritical regard for it. He was conscious of its use by monkish writers as a projection of their prejudices into the past. Milton, also, is sceptical of history but not for the same reason:

> . . . our homebred Monks in their Histories blanch the Kings their Benefactors, and brand those that went about to be their Correctors . . .[1]

Although a small point, it emphasizes the difference between those concerned with clerical hostility to monarchy and those concerned with clerical exaltation of monarchy. Both Milton and Prynne are sceptical, not merely of history in a general sense, but of a particular interpretation of history. The triumph of Laudianism struck at the omniscience of Foxe. How could it be held that this triumph was merely the effort of a corrupt minority against the sure traditions of the Church, when all the evidence suggested that even the more enlightened Anglicans equated her traditions with those of her supposed corrupters? The Laudian triumph within Anglicanism suggested that Foxe had miscalculated on some points: that he had not realized that episcopacy itself was tainted; that he had overrated the importance of the Godly Prince, Constantine or Elizabeth; that he had laid too much stress on the worth of the martyrs and the Elizabethan bishops. These are the points developed, with variations in method and emphasis, by Prynne and Milton in 1641.

Milton's work was an inquiry why the light lit by Wycliffe —to Foxe the beginning of the last stage of Church history— was 'but a short blaze soon dampt and stifled'. He showed the frail foundation of the Reformation in England. Henry VIII had broken with the Pope but in the interests of his own supremacy, not of religion. The Tudor bishops 'tho' they had

---

[1] Prynne, *The Antipathie* . . . (London, 1641), i, p. 35; Milton, *Of Reformation* . . . (London, 1641), p. 26.

67

renounc'd the Pope . . . still hugged the Popedome'. Cranmer, Ridley and their colleagues were too conservative. Of them, Milton said:

> . . . But it will be said These men were Martyrs: What then? Tho' every true Christian will be a Martyr when he is called to it; not presently does it follow that every one suffering for Religion, is without exception . . .

Milton complained of the 'ignominious bondage' of Truth 'unlesse shee can bring a Ticket from Cranmer, Latimer and Ridley; nor proove herself a retainer to Constantine and weare his badge'. Milton would have no sophistries about limited guilt: there was 'an universall rottennes, and gangrene in the whole Function'. Nor does he exempt the Elizabethan bishops from these strictures:

> And surely they were moderate Divines indeed, neither hot nor cold, and Grindall the best of them.

What of the argument that the Church in its earliest times had been incomplete until the coming of the Christian Emperor? This Foxian answer was rejected by Milton. The coming of the overrated Constantine had reinforced, not eliminated, the pristine impurities:

> . . . the Church that before by insensible degrees welk't and impair'd, now with large steps went downhill decaying . . .

Milton spoke eloquently of the long affection of the people for a divinely-warranted Reformation. He cited the agitation in Parliament itself from the first years of Elizabeth's reign; even Elizabeth's reign was the negation, not inspiration, of reform.[1]

Like Milton, Prynne avoided a frontal attack on Foxe: as late as November, 1641, he presented his local church at Swainswick with a gift of Foxe's works.[2] But like Milton, his historical analysis was intended as a corrective to Foxe's account; as such, it contrasted markedly with the dependence on Foxe which characterized his earlier writings. A cataclysmic view of the change in 1641 would, however, be false. *The Antipathie*, it is true, marks the first open renunciation of the principle of moderation and of the historical philosophy that

[1] Milton, *Of Reformation* . . . ., pp. 7, 8, 11, 12, 15, 73.
[2] (Bodl. Lib.) Tanner MSS. 69, f. 1.

supported it, but Prynne's dependence on Foxe had weakened perceptibly before 1641. The beginnings of disenchantment with Foxe can be traced in some of the pamphlets as early as 1637, in one of which he uses apocalyptic prophecies from Scripture as portents of the destruction of episcopacy. But in 1637 his attack was still limited to a group within the episcopate; in 1641, his attack was on episcopacy itself. In 1636, when Prynne referred to the use of force by bishops, he said: 'as the *Bookes of Martirs*, and present experience plentifully evidence, to their shame.' Of their cruelty, he said: 'all which our *Booke of Martyrs* and dayly experience witnesse to the full.'[1] Thus, in 1636, he used 'present' or 'dayly' experience as a supplement to Foxe; in 1641, he used such experience as a substitute for Foxe.

Prynne defined his aim in writing *The Antipathie* as the refutation of Archbishop Bancroft's apopthegm, which, he said, had been wrongly fathered on James I, 'No Bishop, No King'. If this had been his only aim, the pamphlet would not have differed from his earlier attacks upon anti-monarchical bishops. But the attack had broadened in scope in 1641, and in so doing had changed its nature. In 1641, Prynne does not argue merely, that monarchy can exist without bishops, nor even that certain bishops are working to overthrow monarchy; he argues that monarchy cannot exist with bishops, and that all bishops, at all times, are working to overthrow monarchy. This anti-royalism is not a question of person but of function: it clings inseparably to the office. He abandons his qualified attack on the bishops: the elimination of the Laudian clique will not in itself restore the well-being of religion. He attacks the bishops' *iure divino* claims, but no longer from an Erastian position:

> ... their Function, which though their many late published Pamphlets would prove to be of Divine Right, yet the pernicious evill fruits thereof infallibly proclaime to be of mere humane wronge ...

The bishops do not rule by divine right: nor now do they rule by human right: they rule by human wrong.

[1] Prynne, *A Catalogue of Such Testimonies* ... (London, 1637), p. 22; Prynne, *A Looking Glasse for All Lordly Prelates* ... (London, 1636), pp. 62, 64.

Prynne claims that 'Divine Providence' set him on the task —the most exhaustive essay in special pleading that even Prynne had ever undertaken—of showing historically that every bishop who had ever held office had been anti-monarchical. He acknowledges—after God—his debt to Thomas Gibson, a reference to whose history of the treacheries of bishops from the time of the Conquest he had first come across in John Bale's works. To compare Gibson with Prynne is to realize how little indebted was Prynne to the earlier writer for his radicalism. Gibson's analysis in 1550 was optimistic: although he recounted many instances of clerical insubordination, he emphasized the altered position at the Reformation, when bishops recognized the Royal Supremacy.[1] *The Antipathie*, by way of contrast, is a tale of unrelieved guilt within the episcopate to be expiated by its total abolition. Foxe's history had been born of compassion for the seemingly needless suffering of godly men; in showing their suffering as part of the divine plan, Foxe emphasized that persecutions and sufferings within the Church had an appointed end. No such compassion relieves Prynne's description of an episcopate which, by 1641, he would call Antichristian, and whose corruptions would continue until it was destroyed completely. In tracing the history of the Church, Foxe showed that Satan had been bound for a thousand years and that 'no universal murdering prosecution was stirring before the preaching of John Wycliff, Huss and such others.'[2] No such reading was possible to Prynne in 1641: the conflicts within the Church were products of that universal unrest that derived from its original foundation in Satan. The prelates' treachery towards their sovereign had been obscured hitherto only by 'the immoderate panegyricall applause of their Parasites (who almost deifie them in Presse, in Pulpit, especially in Court Sermons)': a belated, and then only parenthetical, recognition of Anglican absolutism.[3]

[1] Prynne, *The Antipathie* . . ., i, dedicatory epistle; Thomas Gibson, 'A breve cronycle of the Byshope of Romes Blessing', *Fugitive Tracts, First Series, 1493–1600* (London, 1875), p. 13; for Prynne's reliance on Bale, see: J. W. Harris, 'John Bale', *Illinois Studies in Language and Literature*, xxv, no. 4 (Urbana, 1940), p. 109.

[2] John Foxe, *Acts and Monuments* . . ., ed. S. R. Catley (London, 1837–41), i, pp. 289, 292.

[3] Prynne, *The Antipathie* . . ., i, dedicatory epistle.

In a pamphlet which set out to show the universal depravity of bishops, there were obvious differences from his earlier pamphlets when he had set, against the innovations of the corrupt few, 'the uninterrupted streame' of Anglican tradition.[1] These developments become clear in his treatment of the martyrs and moderate bishops in general, and of Archbishop Cranmer in particular. Cranmer's royalism made him a key figure. The very reason for which Prynne had revered him in the earlier period—an awe of magistracy that almost blurred for him the distinction between *rex* and *sacerdos*—made the destruction of his prestige essential in a thesis on the total corruption of episcopacy. Foxe had quoted Thomas Cromwell's praise of Cranmer that on no point could he be discredited with the King: if Cranmer could therefore be shown to be corrupt and anti-royal, then *a fortiori* these qualities were present in other bishops.[2] Thus Cranmer, extolled by Prynne in 1630 as 'our religious Martyr', is made the main object of attack in 1641. Prynne claims that he has no wish to detract from Cranmer's martyrdom, and then qualifies it in nine ways. Cranmer condemned Lambert and Frith before he was thoroughly instructed in his religion; he brought about the divorce between Henry VIII and Catherine; the Lincolnshire rebels complained of his attitude; pious writers of the time like Barnes, wrote against bishops; he bore a responsibility for the Six Acts; he was the only real martyr-bishop; his martyrdom came after his bishopric; he was not a very good martyr (witness his recantation); he was martyred for his religion as a private Christian after he had been removed from his bishopric, yet—this is the vital point—he was justly condemned for treason for his action as Archbishop in defying the Crown. Prynne was particularly wilful in his reference to the Six Acts, 'made and devised in this Archbishops time', which he called 'worthy of no memory among Christian men, but rather to be buried in perpetuall silence of oblivion, as Mr. Foxe determines'. This is typical of Prynne's treatment of Foxe in 1641: he praised him and revised his ideas at the same time. What he quoted from

---

[1] Prynne, *Anti-Arminianisme . . .*, p. 77.

[2] Foxe, op. cit., viii, p. 27. Cf. E. T. Davies, *Episcopacy and The Royal Supremacy in the Church of England in the Sixteenth Century* (Oxford, 1950), p. 137.

Foxe was true; what he did not quote was devastating. Foxe
had been at pains, in point of fact, to vindicate Cranmer. He
praised Cranmer as 'an example for ecclesiastical pastors' in
his defiance of Gardiner and Henry VIII himself in opposing
the Six Acts:

> . . . let us pray that both the like stoutness may be perceived in
> all ecclesiastical and learned men, where the truth ought to be
> defended, and also the like relenting and flexibility may take
> place in princes . . . so that they utterly overwhelm not the truth
> by self-will, power, and authority . . .

In this passage Foxe showed a concern for the abuse of power
by a magistrate, absent in Prynne, and which would have
robbed Prynne's historical survey of the 'Antipathie' of magistrate and bishop of much of its point. Prynne does acknowledge
the existence of a belief that Cranmer had opposed the Six Acts.
For evidence to support this, however, he refers to Matthew
Parker—a tainted source that he later discredits—and brushes
the belief aside in the comment that 'others seeme to imply
that he gave consent thereunto at first'. Thus he cites Foxe for
a reference to the Six Acts, but not to Cranmer's opposition to
them. Similarly, he quotes Foxe's condemnation of Cranmer's
recantation but not his charitable judgment that tempered it:

> . . . so it pleaseth God that so great virtues in the archbishop
> should not be had in too much admiration of us without some
> blemish . . .[1]

Ridley was similarly maltreated by Prynne in 1641. Prynne
points out that Ridley's martyrdom, like Cranmer's, dates
from the time after his deprivation from his bishopric. Although
Prynne does not 'dismartyr' Ridley to the same extent as
Cranmer, he does point out that Ridley suffered primarily
because he was anti-monarchical: he had preferred Lady Jane
Grey to his rightful Queen. Tunstall, too, is a 'dabbling hypocrite', and Prynne claims that it is inevitable:

---

[1] Prynne, *Anti-Arminianisme* . . ., p. 81; Prynne, *The Antipathie* . . ., i,
pp. 132, 133, 147; Foxe, op. cit., viii, pp. 147, 81–2. Although Prynne
abandoned radicalism later, he did not abandon his contempt for Cranmer's
cowardice: Prynne, *Summary Reasons Against the New Oath and Engagement
. . . .* (London, 1649), p. 15; Prynne, *A Briefe Apologie for all Non-Subscribers
. . .* (London, 1650), p. 6.

Neither is it possible naturally (pray marke this passage) that there should be any good Bishop, so long as the Bishoprickes be nothing save wordly Pompe.

Prynne's criticisms of Cranmer, Ridley and Tunstall show that, for him, no change took place at the Reformation in the bishops' hostility to the Crown. This is true also of Elizabethan bishops. Matthew Parker may have been better than Cardinal Pole, but was 'over-Pontificall and Princely in his buildings, feasts'. He acknowledges the piety and gravity of Grindal—even Milton had thought him the best of the Elizabethan bishops— but emphasizes that he had lost his office for opposition to the Crown. Prynne wilfully ignores the fact that Grindal lost favour with the Queen because of his Puritanism; it serves his thesis to show that he was anti-monarchical.

Even Whitgift, whom Prynne had sided with against Cartwright earlier, is now attacked. Before 1641, he had praised Whitgift's refusal of the *iure divino* claim for episcopacy, but now he called him:

> . . . a stately Pontificall Bishop . . . (who) contested much for the authority and Lordly Jurisdiction of Prelates, in defence where of hee then writ, though hee durst not averre our Archbishops to be of divine institution . . .[1]

Thomas Fuller thought Whitgift to be 'one of the worthiest men that ever the English hierarchy did enjoy', and defended him from Prynne's attack:

> But a modern writer, in his voluminous book against the practices of English prelates, bitterly inveigheth against him, whom he termeth a pontifical (meaneth he paganish or popish?) bishop, and chargeth him with many misdemeanours . . .

Fuller, aware of Prynne's earlier admiration for Whitgift, treated his unfairness to Whitgift as symbolic of the selective unfairness of the entire pamphlet:

> Thus he weeds men's lives, and makes use only to their disgrace, of their infirmities; meantime suppressing many eminent actions, which his own conscience knows were performed by them.

Fuller stressed the hypocrisy of the claim that Whitgift, most royal of bishops, was anti-royal and concluded with a neat

[1] Prynne, *The Antipathie* . . ., i, pp. 238, 304–5, 147, 149.

thrust at Prynne's later distance from the transient radicalism of *The Antipathie*:

> More might be said in the vindication of this worthy prelate from his reproachful pen; but I purposely forbear, the rather because it is possible that the learned gentleman since, upon a serious review of his own book, and experimental observation of the passages of this age, may be more offended with his own writing herein, than others just take exception thereat.[1]

Bancroft is discredited by Prynne on three counts: he was the first advocate of the *iure divino* claim for episcopacy; he sought to extend the ecclesiastical jurisdiction at the expense of the civil; he was implicated in the Gunpowder Plot.[2]

One might have expected Abbott to escape the general censure of Archbishops of Canterbury. Heylyn noted in the thirties Prynne's understanding with Abbott, 'with whom he was grown very gracious',[3] and even in 1643 Abbott did not share the calumny which Prynne heaped on other former favourites, such as James I, Charles I and John Williams. But Prynne had to discredit Abbott if the episcopate were wholly corrupt. Thus Prynne calls Abbott 'a man of better temper' than Bancroft, but too fond of shooting deer. Prynne points out that Abbott had alienated the King by his accidental homicide while hunting and had been debarred from Court. Thus even the ostensibly moderate bishops are against the Crown. But in 1644 Prynne interpreted Abbott's disgrace in a different way. The commission that sequestered Abbott represented then the triumph of Laud's envy:

> . . . which Commission being of his owne procurement, in malice and envy against Archbishop Abbott (for his casual homicide of his keeper, in shooting at a Buck, many years after the fact done) . . .[4]

In 1641 nothing must extenuate the total guilt of the episcopate; the whole line had been infected by its original bequest from Pope Gregory and none might escape it:

[1] Thomas Fuller, *The Church History of Britain* . . ., ed. J. Brewer, (Oxford, 1845), v, pp. 316–19.

[2] Prynne, *The Antipathie* . . ., i, p. 151.

[3] Peter Heylyn, *Cyprianus Anglicus* (London, 1668), p. 230.

[4] Prynne, *The Antipathie* . . ., i, p. 152; Prynne, *A Breviate of the Life of William Laud* . . . (London, 1644), p. 11.

This its unhappy derivation from such a Trecherous and rebellious parentage, hath tainted the whole line of our Canterburian Arch-Prelates and infused such an occult pernicious quality into this See as hath made it a very chaire of Pestilence.

Prynne's intention in the rest of the pamphlet was to examine other bishoprics in the same way as he had examined Canterbury in order to produce the same conclusion: a condemnation of episcopacy as totally anti-monarchical and corrupt. Prynne's achievements did not match his aim: frequently his general analysis broke down on points of detail. Although he spoke in general terms of a total depravity in episcopacy, he did not always succeed, in his examination of individual cases, in shaking off earlier influences to the extent which he had done successfully with Grindal, Whitgift, Abbott and the martyrs. He related with relish the crimes of Popish bishops, but became evasive when he reached the Elizabethan bishops. For instance, he said that he would omit further tales of treachery in the see of Bath and Wells after Mary's reign in the interests of brevity: from Prynne of all people, no argument could have carried less conviction.

In 1641 Prynne accepted the 'root and branch' thesis; *The Antipathie* was meant to provide its historical rationale. Prynne, in his dedicatory epistle to the Commons, referred directly to the link between his work and the Root and Branch petitions which they had received:

. . . which long efflagitated difficult worke (which your Honours have now set upon) I conceive the publishing of this Antipathy, will much facilitate and advance . . .[1]

*The Antipathie* was a failure, if its achievement was to be measured against its aim. Its inconsistencies and equivocations prompted Bishop Goodman to note, how unsatisfactory really *The Anthipathie* was, as the total condemnation of episcopacy that it set out to be. As Symmons pointed out in 1645, it was hardly sensible to hold that men should deserve punishment for sins committed by predecessors hundreds of years before they were born, and which they might have expressly repudiated. What logic the narration of past treacheries had was very much dependent on a clear demonstration that these same tendencies

[1] Prynne, *The Antipathie* . . ., i, pp. 153, 220, 221, 280, 281, 334, 343, dedicatory epistle.

75

were apparent in more recent predecessors; it is this which is lacking in Prynne's history.[1] Prynne's thesis of a totally corrupt episcopacy, if it were to carry conviction, required the destruction of the prestige of the 'good bishops', such as the martyrs and the Elizabethan moderates. It is precisely at these points that Prynne falters, because his views are still coloured by the Elizabethan preconceptions which—in theory—he has rejected. Thus a large section of his second volume is a refutation of the *iure divino* claims by bishops. Once more he turns to the martyrs and moderate bishops whom he had repudiated in the first volume: Jewel, 'the incomperable Bishop of Salisbury'; 'Tyndale our famous Martyr'; Barnes, 'our godly Martyr'; Frith, 'our learned English Martyr'; Latimer, and even Tunstall, whom he had rejected earlier expressly because a good bishop was an impossibility.[2] *The Antipathie* is not a systematic corrective of Foxe, but it attempts to be. In terms of Prynne's attitude, his aim is more relevant than his achievement.

Behind that radical aim lay a profound disillusionment with the moderate bishops of his own time. Francis White provided Prynne, in *The Antipathie*, with the example of a man who 'had gained great fame and reputation in our Church for his learning and Books against the Papists whilst he continued an ordinary Minister' but who 'soone lost all his honour and reputation after he became a bishop'. As early as 1637 Prynne had seen the significance of White's decline. He pointed out then that when White had been only Dean of Carlisle he had written spiritedly against Popery, but once he became Bishop of Ely he wrote against sabbatarianism. The punning moral that Prynne drew for bishops from White's case was that 'they have in a short time altered their colour for the worse and . . . growne blacke in their old age, when as they were white in their youth'. Underlying the play on words was a serious suggestion that had hardened into belief in 1641: 'none growing better men, but most farre worse by their Sees.'[3]

---

[1] Godfrey Goodman, *The Two Great Mysteries of Christian Religion* . . . (London, 1653), dedicatory epistle; Edward Symmons, *Scripture Vindicated* . . . (Oxford, 1645), p. 61.

[2] Prynne, *The Antipathie* . . ., ii, pp. 351, 352, 363, 375, 377, 386, 452.

[3] Prynne, *The Antipathie* . . ., ii, pp. 265, 312; Prynne, *A Quench-Coale* . . . (London, 1637), p. 288.

Prynne's reference to White in 1637 almost immediately preceded his explanation of Morton. That explanation was along lines that were compatible with Prynne's faith in moderate bishops: that passages in Morton's works which seemed to approve of ceremonial innovations must have been fathered on him by Laudians, such as Cosin, Pocklington and Widdowes. He rejected the ascription of one passage to Morton because it 'savours neither of his judgement, learning nor acutenes'. But was there another interpretation possible of Morton's behaviour? Prynne's comments on White might have been intended as an explanation of Morton's lapse: that his 'judgement' and 'learning' had been clouded—not by Laudian intrigue—but by his own retention of a bishopric. Whether, by the juxtaposition of the two passages, Prynne intended such an inference to be drawn, is difficult to say. It certainly cannot be taken for granted that the suggestion of Laudian intrigue was meant to be discounted as irony, under cover of which the real thrust against Morton was delivered. Prynne's belief in the existence of wide-spread plots by Laud and his agents was too firmly rooted for that assumption to be safe. But it is possible that, even in 1637, the Laudian scapegoat did not resolve all Prynne's doubts and that he was beginning to consider a less superficial explanation for corruptions within the episcopate.[1]

What Prynne may have felt about Morton in 1637, he certainly felt about Usher in 1641; he would have agreed with the judgment of a news journal that 'he was a very brave Scholar, and an excellent preacher; had he not beene poysoned with the Office of a Bishop . . . he had beene one of ten thousand.' Prynne's attitude to Usher faithfully charts his changing moods about moderate bishops: enthusiastic praise in 1630; pained criticism in 1641; violent abuse in 1646; cautious respect in 1660.[2] Prynne had admired Hall in the earlier period for his views on moral questions as much as for his Calvinism, but in *The Antipathie* Prynne's disillusionment with

[1] Prynne, *A Quench-Coale* . . ., p. 294. Cf. Prynne, *The Soveraigne Power of Parliaments* . . . (London, 1643), iii, p. 115, for a later, sceptical view of Morton.

[2] *The Scottish Dove*, Numb. 113, 10–17 December, 1645; Prynne, *Anti-Arminianisme* . . ., p. 217; Prynne, *The Antipathie* . . ., ii, p. 479; Prynne, *Canterburies Doome* . . . (London, 1646), dedicatory epistle; Prynne, *The Second Part of the Signal Loyalty* . . . (London, 1660), p. 92.

him is clearly expressed. Prynne attributes Hall's decline to his being blinded by episcopal pomp:

> . . . a man formerly much honored and deservedly respected, both for his Writing and Preaching before he became a Bishop. He hath much degenerated and lost himselfe of late, not onely by his too much worldinesse but by his overconfident defence of Episcopacy to be *Iure Divino*, in some late Bookes he hath published . . .[1]

Prynne noted also, in 1641, that John Williams 'hath much eclipsed all the honour and reputation he had gained by his former sufferings', and that Wright had proceeded with zeal against Puritans in his see at Chester. Pointing out that Wright had once been revered as one of the 'old Puritanes', Prynne commented bitterly: 'it seemes you played but the hypocrite.' Daniel Featley had acknowledged that the Beckets and Bonners were 'bitter Almondes' but on behalf of Anglicanism cited 'our learned and every way accomplished Ushers, Mortons, Halls and Prideauxes'. In 1641 these names had lost their charm for Prynne.[2]

Featley had another line of defence against Prynne: that the fault of the Beckets and Bonners lay in their Popery, not in their Prelacy. But Prynne maintained that the sedition came from their prelatical, not papal, status and pointed to Laud, Wren and Mountague as proof of this thesis. This was a rare case where Prynne found it profitable to dissociate the Laudians from the Papists. He acknowledged that obedience to the Pope had made some of the earlier bishops more disloyal than otherwise they would have been, as when the Pope sided with Stephen Langton against poor King John, but he went on:

> . . . but yet afterward when the Pope sided with King John and Henry III against Langton, and the other Bishops who stirred up the Barons Warres, these Bishops continued as trayterous and rebellious to these Kings as ever they were before whiles they adhered to the Pope, and the Pope to them; therefore their Hierarchy (the cause of all these stirs) not their Popery was the ground work of their Treachery and enormities . . .[3]

[1] Prynne, *The Antipathie* . . ., ii, pp. 226–7.
[2] Ibid., ii, p. 334; Prynne, *A New Discovery* . . . (London, 1641), p. 225; Daniel Featley, *The League Illegal* . . . (London, 1643), p. 40.
[3] Prynne, *The Antipathie* . . ., ii, p. 515.

This curious inversion of a traditional view of history reinforced Prynne's thesis of a totally corrupt episcopacy that must
be totally removed.

Prynne's loss of faith in the moderate bishops was a cause,
not merely an effect, of his swing to radicalism in 1641. But it
was not the only cause, nor even the more important one: at
the root of his radicalism in 1641 lay, not despair, but hope. His
personal sufferings; his changed attitude to the King; the fresh
proof of Laudian intransigence in the Scottish Wars: all these
may have contributed to his break with moderation.[1] Yet the
mood of *The Antipathie* is not one of bitter disillusionment, but
rather one of expectant rejoicing at the radical reconstruction
that lay ahead.

Prynne makes it clear in *The Antipathie* that future reform is
to be linked closely with the Scottish Presbyterians. He speaks
of their government with affection and defends their claims to
powers of excommunication. He even sees merit in their anti-
monarchical tendencies.[2] Such violation of his constitutional
principles of the earlier 'royal' period is only to be explained in
terms of the overriding priority that he gave to ethical issues in
1641. Philip Hunton, with his remorseless logic, could see that
the ethical and the constitutional must not be confused: 'the
expurgation of in-crept corruptions in Church and State' was
irrelevant when set beside the constitutional issues. Prynne
argues a contrary view in *The Antipathie*:

> I shall be a daily Oratour to the Throne of Grace . . . til you
> have cleansed both our Church and State from all Corruptions
> which infect them . . .

Throughout *The Antipathie* the desire for a moral reform is
expressed. Prynne attacks the Laudians for their neglect of
preaching, 'this principle part of their office' and even attacks
their *iure divino* claims on ethical rather than constitutional
grounds:

> . . . the first thing that caused me to suspect our Prelates calling,
> not to be divine . . was the pravity of their actions, and enormity
> of their lives . . .

[1] For his changed attitude to the King, see: Prynne, *The Antipathie* . . .,
ii, pp. 309–10.
[2] Prynne, *The Antipathie* . . ., ii, pp. 343, 312–13, 310.

Prynne points out that in the Reformed Churches such as France and Geneva, where there were no bishops, there was a more orderly moral code than in England, whose bishops' crimes included 'commutations of penance, admission of prophane and scandalous persons to the Sacrament, toleration of scandalous, superstitious, lasie, non-preaching and insufficient Ministers'. Prynne clearly lays down the mandate for an alternative government to this:

> . . . there is no neede at all to continue our Lordly Prelates to suppresse these mischiefes, which may be better reformed, and suppressed by others, than by our Bishops and their officers . . .

Prynne's attraction to the Scottish solution is not the result of ignorance of its clericalist potentialities. He denies that Presbyterianism is inimical to monarchy in the way that episcopacy has been, and boldly faces the question whether the clerical powers claimed in excommunication by Presbyterian ministers will encroach on the powers of the laity in general and on monarchy in particular. His conclusion is that they will not; but an argument which he develops later in the pamphlet shows that he does not really care, one way or the other. The experience that he had belatedly learnt in 1641 was that sympathy between prelate and monarch could be as potentially dangerous as antipathy. Events of 1641 had taught him 'how easily might our Church and Religion by one over-potent Arch-bishop, or Prelate, backed by his Soveraigne, be undermined, suppressed and eradicated in a short space'. Such reasoning led him to defend Presbyterianism for its lack of dependence on the monarch:

> . . . whereas if this jurisdiction were devested from the Bishops (which are but 26 and depend on one Arch-Prelate) and settled in the Ministers which are many, and more independent on the Prince then they, our Religion, would be farre more secure . . .[1]

This passage represents an extraordinary, but ephemeral, phase in the development of Prynne's ideas: so far had he moved from the 'royal' position of his earlier years that he now valued clerical independence of monarchy as one of the most attractive features of Presbyterianism. Practical experience had taught

[1] Philip Hunton, *A Treatise of Monarchie* (London, 1643), p. 75; Prynne, *The Antipathie* . . ., i, dedicatory epistle; ii, pp. 308, 505–7, 313, 309–10.

him how much harm a King, seduced by a cleric, could cause. This lesson destroyed the philosophical basis of *The Antipathie* as surely as his respect for the martyrs and Elizabethan bishops had destroyed its historical basis. Prynne's philosophical attack on clerical dependence on the Crown, and his historical attack on clerical independence of the Crown were reconcilable only in their ultimate aim; admiration for the Scots and a belief in the total corruption of episcopacy testified alike to his radical sympathies in 1641.

Such sympathies brought him closer in 1641 to Leighton's position in the thirties, from which he had then markedly dissociated himself. Although Prynne pays no formal acknowledgment to Leighton in *The Antipathie*—as he did to Gibson—his debt is clear. Leighton, in his *An Appeal to the Parliament*, specifically attacks Whitgift, Downame and Morton: three moderate bishops that Prynne revered then, but attacked in 1641. Leighton calls for the total removal of bishops and turns to history for support:

> ... of all the evills inflicted, and of all the good hindred, since Anno 600 one or more of the Hierarchie have been a principall cause... The proofe of this point must be by induction of particular instances, selected from the Histories of the Kingdome ...

Leighton then proceeds to make an historical sketch very much along the lines that Prynne adopted in 1641—briefer, but no less partial. The bishops were tainted from the start because St. Augustine was their founder. Becket typifies their pride whilst King John was a victim of their intrigues. It is no defence to say that they were Popish bishops—'they are garments cut out of the same cloth'. Edward VI had sincerely wanted a full Reformation but had been held back by the conservatism of the bishops. Leighton was forced to concede their worth to some extent:

> At the beginning of Reformation, our Bishops did not see the evill of the things. Manie of them were painfull in labours, rich in works of mercie, and in the end some of them sealed their Repentance with their blood ...[1]

Yet Leighton refused to be blinded by their martyrdom: their conservatism had caused the retention of abominations, such

[1] Alexander Leighton, *An Appeal to the Parliament* ... (London, 1628), pp. 28, 160, 51, 56–8, 69, 150, 70, 72.

as kneeling at the receiving of the Sacrament. In Elizabeth's reign these evil tendencies, unmitigated by personal heroism, reached their height. Reynolds, against Downame, had defended the Elizabethan bishops by denying that they had presented the Queen with an '*Omnia bene*'; Leighton attacked them by asserting, in those very words, that they did.[1] This is the distance between Jacobean nonconformity and later radicalism. Leighton defended Cartwright against Whitgift; Prynne only came to do so in 1641. Leighton accused Bancroft of complicity in the Gunpowder Plot: an unusual charge, borrowed by Prynne in *The Antipathie*, but at no other time in his career.[2] Leighton anticipated Prynne in two other important assertions: that a good bishop is an impossibility: that episcopacy is neither divine nor human, but Antichristian and totally corrupt. A comparison between *The Antipathie* and Leighton's pamphlet brings out the radical aims of Prynne in 1641.[3]

This radicalism was recognized by contemporaries. Edward Symmons, an Anglican, wished to explain in 1645 why the 'root and branch' thesis had triumphed in 1641 over the moderate traditions of English nonconformity. He saw that such a thesis was dependent on a belief that English bishops after the Reformation were tainted with the guilt of their Popish predecessors. For this reason he saw Leighton's *An Appeal to the Parliament* as a landmark in anti-episcopal thought. In that work, Leighton had enumerated the faults of Popish bishops since the Conquest: a theme that was developed by Smectymnuus in 1641:

> . . . they there doe Laytonize up many of the miscarriages of the Popish Bishops, as if they were the fault of ours, so endeavouring to imbitter peoples spirits against that Sacred Order . . . as against Antichristian men, and maintainers of the same evills, practiced by men of another Religion, many Hundreds of Years before they were borne . . .

---

[1] Ibid., p. 72; John Reynolds, *Mr. Downames Sermon Answered and Refuted* (London, 1609), p. 46.

[2] Leighton, op. cit., pp. 80, 76, 77; Prynne, *The Antipathie* . . ., i, p. 151. When Prynne condemned Jesuit responsibility for the Gunpowder Plot in 1655, he did not revive the charge against Bancroft: Prynne, *A Seasonable, Legal, and Historical Vindication* . . . (London, 1655), dedicatory epistle.

[3] Leighton, op. cit., pp. 153, 88.

Symmons saw *The Antipathie* as the logical culmination of the ideas of Leighton and Smectymnuus:

> . . . But then comes William Pryn with his 2 Volumnes, and speaks over the same thing the third time, with many more words, though with as little Conscience, and Honesty as the rest; and he strikes the matter dead; for by the mouth of 3 such witnesses the thing is so established, that people should be worse than Infiddels if they believe it not . . . it being so; the Bishops must be pluckt up Root and Branch, and all that approve of them, be they who will, must (like welwillers to Babylon as they be) be caste down, and rooted out with them, what effusion of blood soever it cost, for 'tis the Lords work against Babilon . . .[1]

This was a first-class analysis by Symmons. He had identified Prynne with the Smectymnuan radicals in 1641; he had stressed the affinity between Prynne in 1641 and Leighton (in marked contrast to Prynne's attitude to Leighton before 1641); he had acknowledged the service that Prynne's 'Laytonizing' of episcopacy had rendered to the cause of 'root and branch'.

Another pamphlet provided evidence of a more oblique nature. It was an attack on Prynne in 1649. The date is important: it was written at a time when Army sympathizers felt the need to discredit the eloquent champion of negotiations with the King. One of the points that the author of the pamphlet made was cryptic, but suggestive. He pointed out that Prynne, despite his rehabilitation in 1641, had not remained content with a passive rôle:

> But as a Dog to his Vomit, he returns to scribbling, and having catch at the desires of wisemen (who admitted him, because of his sufferings to their company) fit some years after for publication, he not being able to hold any longer, untimely acquaints the people with what they were not then enabled to understand, by which means, divers persons staggering betwixt honesty and malignancy, quite fell off; and many others pretty well inclined to the publike, began to waver: and thus fitted for temptation, soon found an opportunity of departing from us. Thus was the common enemy furnish't with friends by the folly and letchery of writing of Mr. William Prynne, and his companions . . .[2]

[1] Symmons, *Scripture Vindicated* . . . (Oxford, 1645), p. 61; Smectymnuus, *A Vindication of the Answer* . . . (London, 1641), p. 89.

[2] (Anon.), *A Word to Mr. Wil Pryn Esq.*, . . . (London, 1649), p. 4.

The author had a definite grievance against Prynne, and although unfortunately he did not state it specifically, it is still possible to guess at his meaning. *The Antipathie* is the only work at this period written by Prynne that is susceptible to the author's interpretation, and the only counsels that it could divulge prematurely were those of the ecclesiastical radicals. The cause of the 'falling off', which the writer bemoans, may well have been the recognition of ecclesiastical radicalism that played so large a part in the 'departing' in 1641 of men like Clarendon, Falkland, Bagshaw and Gauden. The 'wisemen', on this hypothesis, were 'root and branch' advocates who admitted Prynne to their counsels. That the passage in the pamphlet was a criticism of *The Antipathie* for its premature radicalism is only an hypothesis, but it seems a plausible one in the light of the other evidence.

In one other way, too, the hypothesis rings true: it faithfully captures Prynne's mood in 1641. *The Antipathie* is the testament of a radical; its pages breathe a messianic recklessness. Prynne, in his views on church government, was an Erastian; in his concern for moral issues, a Puritan. The two positions fused, in the period from 1626 to 1640, in antipathy to a church government that seemed to Prynne to be both clericalist and immoral. In 1641, however, the two positions seemed to be poised as antitheses. The London ministers, preaching Brightman and a godly discipline, won Prynne to a programme that was potentially clericalist in nature. Prynne, said one writer, would at this time have 'plucked out his eies for the godly Ministers zealous of Reformation'.[1] He did more for them than that: he plucked out Foxe from his heart.

---

[1] 'S.S.', *Holy Things for Holy Men* . . . (London, 1658), preface.

# V

# THE CIVIL WAR

PRYNNE wrote his defence of the sovereignty of Parliament in 1643.[1] In an introduction to the appendix which he inserted at the end of the last part of this work, Prynne apologized for its confused construction and hasty compilation.[2] True of the appendix, the criticism was equally valid of the work as a whole. Prynne had been commissioned by Parliament to justify its actions and his work came out in piecemeal fashion in four parts in 1643. His work bore the mark of its origins: Prynne was more concerned with the defence of what Parliament had already claimed than with an analysis of how much it ought to claim. One anonymous critic noted that singularly absent in Prynne's work was an appeal to 'those Generall and Royall Laws of Reason, Nature, Nations and Necessity that must be appealed to'. Instead, Prynne had contented himself with the inferior authority of mutable 'bare municipall Laws of a Country'. Prynne had rejected the speculative approach in favour of the empirical:

> . . . instead thereof you decline, all examinations of Governments and their ends . . .[3]

[1] Prynne, *The Soveraigne Power of Parliaments* . . . (London, 1643): this abbreviated title, by which the work was generally known, has been used throughout the chapter.

[2] Ibid., iv, dedicatory epistle. Cf. William Haller, *Tracts on Liberty in the Puritan Revolution 1638–47* (New York, 1934), i, p. 25: 'Few if any readers could have followed Prynne with understanding. But . . . many an earnest if simple mind must have been persuaded that truth must surely lie where, in so good a cause, appeared so much zeal and learning.'

[3] (Anon.), *A Serious Epistle to Mr. William Prynne* . . . (London, 1649), pp. 9–10. Haller, op. cit., i, p. 25 contrasts Prynne's disorderly dogmatism with Henry Parker's appeal to reason.

The low level of reasoning in Prynne's work was a more serious restriction upon its popularity and influence than one might have expected in a polemical work written in the distractions of a Civil War. For Prynne was addressing many men who were Puritans, and who had, therefore, been accustomed to the analytical, rational sermons of ministers trained in Ramist logic. Ames had looked for the accomplishment of Scriptural analysis 'by right application of the precepts of Logic'. To Preston, the insight which men derived from analytical reasoning provided not the Arminian passport to redemption but the perception of the justice of their damnation.[1] Most sermons and pamphlets written on behalf of Parliament in the early stages of the Civil War (before the emergence of more radical and mystical thought), paid lip-service to logical construction, even if their logical grasp of the issues at stake was suspect.[2] Henry Parker complained bitterly of the low intellectual calibre of his colleagues in comparison with their opponents, yet the popularity of his own writings, and the controversies which they aroused, indicated that this was only a reflection upon their quality of mind, not upon the values which they respected.[3] It was otherwise with Prynne: he differs from most other writers on the great constitutional controversy at this time, in that the low priority which he gives to reasoning is deliberate.

In an introduction to the first part of his work, Prynne explained his motive in writing the pamphlet in this way:

[1] Perry Miller, *The New England Mind: The Seventeenth Century* (New York, 1939), pp. 111–53, 189, 215. This work is the classic statement of the Puritan paradox: that, however emotionally-charged in tone, the Puritan sermons and pamphlets were generally logical and analytical to the point of pedantry, in construction. Cf. also W. Fraser Mitchell *English Pulpit Oratory from Andrewes to Tillotson* (London, 1932), *passim*.

[2] Although for purpose of comparison or illumination, reference is made throughout the chapter to the constitutional contribution of other writers than Prynne at this time, a detailed analysis of their works has been avoided. This is partly because it lies outside the main theme of discussion, and partly because such analysis has been well undertaken by recent scholars (most notably by M. A. Judson).

[3] Henry Parker, *The Contra-Replicant* . . . (London, 1643), p. 3: 'though too many papers are scattered of both sides, yet those of the Kings are most of them serious, and done by able men, whereas those of the Parliaments side for the most part are ridiculous done by Sots, or prevaricators to the disadvantage of the partie.'

... the insufficiency and unsatisfactorinesse of all late Printed Pleas for the Parliaments Interest, through defect of punctuall Precedents, any Authorities to backe their rationall Discourse ...[1]

Philip Hunton had, by subtle reasoning and sensitive insight, constructed a cogent plea for personal action by the subject on behalf of Parliament, but he had incidentally destroyed the formal authoritative case for Parliament.[2] To Prynne, this might well read as the nemesis of too great a reliance upon reason. Hunton himself had complained that Henry Ferne, on the Royalist side, 'slights my endeavour because I bring not History and Antiquity but doe go about to reason him into a belief of these Assertions'.[3] When Hobbes discussed the question of the legality of commissions of array, he acknowledged that the issue was, to him, academic and meaningless; self-preservation was the best title for war. Yet he recognized, at the same time, that such had been the influence of legal pre-conceptions upon the class of members represented in Parliament, that these issues were neither academic nor meaningless to them:

> ... For the lawyers, I mean the judges of the courts at West-minster, and some few others, though but advocates, yet of great reputation for their skill in the common-laws and statutes of England had infected most of the gentry of England with their maxims and cases prejudged, which they call precedents; and made them think so well of their own knowledge in the law, that they were very glad of this occasion to shew it against the King, and thereby to gain a reputation with the Parliament of being good patriots, and wise statesmen ...[4]

Prynne believed that he was satisfying a genuine need by demonstrating, from precedents, the legality of the claims which Parliament came to make in the course of the war; in the context of the debates upon Ship Money, and Hobbes' observations, the belief seems tenable. A critic ridiculed Prynne for

[1] Prynne, *The Soveraigne Power of Parliaments* ..., i, dedicatory epistle.
[2] Philip Hunton, *A Treatise of Monarchie* ... (London, 1643): especially pp. 17, 69, 73.
[3] Hunton, *A Vindication of the Treatise of Monarchy* (London, 1644), p. 36.
[4] Thomas Hobbes, *English Works* ..., ed. W. Molesworth (London, 1839–45), vi, pp. 311–12. Cf. J. G. A. Pocock, *The Ancient Constitution and The Feudal Law* (Cambridge, 1957), p. 47, on the significance of claims from precedent.

seeking to prove the sovereignty of Parliament from 'morall sentences out of Seneca', but Prynne's exhaustive citations of authorities from almost every source had their vindication in Herle's comment:

> . . . the civill Lawyer when he pleads doth not he carry it when he quotes the most Authours.[1]

For Prynne's defence of the sovereignty of Parliament was essentially a lawyer's brief; it was on these terms that Prynne undertook the case, and it was on these terms that his writings should be discussed. His was not an attempt to analyse the causes of breakdown, nor even inferentially to point to the solution, but it was an attempt to justify legally the position which Parliament had maintained up to the time of his writing. The empirical nature of this approach was evident in 1649 when he justified an assertion, which he had made in his defence of the sovereignty of Parliament earlier, that Parliament was not challenging the person of the King. He said that he had good reason to write this in 1643, not because of the grasp of the constitutional relationships which it revealed, but 'because the Lords and Commons in their Answer to his Majesties Declaration, after his late victory against the Rebels on Sunday the 23 of October 1642' had a few months before his writing put forward precisely this denial.[2] One cannot discount the respective popularity of his work, and the controversy which it excited, simply in terms of the prestige which he had enjoyed through his sufferings, and the retrospective significance which his work acquired in 1649 when he attacked the regicides.[3] The appeal of his work to his contemporaries must, in part at least, be attributed to the support which it gave to the argument of legality from precedent; his contemporaries recognized in Prynne its most extreme exponent.[4]

[1] (Anon.), *A Serious Epistle to Mr. William Prynne* . . . (London, 1649), p. 9; Charles Herle, *An Answer to Mis-Led Doctor Fearne* . . . (London, 1649), p. 19.

[2] Prynne, *Prynne the Member Reconciled to Prynne the Barrester* . . . (London, 1649), p. 11.

[3] Prynne, *The Substance of a Speech* . . . (London, 1649), *passim*.

[4] (Anon.), *The Fallacies of Mr. William Prynne* . . . (Oxford, 1644), p. 1 compared Prynne's popularity with that of the preachers: 'Mr. Prynne's books are more prevalent than their Sermons.'

If Prynne's work had been developed consistently along the lines of a legal brief, criticism of it for its lack of method, weakness of analysis and reluctance to argue general principles, would have been unfair; Prynne then would have been criticized for doing what he had set out to do. The most damaging criticism of Prynne's work is that it does not rely consistently upon precedent: that he fails to do what he set out to do, by seeking to do more. There is an ambiguity latent in the original title: *The Treachery and Disloyalty of Papists to their Soveraignes, in Doctrine and Practise, Together with the First Part of the Soveraigne Power of Parliaments and Kingdomes*... The question which Prynne never really satisfactorily resolved was: are Parliament's proceedings against Kings in former times to be revered as precedents, or reviled as Papist? A critic seized upon the ambiguity, when he commented upon Prynne's citation of the actions of Popish Barons, Prelates and Commons against such figures as John, Edward II, Richard II, and Henry VI:

> If any will wash the Black-Moore white, and excuse Mr. Prynne that he delivereth all these Examples, onely historically; but that he determineth nothing Dogmatically... Wherefore doth he then print such Presidents under such a Title, as *The Soveraigne Power of Parliaments* ...[1]

When Prynne attacked the regicides in 1649, he denied the relevance of precedents drawn from the reigns of such Kings as John, Edward II, or Richard II:

> ... those proceedings were only by Popish parliaments in time of ignorance ...[2]

But a critic, writing in that year, could justly point out that Prynne did not draw such an inference in 1643 from these same precedents.[3]

At the root of Prynne's ambiguous attitude to precedents was an uncertainty about sovereignty. Professor Judson has shown how the ideal of a 'balanced polity' resting upon law was basic

---

[1] (Anon.), *The Fallacies of Mr. William Prynne* ... (Oxford, 1644), p. 21. Cf. H.M.C. *5th. Report*, p. 177, for comment by a critic on Prynne's ability to use titles which were misleading, but sold well.

[2] Prynne, *A Briefe Memento to the Present Unparliamentary Junto* ... (London, 1649), p. 14.

[3] (Anon.), *Prynn Against Prinn* ... (London, 1649), p. 7.

to both sides until late in the Civil War; she praises the contribution of writers, such as Parker, Digges and Hunton, who emancipated themselves from these legalistic preconceptions in order to proclaim the necessity of sovereignty: of a single, uncontrollable power which was not simply based upon, but which controlled, law.[1] Prynne's attempt to prove the sovereignty of Parliament by showing, from past precedents, that its actions were based upon the law, seemed therefore to indicate that Prynne had not grasped the concept of sovereignty; Professor Judson thus can ignore Prynne's contribution to her discussion. When Prynne wished to justify the Militia Ordinance, he cited innumerable legal precedents; Hobbes, on the other hand, could say of it, simply, that: 'Which power, whosoever has, has also, without doubt, the whole sovereignty.'[2] But Prynne did not rest content with argument exclusively from precedent, and in his search for a higher sanction he touched upon sovereignty. A critic emphasized the confusion:

> . . . In one side he calls his Theame (The Soveraigntie of the Parliament) a practice as old as Adam; in the very next a Truth newly discovered . . .[3]

Prynne's approach has less in common with his legalistically-minded colleagues, who failed to understand the concept of sovereignty, and with Parker and Herle, who came to recognize it as the solution of the crisis, than it has with Hunton, who understood the concept but who would not ultimately accept it as the solution. Prynne's motives, however, differ entirely from Hunton's in reaching this position, and they are worth examining in detail for the light which they throw upon the development of his thought from his 'royal' pamphleteering of 1626–40.

Academically, theologically, and, above all, constitutionally, Prynne was better equipped than most of his colleagues to

[1] Judson, op. cit., *passim*; Parker, *Observations Upon Some of His Majesties Late Answers and Expresses* . . ., pp. 34–5; Parker, *The Contra-Replicant* . . ., p. 19; Parker, *A Letter of Due Censure* . . . (London, 1650), p. 28; Dudley Digges, *The Unlawfulnesse of Subject Taking up Arms* . . . (Oxford, 1643), pp. 40, 69; Hunton, *A Treatise of Monarchie* . . ., pp. 28–9.

[2] Prynne, *The Soveraigne Power of Parliaments* . . ., ii, *passim*; Hobbes, *Works* . . ., vi, p. 263.

[3] (Anon.), *The Fallacies of Mr. William Prynne* . . ., p. 13.

understand sympathetically the concept of sovereignty. Academically, Prynne had read Bodin, and understood from his writings the importance of legislative sovereignty; that the sovereign was not to be defined as a mosaic of legally defined rights but as the power to make law. Prynne could thus say:

> John Bodin that great Lawyer and Polititian, resolves, that the chiefe mark of an absolute and Soveraigne Prince is to give Lawes to all his Subjects in generall, and to every one of them in particular without consent of any other greater, equall or lesse than himself . . .[1]

Professor Miller has emphasized the importance of the connection between theology and politics in this period: of the interaction of views of God and the civil magistrate as an influence upon political thinking. The 'Covenant theology' taught by English Puritans such as Sibbes, Preston and Ball had substituted for the remote, unaccountable deity, essential to strict Calvinist doctrine, the concept of a Merciful God who had entered into a Covenant with His People, almost on a *quid pro quo* basis. Professor Miller pointed out that, by taking the Covenant upon Himself, 'God had become the kind of sovereign every Puritan in the House of Commons was hoping to behold in Westminster'. The analogies which these divines used, show that such was the inference intended. Cotton emphasized that the mutual obligation of King and people had its counterpart in the Covenant between God and people: '. . . a Governour, a Provider for, and a protector of his people . . . and the people undertake to be obedient to his Lawes. . .' Similarly, Thomas Hooker likened the Covenant to '. . . a Parliament Consultation, they must profound all to the King, and he must ratifie, and confirme it. . . .'[2] Acceptance of this contractual theory, on a theological level, stimulated the orthodox constitutional opposition before the Civil War to a King, who was moving beyond the bounds of law; faithful obedience by the subject was one part of the Covenant, and righteous government by

[1] Prynne, *The Soveraigne Power of Parliaments* . . ., i, p. 46. A good discussion of Bodin's views upon sovereignty is contained in: W. F. Church, *Constitutional Thought in Sixteenth Century France: A Study in the Evolution of Ideas* (Camb., Mass., 1941).

[2] Miller, op. cit., p. 413. His whole section upon the Covenant of Grace (pp. 365–97), is most helpful.

the magistrate was the other. Professor Miller pointed to the significance of Preston's position in this context:

> . . . the concept was essentially legal . . It seems significant that Preston . . . its greater popularizer, should have been, as Master of Emmanuel, the leading politician among Puritan divines just when the union between religious reformers and the lawyers was being cemented . . .[1]

One of the lawyers who came directly under Preston's influence at Lincoln's Inn was William Prynne. In view of the belief that Prynne was the mouthpiece of Preston in the early part of his career, it is important to realize that in one significant respect at least, the doctrinal teachings, Prynne's views are singularly uninfluenced by Preston's theological compromise.[2] Prynne went back to Calvin, to the view of a God who was omnipotent and inscrutable: a view which coloured his constitutional thinking as markedly as the theology of the 'Covenant' school coloured theirs. For, when Prynne draws the analogy between God and King, a different image is evoked. He says that: 'We see that earthly Monarchs doe oft dispence, and cast their honours, favours and disfavours upon men . . . upon no other grounds at all, but that it is their pleasure.' Likewise, he claims, God's sovereignty is 'an absolute, a free, a just Prerogative'.[3]

The King's sovereignty, no more than God's, was to be questioned by men. The sovereignty which Prynne valued in the civil magistrate was that which was exercised by God in the Old Testament: capricious, uncensurable and capable of bringing order and a 'godly discipline' to the reprobate majority. Prynne had little sympathy with the legal shibboleths of 'balance' and of limiting the power of the monarch: this accounts for Prynne's distance from the preoccupations of his legally-minded colleagues in the years before the Civil War. Yet this distance must not be exaggerated. Although Prynne did not think in 'covenant' terms of the rights of the subject, he did think in somewhat similar terms of the obligations of the ruler. Absolute power was not surrendered absolutely, but,

[1] Ibid., p. 374.
[2] Prynne, *Anti-Arminianisme* . . . (London, 1630), *passim*.
[3] Prynne, *God No Imposter* . . ., pp. 28-9.

conditionally, on the ruler's ability to effect God's will.[1] This loop-hole lessened the arbitrary nature of the rule: absolute power was not in itself to be questioned, but its location was, if it became obvious that the ends, for which Christian magistracy existed, were being frustrated. The failure to effect moral reform in the years immediately prior to the Civil War has already—in the previous chapter—been seen as a major factor in Prynne's renunciation of moderate episcopacy: that failure similarly reflected upon the Crown, not upon the limits of its power. The absolute power, which had been misdirected by Charles I, should be transferred to Parliament: a critic noted in 1644 alarming traits in Prynne—'two grosse points of Poperie, Implicite Faith and Blinde Obedience'—in claiming in his defence of the sovereignty of Parliament 'a supreme unlimited Authority, that is supreme, above the Kings: and Unlimited, above the Lawes of this Land'.[2] Prynne did not turn to Parliament out of concern for the law, nor out of a desire to see that the people's part in their Covenant with the King was honoured, but primarily out of a search for a sovereign power which could command the absolute obedience which 'men of Augustinian piety' were anxious to pay to an authority which they could trust to implement God's will on earth.[3]

But the greatest obstacle to an understanding of sovereignty which the legal mind faced was the reverence which Coke and his colleagues had inculcated for Magna Carta as the embodiment of law. Even Philip Hunton, who had seen that the struggle for sovereignty was the great issue at stake, could not regard the claims by either side to it as anything other than bogus. Hunton saw in the concessions embodied in Magna Carta the proof that 'the sovereignty of our Kings is radically and fundamentally limited'.[4]

[1] As will be shown later in the chapter, this became more narrowly identified with the ruler's fulfilment of his imperial rôle.

[2] (Anon.), *The Fallacies of Mr. William Prynne* . . ., p. 15.

[3] Miller, op. cit., pp. 416–17, contrasted the contractual theory of obligation with the strict Calvinist reasoning, on which, 'as long as they were men of Augustinian piety they had to agree that God enjoined obedience to magistrates as a religious duty, that civil powers were divinely appointed to keep the world from becoming "a great Den of Thieves and Robbers".'

[4] Hunton, *A Treatise of Monarchie* . . ., p. 31.

Mrs. Kirby equates Prynne's position with that of the majority of his lawyer-colleagues, when she says that 'in Magna Charta and such documents they found the means of preserving the traditional liberties of Englishmen'.[1] But Prynne had learnt his views of Magna Carta not from Coke but from Foxe and Bilson. His admiration of Coke was not uncritical, even in 1643; in view of Prynne's important challenge later to Coke's scholarship on the origins of the Commons, it is worth noting that Prynne could write thus in 1643:

> . . . Sir Edward Cooke, in his Institutes on Magna Charta, proves that the Lords and Peers in many Charters and Acts, are included under the name of the Commons and Commonalty of England. But we need not returne to this last doubtfull refuge . . .[2]

Foxe could not share Coke's concern with a King who encroached upon the law; as an imperial historian, he saw King John as an heroic, Promethean figure in his defiance of the Pope. Magna Carta was the victory of clerical intrigue over a King, described by Foxe as 'the noble personage . . . being far from the superstition which Kings at that time were commonly subject to, he regarded not the popish mass'.[3] Bilson, eclectic as ever, gave the orthodox vindication of Magna Carta in language which was echoed in many Civil War pamphlets, when he asked whether a King could subject his realm to tyranny:

> I thinke Lawyers will say no, as well as divines: sure I am the Barons of this Realme thought no.

Yet Bilson's historical interpretation of King John's reign is much nearer to Foxe's than it is to Coke's: Stephen Langton is the villain of the piece, who 'set all the Barons of this Realme in an open rebellion against the King, that never ceased till the King was poysoned'.[4]

It is this interpretation which is taken over by Prynne. He deplored the way in which John had been maligned by clerical historians, such as Matthew Paris; he could sympathize with

---

[1] Kirby, *William Prynne . . .*, p. 182.

[2] Prynne, *The Soveraigne Power of Parliaments . . .*, i, p. 44.

[3] Foxe, op. cit., ii, p. 340.

[4] Bilson, *The True Difference betweene Christian Subjection and Unchristian Rebellion . . .*, pp. 479–80, 475.

John, because anti-clericalism, not respect for the law, was his criterion of good kingship. Conversely, the barons' resistance was not the defence of legal rights but the expression of clerical influence:

> ... For the King ... began to curbe the Arch-Bishop and his Faction; who finding the King stronger in the Popes favour then they thereupon stirred up the Barons to rebell and take Armes against the King ... To obscure whose Treason and Rebellion, our Monkes, who writ the Histories of these times, have raised up many slanders and lyes of the poysoned King John, to his great defamation ...[1]

This historical interpretation encouraged the idea of Magna Carta as the triumph of clerical extortion: an idea which co-exists in controversial literature alongside the reverential approach. Henry Parker, for instance, showed an awareness of the limited value of Magna Carta, 'as having been penned by Popish Bishops': an awareness which may have facilitated his grasp of sovereignty.[2] When the High Churchman, Edward Boughen, appealed to Magna Carta as a protection for episcopacy, John Geree answered by an appeal to the sovereignty of Parliament.[3] John Lilburne came to share Prynne's scepticism of a document which guaranteed freedom of the Church. The fact that Parliament had extirpated government of the Church by bishops, 'who have their foundation in Magna Carta', did not establish, as it did for Prynne and Geree, the sovereignty of the body which had over-ridden Magna Carta to make the alteration. To Lilburne, it emphasized instead the limited authority of Magna Carta in those parts where it failed to express the spirit of reason, equity and common sense.[4]

Prynne's attitude to Magna Carta placed him at a distance from the majority of his legally-minded colleagues. Herle typifies the orthodox Parliamentary interpretation when he justifies the barons' resistance:

> ... if publike resistance should not be lawfull in such a case, the

[1] Prynne, *The Antipathie* . . ., i, pp. 39–41.
[2] Parker, *Observations Upon Some of His Majesties Late Answers and Expresses* . . ., p. 4.
[3] Geree, *The Sifters Sieve Broken* . . ., p. 102. Cf. Laud, *Works* . . ., iv, p. 352 for similar reasoning.
[4] John Lilburne, *Englands Birth-Right Justified* . . . (London, 1645), p. 5.

tyranny of Kings would grow infinite, by which all civill societie would be destroyed . . .[1]

The difference in historical interpretation is fundamental. Prynne saw Laud as a Stephen Langton, against whom he must fight to rescue the King; his colleagues saw Charles I (who had been encouraged to think in such terms by Laud and his bishops), as a King John, against whom they must fight to preserve Magna Carta.

It was easier for Prynne to think of Charles I as the innocent victim of clerical intrigue in the years before the Civil War, and it is in that period that this antithesis is most valid. But Prynne's loss of faith in the monarch's good intentions—which will be shown to be the key to Prynne's attitude in this period—only strengthened his scepticism of the value of Magna Carta. For Magna Carta was no more a guarantee against a perfidious King than the Petition of Right had been against Charles I. Legalism was not enough: the legislation of the Long Parliament, intrinsically admirable, had been unable to protect the security of the subject. Prynne was clear-sighted enough to see that such legislation was mere 'Spiders Webbs . . . already undermined in action or intention'. He cited examples of Kings wriggling out of the consequences of Magna Carta by devious means, and commented:

> What weak assurances then are Lawes alone, to binde Princes hands, or secure Subjects Liberties, let all men judge.

Prynne ridiculed the shibboleths of legalism:

> . . . the ignorant vulgar . . . deceived with these specious fruitlesse Protestations and the bare grant only of some good Laws (already highly violated), without any apparent intention to observe them . . .[2]

One anonymous critic saw that, despite the legalistic platitudes which abounded in his work, Prynne's defence of the sovereignty of Parliament was essentially founded upon a contempt for fundamental law, which was expressed in his attitude to John and Magna Carta:

[1] Charles Herle, *An Answer to Mis-Led Doctor Fearne* . . . (London, 1642), p. 35. Cf. James Howell, *The Preheminence . . . of Parliament* . . . (London 1643), p. 4, for a similar view.

[2] Prynne, *The Soveraigne Power of Parliaments* . . ., ii, p. 39.

This blemish which Mr. Prynne casts upon our Grand Law, the Magna Carta of England is observable. Mr. Prynne tells us, The Parliament by force of arms compelled King John and Henry III to confirm Magna Carta . . . Now most of the people thought hitherto, that, That Fundamentall Law of England, the Magna Carta, had been our lawfull, indisputable, indubitable, inheritance; if not originally from the Right of the People, yet at least derivatively, from the Grace of our Princes. But when they shall understand, that our interest to our prime Priviledges depend upon force and compulsion, it will smite simple men with the fear of vain proverbs and predictions: That which is gotten by force, may be lost by force.[1]

Prynne, writing as a 'royal' pamphleteer in 1649, denied that such an inference was fair: the origin of an authority in force did not remove the obligation to obey that authority.[2] This defence is less impressive in the context of its time: the intense controversy about 'the Norman Yoke' testifies obliquely to the soundness of the critic's point.[3]

It is his scepticism of Magna Carta which provides Prynne with the basis for his claim for the sovereignty of Parliament. He is able to brush aside the Royalists' legalistic scruple, that Parliament's claim to a taxing power infringed Magna Carta, with the words:

Parliament is the absolute soveraigne power within the realme, not subject to, or obliged by the letter, or intendment of any laws, being in truth the sole law-maker, and having an absolute sovereignty over the laws themselves (yea, over Magna Carta and all other objected acts) to repeale, alter, determine and suspend when there is cause, as is undeniable by its altering the very common law in many cases . . .[4]

---

[1] (Anon.), *The Fallacies of Mr. William Prynne* . . ., pp. 24–5.

[2] Prynne, *The Substance of a Speech* . . ., p. 76. But when Prynne was engaged in controversy in 1659 on behalf of the secluded members, an opponent argued that 'Free Parliament' was a shibboleth as meaningless as Magna Carta: 'nor was Magna Carta neither free. Was not that a forced Charter in its creation?' (Anon.), *A Declaration of Many Thousand Well-Affected Persons . . . Expressing their Adherence to this Present Parliament . . .* (London, 1659), no pagination.

[3] For which, see the important essay with that title in Christopher Hill, *Puritanism and Revolution* (London, 1958).

[4] Prynne, *The Soveraigne Power of Parliament* . . ., iv, p. 15.

This is as clear and unequivocal an assertion of the sovereignty of Parliament as is to be found in the pages of Parker, Hunton, or Herle. It was a Royalist judge who was to chide Prynne for this lack of reverence for the law, implicit in his concept of sovereignty: Jenkins pointed out that Magna Carta stipulated that justice should not be sold, delayed or denied to any man, 'but by this Argument the Parliament may make Lawe to delay, deny and to sell Justice, which surely is a very ill position to maintaine. . .'[1]

Prynne's failure to develop sovereignty as the coherent theme of his work is more surprising, therefore, than a superficial view of it would suggest. The explanation of his failure is partly to be found in the incompatibility of the concept with the search for legal precedents, which he had defined as his main task. Partly, too, his eclecticism fatally weakens the case which he had made for the sovereignty of Parliament. In his anxiety to take up any arguments to support the cause he borrowed ideas alien to those of his main theme. This is true even of his interpretation of John and Magna Carta which, at times, is developed in the pamphlet along lines which were familiar to Herle and his colleagues. Thus he can defend the legality of subjects' invoking foreign aid against tyranny by reference to the barons' action against John; he can deride the King-flattering historians, such as John Speed, who called the barons' wars treasonous, and overwhelm them by reference to 'the judgment of our ancienter Chroniclers, and Matthew Paris'; he can even directly draw the analogy between Charles I and John, 'spoyling, robbing, destroying his people everywhere, in the self-same manner as we now are plundered'.[2] But Prynne's failure to develop the concept of sovereignty with any consistency is, in addition to these points, an expression of personal choice; as such, it represents an important stage in the development of his ideas, which is to be understood by closer study of his writings.

The origins of Prynne's defence of the sovereignty of Parliament are probably to be found in a controversy in which he engaged in 1642. In that year, he offered his first thoughts upon

[1] David Jenkins, *Lex Terrae* . . . (London, 1647), p. 33.
[2] Prynne, *The Soveraigne Power of Parliaments* . . ., iii, p. 22; iii, p. 23; i, p. 55.

the constitutional conflict: he sought to prove that the Biblical text, forbidding the touching of the Lord's Anointed, was really a caveat against Kings, not against subjects. Therefore, Prynne argued that it was more unlawful for Kings to make offensive war upon their subjects than it was for subjects to take up defensive arms against Kings.[1] With justice, an opponent pointed out how many questions were begged by this proposition:

> . . . this very point was worth a treatise: which is not to be lookt for in a pamphlets refutation . . . he shall never resolve nor perswade wise men and consciencious; unless he will take pains not to determine rashly, but to discusse orderly, and instruct soundly, in these three points at least, 1. What warre offensive, and defensive is. 2. How farre forth a man may be defensive onely, and yet not offensive. 3. Whether the defensive, or offensive, be on this side, or that . . .[2]

Prynne's defence of the sovereignty of Parliament must be seen in part at least, as a response to this challenge.

At the opening of the work, Prynne made it clear that lack of public-spiritedness among public persons had brought about the crisis; that the intellectual root of this moral error was ignorance about the extent of Parliament's privileges and King's prerogatives. He claimed that, in this work, he would eschew 'dangerous Paradoxes and upstart Enthusiasmes', and went on to argue that the 'High Court of Parliament' should properly be regarded as 'the Highest Soveraigne power of all others, and above the King himself'. He promised to develop this argument in full, precisely because 'it may seeme a dangerous paradox'.[3] Prynne conceded that the King was a principal

---

[1] Prynne, *A Vindication of Psalme 105, 15 (Touch Not Mine Anointed and Doe My Prophets No Harm* . . . (London, 1642), no pagination.  Another pamphlet, *Vox Populi* . . . which appeared in two parts in 1642 has been attributed to Prynne, in his bibliography of his writings, by Mrs. Kirby (op. cit.).  This attribution is questioned in: Mary Isabel Fry and Godfrey Davies, 'Notes and Documents . . .,' *Huntington Library Quarterly*, xx, No. 11 (1956), p. 92; there is nothing in its manner or matter to suggest Prynne's authorship.

[2] (Anon.) *A Revindication of Psalme 105.15* . . . (Cambridge, 1643), p. 9. Mrs. Kirby (op. cit.), included this attack upon Prynne by a Royalist among Prynne's works; a mistake which is repeated in William Haller, *Tracts on Liberty in the Puritan Revolution* . . ., i, pp. 25–6.

[3] Prynne, *The Soveraigne Power of Parliaments* . . ., i, dedicatory epistle; p. 33.

member, but only one, of the High Court of Parliament. The Lords and the Commons were the greatest and most important estates, because they represented the entire body of the Kingdom. Regal power itself only existed for the welfare of the people: *salus populi* was 'not only that *Suprema Lex* but principall end for which all royal power was instituted by God and Man'. He shrinks, however, from a straightforward defence of supremacy of the Commons on the basis of representation: a few lines later he has modified his position to the unexceptionable, and unexciting, claim that one of the three estates (the King), is inferior to the three estates together (Lords, Commons, and a King legally present, although personally absent), because they are 'co-ordinate parts of the same great Common Council of the Kingdome'. These stock legal platitudes seemed to give the lie to the claims of the title.[1]

The absence of the King from Parliament is the greatest injustice which a Prince can offer to his people. The Lords' absence is not similarly disastrous. The King can hold Parliament with the Commons alone, 'every one of which hath a greater voyce in Parliament than the greatest Earl in England, because he represents a whole county, towne or city, the other himself alone'.[2] The Commons' absence destroys the essence of Parliament, which cannot exist with Kings and Lords alone. Historically, Prynne turns to Coke's authority to claim that there were no Prelates or Barons when Parliament first began; philosophically, his justification is that every Commons man speaks for all for whom he is sent.

Prynne does not claim for the Commons sovereignty through legislation: he accepted that legislation was dependent upon the co-operation of the estates who, together in Parliament, had a power which was above the Common Law, and also above the King—outside—Parliament. When Prynne went on to argue, therefore, that Parliament was the sovereign authority above the King through legislation, he was saying less than he appeared to. For, when he quoted Bodin's concept of legislative sovereignty, he did so to show its inapplicability to English Kings, but it also told against the authority of Lords and Commons

[1] Ibid., i, pp. 40–1.
[2] Ibid., i, p. 41; an argument noted by a contemporary: see (B.M.) Harleian MSS. 980, f. 411.

without King. Prynne accepted that legislative power was still dependent upon the King; he had not rejected the legalistic ideal of the co-operative harmony of the three estates as the basis of the 'balanced polity'.[1]

In this sense, the sovereignty of Parliament was no more than a restatement of the time-honoured concept of 'balance'. And yet Prynne saw it as something more dynamic and relevant to the crisis than that: this is where the confusion becomes evident in Prynne's mind, which was noted by a critic, as to whether sovereignty was old or new. For Prynne sees the sovereignty of Parliament not simply as the expression of balance, but as the attempt to redress the balance, which had been upset by extravagant claims for monarchy. It is in this light that the claim to sovereignty is most usually seen in the pamphlet; as an extra-legal expedient to sustain a legal ideal. The legal ideal is permanent; the breach with legalism is temporary. But it is the perception of the inadequacy of legal compromise in the crisis which leads Prynne to more radical solutions.

Prynne points out that Popish Parliaments have, in the past, disposed of Crowns themselves: this is not simply precedent to be followed, nor is it Papistry to be shunned, but it is a subtle blend of each, which illustrates that concept of sovereignty which Prynne most often recognized. These actions represented necessary extra-legal expedients in response to provocations which threatened legalism. Prynne commented upon such actions:

> True it is our Protestant Peeres, Commons and Parliaments, never challenged nor exercised such jurisdiction and I presume they will never doe.[2]

But Kings, who acted upon the assumption that they would not, were courting danger; by following the destructive policy of evil counsellors against Parliament, Kings might 'provoke them to use the extremity of their power and revive dead sleeping precedents for their relief'. If the King restrains himself within the bounds of mixed monarchy, then 'neither he nor his Posterity need feare this Supreme Prerogative Power which hath lain dead and buryed for many ages'.[3] Sovereignty was the extreme medicine, not the daily bread, of the English con-

[1] Ibid., i, pp. 45–6.    [2] Ibid., ii, p. 3.    [3] Ibid., i, p. 88.

stitution. In recognizing that, in a crisis, Commons and Lords alone had the power to control the law, even to the point of deposition of the King, Prynne grasped sovereignty. But the grasp was weakened by the fact that Prynne saw it only in terms of temporary police action; that he was anxious to demonstrate that this action was still legal by citation of those 'dead sleeping Precedents'; and that sovereignty was only the means to the end, which was a restoration of the legal harmony of the balanced polity.

Prynne's defence of the sovereignty of Parliament is, there-fore, a rationalization of the empirical claims which had been forced upon Parliament by Royalist imprudence. Prynne cannot—like Hobbes—simply say that control of the militia is a mark of sovereignty and disregard the legal case. Rather, he must concede that, in normal times, the King's interest in the militia would not be disputed; this is not to say that Parlia-ment's present actions are illegal. They are not illegal because, in abnormal times, there are many historical precedents for Parlia-ment's challenge of such interest. This compromise has a double advantage for Prynne. By emphasizing that, in normal cir-cumstances, this claim would not be made, he points to an ultimate solution in the restoration of the position which had existed before Royalist provocation had brought about the change in circumstances. And so he could claim that, in the dispute over the militia, Parliament were 'never desiring, nor intending to devest him of this his soveraigne power over them'.[1] But, at the same time, by emphasizing that abnormal circum-stances justified action, which, although in itself legal (this is the point of the exhaustive citations of precedents), would not have been justified in normal circumstances, Prynne was giving sovereignty to Parliament. For, as Hunton saw, to give to one estate the power of 'finall determination of Fundamental con-troversies arising betwixt them is to demand which of them shall be absolute'.[2] And despite Prynne's quotation of legal pre-cedents, he had sifted the emphasis, by such reasoning, from a question of legality to that of self-preservation.

Thus, Prynne goes on to cite the action of Elizabeth in pro-hibiting the Hanseatic towns and other foreign merchants, over whom she had no jurisdiction, from transporting war

[1] Ibid., ii, p. 3.　　　[2] Hunton, *A Treatise of Monarchie* . . ., pp. 28–9.

materials to Spain 'for feare they should be turned against our Kingdome'.[1] Self-preservation, similarly, justifies all Parliamentary actions after 'the eruption of that horrid Popish rebellion in Ireland' and the fears of a similar intention in the 'Malignant Popish Prelaticall party in England'. Prynne uses other arguments to defend the Militia Ordinance: constitutional technicalities, historical examples, appeals to Aristotle and Mariana.[2] Yet self-preservation is the essential vindication of Parliament's actions: Prynne points out that it would be dangerous to resign into the King's sole hands the militia, to which he was legally entitled in normal circumstances, until the Popish party in England and Ireland have been destroyed. He cites the Grand Remonstrance, and the actions of the Crown since 1626 which point to:

> . . . A more than probable long-since resolved designe in his Majesties evill Counsellors, to make him an absolute Soveraigne Monarch and his Subjects as meer vassals . . .[3]

This design was the product of 'the confederacie (ancient) between the Popish and Prelaticall Party in the Kingdome to change Religion and re-establish Popery'. In this confederacy, the King's part is delicately indicated:

> . . . Which Designe hath been vigorously prosecuted long before his Majesties raigne, but more effectually since his marriage with one of that Religion . . .[4]

Prynne's anti-royalism is clear when he discounts the King's protestations, because of the discrepancy already manifest between the King's actions and the professions which he made in his Coronation Oath and the Petition of Right. Prynne's disillusionment is such that he even suggests that perfidy is a quality of kingship. Kings in former times, he stresses, had never kept their oaths or promises to their subjects:

> . . . And shall we dreame of a new world, onely in this dissembling age: when kingcraft is improved to the utmost . . .[5]

Prynne seeks to mitigate the anti-royalism of these remarks by pointing out that it was 'the sway of ill Councellors about

[1] Prynne, *The Soveraigne Power* . . ., ii, p. 16.
[2] Ibid., ii, pp. 22–6.    [3] Ibid., ii, p. 27.
[4] Ibid., ii, p. 33.    [5] Ibid., ii, p. 34.

him' which caused the discrepancy between the King's words and actions. He had drawn attention to the discrepancy in order to demonstrate the disservice performed by the counsellors, not in order 'to staine his Majesties Reputation with his people, and make the breach between them incurable'.[1]

Prynne recognizes that trust is the cement of the body politic, and yet argues that, in the present abnormal circumstances, the people must withhold it from their King. Prynne's solution is that, in this interim period, the sovereign power (and with it, control of the militia) should be exercised by Parliament, until sufficient confidence had been restored in the King to make the balanced polity workable. The same approach is evident when Prynne considers Parliament's claim to the right of nomination and election of privy councillors, state officers and judges. He argues that such action is no more an encroachment upon the royal prerogative than is the election of Members of Parliament. The responsibility of the elected is, in both cases, ultimately to the Kingdom, not to the King; for that reason, the King must be prepared to waive personal claims. Yet Prynne does acknowledge that the King had legality behind such claims: he concedes that the King's best title to the election of officers is by the ancient trust that he will elect such councillors, officers and judges as shall be faithful to the Kingdom, and promote the subjects' good. But from this premise he argues, as in the case of the militia, that the breaking of this trust has justified Parliament's resumption of it, without any injury to the King's authority: a demonstration of Prynne's confused approach to sovereignty.[2] He knew in what terms Bodin would have discussed the issue:

> John Bodin, a grand Polititian, truely determines and prooves at large, That it is not the right of election of great Officers, which declareth the right of sovereignty, because this oft is, and may be in the Subjects, but the Princes approbation and confirmation of them when they are chosen, without which they have no power at all.[3]

If Prynne really wished to assert the sovereignty of Parliament, acceptance of Bodin's view ought to have led to the claim of an absolute right, on behalf of Parliament, in the choice of ministers, even without the King's assent. Instead, Prynne cited

[1] Ibid., ii, p. 39.    [2] Ibid., ii, p. 41.    [3] Ibid., ii, p. 45.

Bodin's comments precisely to show that sovereignty was the concept which Parliament was avoiding in its claim.

The next empirical claim for Parliament which Prynne considered was its interest in the election of officers. This he defended by selective historical precedents from the reign of Kings such as John and Richard III: from the right of impeachment, he argued the right of appointment.[1] When he dealt with the King's power to veto bills, he claimed that this power was restricted to bills 'of meere grace and favour' but not 'of common right and justice'.[2] The bills in the second group, were (he held) those concerning the public safety of the kingdom, the liberty and property of the subjects, the punishment of wrongdoers, the redress of defects in the Common Law, the advancement of trade, the right execution of justice and the reformation of religion. Prynne's justification for such inhibitions upon the King's freedom is very important: denial of the Royal Assent to such bills is against the Law of God which commands the King to do justice to his subjects:

> The King neither can, nor ought by law to do any wrong, seeing he is Gods Vicar, and the fountaine of Justice.[3]

When Prynne considers the question of Parliament's power to impose taxes and to imprison malignants without the King's presence, he argues that the King's presence is not essential for Parliament: 'rather formal than substantiall'.[4] To the question of what precedents he can cite in support of this point, Prynne replies:

> . . . That the Parliament being the Sovereign Power and Counsell in the Realm is not tyed to any Presidents, but hath power to make new Presidents, as well as new Laws in new Cases and mischiefs; where there are no old Presidents, or vary from them though there be ancient ones, if better, and fitter Presidents may be made . . .[5]

This was the concept of sovereignty which knowledge of his academic, theological and constitutional leanings encouraged one to expect Prynne to express. But this is atypical: such an offhand approach to the value of precedents was inimical to

[1] Ibid., ii, p. 72.  [2] Ibid., ii, p. 73.  [3] Ibid., ii, p. 79.
[4] Ibid., iv, p. 19.  [5] Ibid., iv, p. 23.

the aim which he had expressed at the opening of his pamphlet. In point of fact, only a few lines after the bold rejection of precedent, Prynne is citing precedent after precedent of Parliaments' meetings without Kings.[1] The appendix with which he concludes his work is one enormous collection of historical precedents to prove that Kings are not above Parliaments, but are subject to their censure.[2] Prynne is never really at ease with the concept of sovereignty which overrides precedent; he more often reverts to the concept of sovereignty as a reassertion of latent powers in response to an exceptional situation, and for the limited period in which that situation continues. Although Prynne speaks of sovereignty, in either sense, as the justification for Parliament's actions hitherto, in neither sense is it seen as the ultimate solution of the constitutional conflict. For neither claim would have been made, if faith in the King's good intentions had not been undermined. The sovereignty of Parliament, however justified historically or empirically, only fills the vacuum left by the King's desertion of his people; Prynne sees, as the ultimate aim, the restoration of trust in the King in order to make workable once more the old, mixed, legal monarchy. It is in this ultimate aim that Prynne and Hunton come together, despite the disparate nature of their interests and their level of reasoning. Hunton criticized both Ferne and Herle for refusing to face the fact that in a mixed government, there can be no 'legal, constituted judge'. An indeterminate sovereignty was tolerable in a balanced polity, whose continued functioning was dependent upon the agreement of the parties concerned. When the mutual trust, which had made such compromise workable, disappeared, then the absence of sovereignty produced anarchy. But to make any one of the members of the polity the umpire was to create a sovereign power, which was alien to the whole spirit of the compromise. Hunton's remedy is not neutrality, but that 'every Person must aide that Part, which in his best Reason and Judgement stands for publike good, against the destructive'. Hunton's ultimate arbiter is the individual conscience: he vindicates a power of resistance in Parliament against the destructive acts of the King's agents, without giving it the authoritative power to judge when these agents or counsels are destructive. His hopes

[1] Ibid., iv, p. 24.   [2] Ibid., iv, *Appendix*, pp. 1–218.

for the future rest upon an appeal to moderation: the King must remove his evil counsellors; Parliament must content itself with securing the public safety. Legally speaking, Hunton acknowledges, the King has the right to control of the militia, but, to restore trust between King and people, he suggests that the King should surrender the power to Parliament for an interim period, 'satisfying by a condescendent act of grace their Feares from apprehension of present danger'.[1] It is in this sense that Prynne's vindication of the sovereignty of Parliament is more akin to the argument of Hunton who rejected it for the English Constitution than to that of Parker, who accepted it.

Hunton shrank from sovereignty as the solution because of his awareness of the complexity of the constitutional problems; in part at least, Prynne shrank from sovereignty as the solution because of his indifference to such problems. At one point in his pamphlet, Prynne argues that the primitive Christians' antipathy to resistance was no guide to the action which supporters of Parliament should take: the latter were justified in taking defensive action, because not only religion (which was the only issue which confronted the primitive Christian), but constitutional principles, were threatened.[2] It is rare to come across such reasoning in Prynne at this time. More often, he stresses that religion—in particular, the challenge of Popery—dwarfs constitutional considerations. His priority of values is clear when he describes 'This unhappy difference about the Militia' as 'being (next to the interduction of Popery) the spring from whence our uncivill warres have issued'.[3] In the preface which he wrote to his *The Popish Royall Favourite*, in 1643, it is this interpretation of the origins of the Civil War which is expressed. The Irish had rebelled because Parliament had threatened the Papists; the Queen had left in order to help them; the King had deserted Parliament and gathered malignants around him: it is in such stark simplifications that Prynne sustained the case against the King.[4] It is worth noting that this version minimizes the part played by a constitutional opposition to an arbitrary King in favour of emphasis upon a

[1] Hunton, *A Treatise of Monarchie* . . ., pp. 69, 73, 77.
[2] Ibid., ii, p. 1.                                   [3] Idem.
[4] Prynne, *The Popish Royall Favourite* . . . (London, 1643), preface.

Protestant opposition to a Papist-influenced King. In this sense the distance between Prynne and the orthodox constitutional critics is as marked in 1643 as it was in the period 1626–40. Because Prynne sees the Civil War as essentially a quarrel about religion, he can describe 'Religion and Justice' as the 'reall Causes' of the Parliament fight.[1] Henry Parker, despite his constitutional analysis, could also say that:

> The maine Engineers in this Civill Warre are Papists, the most poysonous, serpentine, Jesuited Papists of the world . . .[2]

Parker may have been sincere in his rhetoric, but his other pamphlets clearly reflected the priority which he gave to constitutional issues. For Prynne, on the other hand, the crusade against Popery was not peripheral: a topic, which lent itself tactically to emphasis, because of its emotive associations. It was the growth of Popery, and the encouragement which it received from royal favour, which caused Prynne to reappraise critically his former views of magistracy. He claimed that Parliament had not originally thought of resistance: the rescue of the King from his evil counsellors was the limit of its aim. But, by 1643, Prynne contended that the Royalist Army was Papist-ridden, and that, therefore, the issue had changed. There was a grand conspiracy against the Protestant Religion, 'the very Embrio and primitive cause of this deplorable warre':[3] a conspiracy on a scale extensive enough to justify resistance.

On what did Prynne base his fears of a conspiracy? The answer is to be found in his *The Popish Royall Favourite* . . ., where previous sovereigns' complicities in Popish Plots provide the explanatory background to Charles I's actions:

> Judge then whether the Kings departure from, and taking up Armes against the Parliament, be not only and wholly to maintaine his Roman Catholikes and their Religion . . . what ever he pretended, protested to the contrary . . .[4]

Essential to Prynne's attitude to the King in the earlier period was the belief that royal passivity in the face of the sufferings of martyrs, such as Bastwick, Burton and himself, was the result

[1] Idem.    [2] Parker, *The Contra-Replicant* . . ., p. 9.
[3] Prynne, *The Soveraigne Power of Parliaments* . . ., iii, p. 2.
[4] Prynne, *The Popish Royall Favourite* . . ., preface.

of episcopal influence.[1] Once Prynne had scrutinized documents of the period, in relation to such matters as dispensations, he harboured no illusions about the sympathies of the monarch. To set against the literature showing sympathy between King and Papist, on the subject of the 'triumvirs' Prynne complained that 'not one Royal Letter (for ought appeares to me) could ever be produced att that time to any Courts of Justice in the lawfull favour of any of them.'[2]

Prynne was not repelled by the absolutist pretensions of the monarch; as an imperialist, he put the rights of the Christian Emperor very high. But such rights were given on the understanding that he fulfilled the imperial mission: the maintenance of his authority against the claims of the Pope and the establishment of good order and a godly discipline in his kingdom. Thus Prynne was concerned when he was confronted with evidence that not only the King's advisers were culpable, but that the King himself was bent on the destruction of his imperial authority by acceptance of subordination to the Pope. When Howell sought to exculpate James I from complicity with 'evil counsellors' in the negotiations for the Spanish Marriage, Prynne angrily rebuked him:

> King James, and some of his great Ministers of State . . . have had overmuch commerce with Rome, which is now no time to palliate.[3]

Prynne cited a list of Papists given dispensations by Charles I, the Privy Council, and Windebank, 'most likely by his Royall direction'; he pointed to the persecutions which he and his colleagues had endured, because of their unmasking of the Popish plans; he mentioned the Habernfeld Plot.[4] To Prynne, these were all pointers to 'a most strong cunning desperate confederacie prosecuted (wherein the Queen Majestie hath been chiefe) to set up Popery in perfection.'[5]

Prynne was outraged when Charles I, then Prince of Wales, referred to his predecessors in a letter to the Pope:

[1] Prynne, *The Quench-Coale* . . ., dedicatory epistle.
[2] Prynne, *The Popish Royall Favourite* . . ., dedicatory epistle.
[3] James Howell, *The Preheminence . . . of Parliament* . . . (London, 1643), p. 8; Prynne, *A Moderate Apology Against a Pretended Calumny* . . . (London, 1643), p. 6.
[4] Prynne, *The Popish Royall Favourite* . . ., pp. 18, 25.      [5] Ibid., p. 33.

*. . . Car à la vente ils ont exposé souvent leur Estat e leurs Vieus pour l'exaltation du Saint Seige . . .*[1]

No phrase could have been more inimical to imperial ideals than: '*pour l'exaltation du Saint Seige.*' Lilly thought that Prynne was excessively fastidious in the prominence which he gave to such points:

> . . . Many also have blamed him (Charles I) for writing unto the Pope when he was in Spain: others think ill of him for the many reprieves he gave unto seminary priests; and Mr. Prynne sweats to purpose in aggravating his offence thereby. Why he might not as well in a civil way write unto the Pope, as write and sende his Ambassador to the great Turk, I know not . . .[2]

To Prynne, such a phrase was more than diplomatic claptrap: it was a renunciation of the imperial mission of the Christian Magistrate. And this renunciation carried with it the vindication of resistance theories.

In the period before the Civil War, more consistently than any other anti-Laudian, Prynne had preserved his royalism, largely through an indifference to the stock constitutional objections of the Parliamentary opposition. After 1641, it was not a transfer of sympathy to that cause which estranged him from the King's cause; his belated recognition of the menace of absolutist views of monarchy is the effect, rather than the cause, of his change of front. The cause is his loss of faith in the Christian Magistrate as the agent of reform and anti-Papalism, which makes the location of absolute power in such hands dangerous, in a way in which it was not before.[3]

---

[1] Ibid., p. 40. Cf. (B.M.) Sloane MSS. 2035 B, f. 12, for evidence of Prynne's interest in information about the negotiations in connection with the Spanish Marriage and such matters in a letter which he wrote in 1643.

[2] *The Lives of . . . Elias Asmole . . . and William Lilly . . .* (London, 1774), p. 191.

[3] This loss of faith left him vulnerable to opponents' taunts against him for anti-royalism. (Anon.), *The Fallacies of Mr. William Prynne . . .*, p. 8, ironically noted Prynne's dilemma: 'he will not put His Majestie to an Open Shame; he doth but onely implie that our King is guiltee of Common Breach of Oaths and Promises; and that he is in his Dotage, not able to governe his Kingdome, nor Himselfe.' In a copy of *The Popish Royall Favourite* which Prynne had presented to the Abbey Library, Bath, a contemporary had commented across the margin of page 58, which described royal intrigues with Papists against Protestants: 'note Mr. Pryns Loyalty'. Cf. also (Anon.), *The Perswasion of Certaine Grave Divines . . .*, (Oxford, 1645), p. 111, where Prynne is bracketed with the Assembly divines who had justified resistance.

Prynne notes the exchange of letters between Williams and James I on the subject of dispensations for Catholics: two former admired models now share in his general disillusionment. He cites Abbott's disapproval of a Popish marriage for Charles I, but not, as formerly, as a sign of episcopacy's worth. He merely points out in the margin that 'Dr. Hackwel and others writ against this Popish match, which divers Bishops approved of as lawful'.[1] And Prynne comes resolutely to face the fact that his earlier admiration of James I may have been not only excessive but entirely misplaced. He now asks:

> . . . Whether King James were really as zealous a Protestant, and anti-Papist, as the ignorant world reputed him, especially in his declining age? . . .[2]

Buckingham he describes as 'the first Grand Favourite . . . who laid the foundation of the Spanish and French Marriage-Treaties.'[3] But at the centre of all intrigues is the Queen:

> . . . all things are subject to the command of Mary . . .[4]

The change which such beliefs engendered in his attitude to monarchy is clear in an attack which he made upon Laud, in his report of the Archbishop's trial. He pointed out that Laud had sheltered behind the King's authority for a change made in the thanksgiving oaths against Roman Catholics. Earlier, it would have been sufficient for Prynne to have exposed this charge as false; now, aware of the influence of Papist upon monarch, Prynne accepted the hypothesis and argued from it that:

> . . . he being by his place and office principally entrusted with the care, honour, safety of our Religion and Church, so much concerned in these alterations; it had been his duty to have disobeyed this command and dissuaded his Majesty from such a dishonourable, scandal and offensive act . . .[5]

Prynne's fear of Popery in the King's circle was leading him to theories of resistance, even of deposition. Acceptance of Beard's philosophy and imperial theory hastened this development.

---

[1] Prynne, *The Popish Royall Favourite* . . ., p. 48.          [2] Ibid., p. 50.
[3] Ibid., p. 56. As early as 1628, Prynne had been interested in the question of Buckingham's complicity with Papists: see (B.M.) Harleian MSS. 980, f. 468.
[4] Idem.                    [5] Prynne, *Canterburies Doome* . . ., p. 248.

The influence of Thomas Beard's writing upon Prynne has already been noted: the didactic reading of history for God's judgments upon rulers who had not fulfilled their divine mission was seen by opponents at Prynne's first trial in 1634 as a dangerous incitement to resistance.[1] This charge had less relevance when Charles I was seen by Prynne as another Constantine; the temptation to assist divine retribution upon a ruler seen in less flattering light, perhaps even as a Nero, seemed to be grave, however. It is notable that Prynne quoted Beard's account of God's judgments upon tax collectors, when he challenged the excise on hops in 1654.[2] Beard had been no less censorious of 'subject Murderers', and claimed that Edward II, for instance, deserved deposition for making war upon his subjects.[3] And when Prynne comes to discuss the question of resistance in his defence of the sovereignty of Parliament, it is Beard whom he quotes to support his claim that:

> Our own Parliaments in all ages have resisted Kings when they have degenerated into tyrants. Because as soon as he ceases to rule by law, he denudes himself of his just regall authority.[4]

Prynne's interpretation of the Royal Supremacy also led him to theories of resistance. Prynne pointed out that the Oath of Supremacy was essentially anti-Papal: 1 Elizabeth I referred to 'No Forraign Power, Person, Prelate, State or Potentate' as having 'any Jurisdiction, Power, SUPERIORITY, PRE-HEMINENCE, or Authority, Ecclesiasticall or Spirituall, within this Realm'.[5] From this, Prynne argues that Supremacy was not thought of by the prescribers of the Oath as a statement of Crown superiority over Parliament; the Supremacy itself was located in Parliament. Rather, the Royal Supremacy was anti-Papal, and Prynne implied that, when this ceased to be true, the Supremacy ceased to be effective. The point of the Supremacy

---

[1] Cf. Maurice Ashley, *The Greatness of Oliver Cromwell* (London, 1958), p. 43, on the influence of Beard upon Cromwell.

[2] Prynne, *A Declaration and Protestation Against the Illegal, Detestable, Oft-Condemned, New Tax and Extortion of Excise in General* . . . (London, 1654), p. 17. Cf. Thomas Beard, *The Theatre of Gods Judgments* . . . (London, 1631), pp. 448–60.

[3] Beard, op. cit., pp. 328–9.

[4] Prynne, *The Soveraigne Power of Parliaments* . . ., iii, p. 4.

[5] Ibid., i, p. 105.

legislation was that 'the Imperial Ecclesiasticall Jurisdiction usurped by the Pope and Prelates' had been restored to the Crown.[1] But what was to happen if a King were to betray the cause for which he was created? It is notable that Prynne's immediate defence of Hotham's action at Hull was that a King who had deserted his imperial mission ought not to be supported.[2] Although in Prynne's eclectic defence later of the sovereignty of Parliament he used many arguments, this was central to his thought. It is to Grotius that he turns in this later work for an expression of this imperial theory of resistance:

> ... That a King who aliens and would actually deliver up possession of all or any part of his Realm to another forraign power without the peoples consents, may lawfully be resisted with force of Arms by his Subjects ...[3]

It is Prynne's attraction towards theories of resistance which largely explains his equivocal attitude to sovereignty: the two concepts were not really compatible. The arguments for resistance put foward by the ministers in 1643 were castigated by Hunton as 'new and over-large grounds for resistance'; they were praised by Prynne, on the other hand, as the 'best and acutest of this kind'.[4] Prynne could not answer the Royalist citations of Romans xiii, forbidding resistance to the higher powers, by a straightforward argument that the powers referred to were Parliament and the Kingdom, as Parker did; instead, Prynne dragged in the support of resistance authorities to claim it as 'a pregnant Text against the tyranny, the boundlesse Prerogatives, the illegal proceedings of Kings, and Higher Powers, if rightly scanned as Pareus and others on it manifest.'[5]

Prynne argued that defensive war was not war, but defence:

---

[1] Ibid., i, p. 100.

[2] Prynne, *A Soveraign Antidote* . . . (London, 1642), p. 5.

[3] Prynne, *The Soveraigne Power of Parliaments* . . ., i, p. 103. Typical examples of Prynne's approval of deposition precedents are to be found in: Ibid., i, pp. 10–11; iii, pp. 23–46.

[4] Philip Hunton, *A Treatise of Monarchie* . . ., p. 63; Prynne, *The Soveraigne Power of Parliaments* . . ., iii, p. 61. The pamphlet under discussion was: *Scripture and Reason Pleaded for Defensive Armes* . . . (London, 1643); its most important critique was: Henry Ferne, *A Reply Unto Severall Treatises* . . . (London, 1643).

[5] Prynne, *The Soveraigne Power of Parliaments* . . ., iii, p. 7.

that subjects, to protect their persons, property and 'Native dearest Countrey', were justified in taking up arms against foreigners. This explains the importance which Prynne attached to Papist infiltrations in the Cavalier Army. Prynne emphasized that Bilson had laid the theoretical foundations of deposition of Kings who were unfit to govern: *a fortiori*, this applied to Kings waging war against their subjects. Self-defence is extanded as a concept by Prynne from the mere repulsion of assault to its intelligent anticipation. The situation is not simply that of two gladiators: kill or be killed. There must be a fine act of judgment as to the extent of the danger.[1] In placing this power of judgment in Parliament, Prynne seemed to entrust it with sovereignty. But the way in which it was done is most instructive. For Prynne turned from reason to 'point of Divinity and Conscience'; he argued that Ferne and the Royalist pamphleteers had misrepresented the situation by attacking, as their opponents' resistance theory, the view that subjects may take up arms against their lawful sovereign, if he is wicked and unjust. Their misrepresentation was in abstracting the King from his Popish forces. Against Ferne, Prynne argues that Christ approved of resistance; He did not practise it, only in order to fulfil 'the Scriptures foretelling his Passion' and 'his Fathers decree', not because He thought that resistance was unlawful. Prynne quotes Biblical authority at length to support resistance and then—almost with an air of apology—brings forward as twelfth in a series of arguments the crucial justification of sovereignty. Romans xiii had sanctioned obedience to the supreme power, which Ferne had falsely identified as the King:

> . . . But this resistance of the Kings Popish malignant, invading forces, is Authorized and Commanded by the expresse Votes and Ordinances of both Houses of Parliament, which I have already undeniably maintained, to be the Supreamest, Lawfull Power and Soveraignest Authority in the Realme, paramount the King himselfe . . .[2]

This is an assertion of sovereignty in Parliament so clear as to shift the onus of justifying resistance upon the Royalists. But there is no evidence that Prynne saw it in such a light: he is far more concerned, in arguing the relevance of Romans xiii,

[1] Ibid., iii, pp. 14, 21, 49, 50.     [2] Ibid., iii, pp. 62, 67, 73.

to show that the obedience prescribed does not extend to tyranny, than to show that Parliament, not King, should command that obedience.

In attacking tyranny, Prynne chides the court divines for their claim that the efficient cause of monarchical power was God, not the people. Morton, besides Ferne, is named as an antagonist: an interesting sidelight upon Prynne's disillusionment with the moderates.[1] Prynne, as a Calvinist, set no limit to God's sovereignty: his distaste for the ascription of monarchy's sanction to God was analogous to his attitude to episcopacy in the earlier period. In both cases, Prynne believed that God had laid down the general lines of government, but He had allowed for the expression of individual differences within that framework. Presbyters were directly ordained by God, but episcopal superiority was derived from the King; civil government was ordained by God, but the monarchical form was derived from the people's consent. Monarchy, in a restricted sense, is therefore of God, although instituted and invented by men, because 'He gave them wisedome to invent and settle it, as most commodious for their republike, till they should see cause to alter it; or because he blessed and approved of it, when invented and received by them.'[2] This was as close as Prynne came to an acceptance of Covenant theology.

Prynne was seen at his weakest when he proceeded to argue that the claim to *iure divino* sanction was not the same as a claim to sovereignty. This was an arguable proposition— Hunton did argue it, although Herle dissented—[3] but Prynne's grounds were lamentable. He argued that the *iure divino* claim for episcopacy by such bishops as Laud and Neale had not prevented their crimes from being censured by Parliament. If the Priests' *iure divino* claim had not meant an exemption from

[1] Ibid., iii, p. 115. Cf. Thomas Morton, *Christus Dei* . . . (Oxford, 1642).

[2] Ibid., iii, p. 116.

[3] Hunton, *A Treatise of Monarchie* . . ., p. 31: 'The derivation of any power from God doth not necessarily infer the non-subjection of the person in whom that power resides to all other men': Herle, *A Fuller Answer to a Treatise by Doctor Ferne* . . . (London, 1643), p. 4: 'The world hath been long abus'd by Court-Preachers . . . first crying up the sole Divinity of Monarchy in generall and then (what must follow) the absoluteness of this in the King's sole person.'

obedience, why then should the King's?[1] Yet Prynne's whole case against the prelates' *iure divino* claim, in the period 1626–40, had been that the claim necessarily involved exemption from imperial obedience. In fact, only a few lines later, Prynne acknowledged, as a 'parting blow' at 'our Prelaticall Clergy', that throughout history the clergy had claimed exemption from obedience to the Emperor: from St. Ambrose to Bridges and Bilson.[2] Prynne knew that the *iure divino* claim was, in essence, a claim to power: for that reason he had attacked its ascription to bishops in the period before the Civil War. If, in that same period, he had shown a marked disinclination to attack the same claim when it was put forward for monarchy, that was because, as a 'royal' pamphleteer of that time, he was prepared to give absolute obedience to a magistrate who worked for reformation against Rome. And while Prynne believed that the Presbyterians could best achieve these goals, he was prepared, in the period 1641–4, to be silent on their *iure divino* clericalism.

Sovereignty was not for Prynne the solution, because constitutional deadlock was not for Prynne the problem. So indifferent was Prynne to the orthodox constitutional arguments that he could regard absolutism in the monarchy as a new Anglican theory. Thus, he could claim that bishops have been ready to follow the lead of Bishop Bilson, 'a fierce Antipuritane', in resisting and excommunicating Emperors whom they thought were ungodly, 'point blank against our Novell Court— Doctors and Royallists'.[3] The Civil War posed for Prynne a moral, not a constitutional problem: how to restore faith in the King's ability to fulfil the imperial mission. Anti-papalism was essential, for Prynne, in the monarch: it was for that purpose that the Royal Supremacy had been bestowed upon him. When Prynne no longer saw in the monarch the necessary bulwark against Rome, his views were radically transformed. His belief in imperialism could lead him to the renunciation of the

[1] Prynne, *The Soveraigne Power of Parliaments* . . ., iii, p. 121. An opponent was to argue from this concession by Prynne that the *iure divino* claim by Presbyterian ministers was not in reality a claim to exemption from obedience to the civil magistrate: J. L., *Illumination to Sion Colledge* . . . (London, 1649), preface.

[2] Ibid., iii, p. 127.                                    [3] Ibid., iii, p. 145.

Christian Emperor who had destroyed his *raison d'être*. Because of this, Prynne is isolated from his fellow advocates of the Parliamentary cause: from Herle and Parker, who defended Parliament's actions on constitutional grounds; from Rutherford and Goodwin, who defended Parliament's actions on Scriptural grounds.[1] Prynne, ever eclectic, combined both arguments in his pamphlets: at times, justifying from Scripture, resistance of the sovereign monarch; at times, justifying from constitutional analysis, non-resistance of the sovereign Parliament. Neither argument commanded his exclusive sympathy, because his imperial thinking of earlier years had led him to place absolute reliance upon the King as the expression of anti-Romanism. Once this identification had broken down, Prynne wavered between two courses: a feeling—inspired by Beard, among other sources—that the King who had betrayed his mission deserved to be resisted, even deposed, as a judgment of God, and a recognition that the solution must ultimately come from a renewal of trust in the King as the instrument of anti-Papalism. The sovereignty of Parliament was, for Prynne, at times, divine retribution upon a wayward monarch, and, at times, an interim expedient until confidence was restored in the King; it was not seen as the solution of the location of powers within the constitution.

No contemporary pamphlet has affinity with this point of view; but there is an anonymous pamphlet of 1689 which might have been written by Prynne. The pamphleteer justified the deposition of James II because he had 'changed the form of Government, and Constitution from an English Monarchy, and Independent; from an Imperial Crown, to a subjection to the Pope, and see of Rome'. The writer cited Coke for an assertion of imperialism: that the Kingdom of England should have no foreign power over it. Imperialism, the writer claims, is an expression of the King's independence of the Pope, not of his subjects; but the writer shows no interest in constitutional questions of royal encroachments upon subjects' liberties. The writer contends that the King has deposed himself from being

---

[1] These are broad generalizations, not absolute distinctions; but for their greater emphasis upon scriptural justification of resistance, see: Samuel Rutherford, *Lex, Rex: The Law and the Prince* . . . (London, 1644); John Goodwin, *Anti-Cavalierisme* . . . (London, 1642).

an independent King of England simply by submitting himself to the Pope, and he concludes with the citation of Jewel and Bilson as imperialists who did not subscribe to tyranny.[1] It is no accident that this 1689 pamphlet should sound the authentic Prynne note; at the height of the Civil War, Prynne's enemy is not the absolutist Charles I whom his colleagues were attacking, but *The Popish Royall Favourite*.

[1] (Anon.), *A Friendly Debate* . . . (London, 1689), pp. 6, 19–20, 34, 52–3.

1. 'The more I am beat down, the more I am lift up.' Prynne wore
   his hair long after 1637 to conceal his disfigurement.

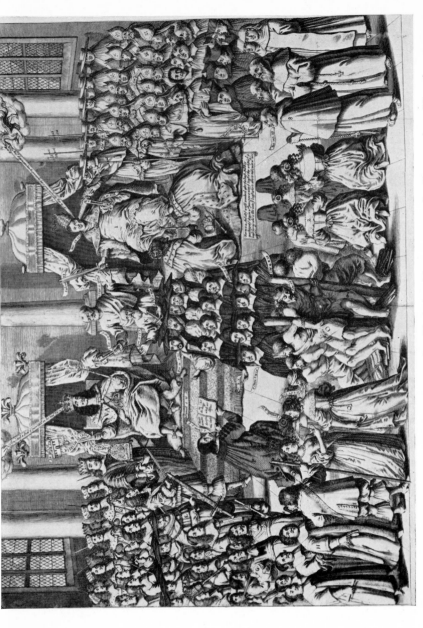

2. Prynne pays homage to Charles II, the Christian Emperor, at the Restoration. How insecure the Pope's Crown is in comparison.

3. Laud on trial with Prynne as prosecutor.

4. 'O Mr. Burton, I am sick at heart': a Puritan caricature of Laud
nauseated by his own misdeeds.

# VI

# THE POPISH PLOT

PRYNNE's account of the trial of Laud throws revealing light upon Prynne, not upon Laud. His *Canterburies Doome* . . ., which was published in 1646, was in no sense an objective record of the trial; in the dedicatory address which he contributed to it, he acknowledged frankly its polemical purpose:

> . . . I presume, the setting forth of this History of his Tryall will will soon Un-Martyr, Un-Saint, Uncrown this Arch-Imposter, by presenting him in his proper Colours, stript of all Disguises . . .[1]

In order to achieve this end, Prynne admitted that he had inserted additional material to that which had been offered at the trial. His defence was that the additional material only substantiated points which had been raised at the trial, without being fully developed through lack of time. Thus he claimed that his fidelity to the spirit rather than the letter of the charge involved not distortion, only enlargement, of the issues which were discussed. His failure to see that enlargement was itself distortion derived from the propagandist purpose behind the work. He could say of the additions that:

> . . . no indifferent persons can justly taxe me with partiality or injustice for inserting them into this History, for the fuller discovery of his Popish intentions in this Kinde . . .[2]

Prynne's record of the trial is not only partisan; it is incomplete. Yet, with the exception of Laud's own account, it was, until

[1] Prynne, *Canterburies Doome* . . . (London, 1646), dedicatory epistle.
[2] Idem.

quite recently, the only major record of the trial. This is no longer true: now that the notes made by John Browne, Clerk of the Parliaments, at Laud's trial are available to scholars, a third source has been provided as a check upon the accuracy of the other two.[1] To collate the rival accounts is to be made aware of the impressive extent of agreement between Browne and Laud. Browne omits some of Laud's answers and his notes are more terse, yet the area of general agreement is surprisingly large when one bears in mind the depressing circumstances in which Laud's account was drawn up. Moreover, Browne was a Puritan: the comments which he has written upon pamphlets of Heylyn and Prynne show where his sympathies lay; Heylyn twice refers angrily to his anti-episcopal spirit.[2] There is ground, therefore, for thinking that, where Browne and Laud speak with one voice, an authoritative check is provided upon Prynne's handling of the issues discussed. It then becomes possible to read significance into the way in which Prynne has distorted the evidence; it even becomes possible to suggest that it was some of Prynne's principles—which were already evident in his previous controversial writings—which determined the strange construction of his account.

Prynne acknowledges that his account does not obey the

[1] Browne's papers were known to be in existence for a considerable time (H.M.C., *10th. Report*, ii), but not until 1953 did they become accessible to scholars, when the House of Lords' Record Office acquired these, and other manuscripts, from Lord Braye (*House of Lords: Record Office Memorandum, No. 11*). Their value was recognized: '. . . none of it appears to have been used by historians. The printed versions of Laud's trial are based on his own diary and on relatively unofficial and slight sources' (*House of Lords: Record Office Pamphlet*, No. 10, p. 5). At the time of writing, a transcript of Browne's account was still in preparation at the House of Lords' Record Office, and I wish to express my thanks for being allowed to consult the original MSS.

[2] Cf. Braye MSS. 110/91, *passim*, for Browne's notes; Heylyn, *Cyprianus Anglicus* . . . (London, 1668), p. 469, on the insulting behaviour of Browne to the bishops: 'The same Clerk at the Reading of such Bills as came in to that House, turned his back toward them in disdain, that they might not distinctly hear what he read; as if their consenting or dissenting to the point in question had been judged unnecessary'; Heylyn, *Extranous Vapulans* . . . (London, 1656), pp. 281–2, on a slip by Hamon L'Estrange on a question of detail: 'We found him in the snare before, when he was fain to rouse up Mr. Prynns Ghost, to help him out of it; and now there is no remedy (for ought that I can see) but to conjure up the silly shaddow of John Brown, that famous *Clericus Parliamentorum* (as he stiled himself) . . .'

chronology of the trial: that he has grouped the separate charges made by the prosecution into one continuous narrative which occupies the greater part of his work, and that he has inserted the Archbishop's replies and the further answer of the Commons in the form of a postscript to the work.[1] But the construction seems suspect logically, even more than chronologically. In the Articles against Laud which Pym had outlined in 1640, six of the fourteen dealt with constitutional objections exclusively; only four touched upon his encouragement of Popery.[2] In the ten Additional Articles which were sent up from the Commons to the Lords in October, 1643, six dealt with constitutional objections exclusively; only one touched upon his encouragement of Popery.[3] When Prynne explained the method behind his construction, he claimed that there was one general charge against Laud:

> That he hath trayterously endeavoured to subvert the fundamentall Lawes and Government of the Kingdome of England, and instead thereof to introduce an Arbitrary and Tyrannical Government.

Prynne divided this charge into four specific branches. First: 'His trayterous endeavours and practises to alter and subvert Gods true religion by Law established in this Realme, and instead thereof, to set up Popish Superstition and Idolatry, and reconcile us to the Church of Rome'. Second: 'His trayterous usurpation of a Papall and Tyranicall power in the Church of England in all Ecclesiasticall affaires in prejudice, and derogation of His Majesties Royall Prerogative and the Subjects Liberties.' Third: 'His trayterous attempts and endeavours to subvert the fundamentall temporall Lawes, Government and Liberties of the Realme and Subjects of England, and instead thereof to introduce an Arbitary and Tyrannical Government against the Law and Subjects liberties.' Fourth: 'His trayterous

---

[1] Prynne, *Canterburies Doome* . . ., dedicatory epistle.

[2] Articles 1, 2, 3, 4, 13, 14 dealt with constitutional objections; Articles 7, 8, 9, 10 dealt with the 'Popery' charge: that he had respectively encouraged Popish idolatry, advanced Papists to office, licensed Popish books, worked for the reconciliation of the Church of England with Rome.

[3] Additional Articles 1, 2, 3, 4, 5, 10 dealt with constitutional objections; Additional Article 7 dealt with the 'Popery' charge: his encouragement of Davenport in schemes for union with Rome.

endeavours to subvert the rights of Parliament, and aunctent Course of Parliamentary proceedings, and by false and malicious slanders to incense his Majesty against Parliaments.'[1]

On Prynne's own reading of the case against Laud, only the first branch deals with his Popery; the second branch deals with his ecclesiastical activities, but mainly in relation to their constitutional effect; the third and fourth branches deal only with his constitutional crimes. It is important, therefore, to see how far *Canterburies Doome* . . . substantiates these charges. In point of fact, Prynne only develops the first branch in his work, and his treatment even within that restricted field reflects his scale of priorities. The greater part of *Canterburies Doome* . . . is taken up with the development of the first part of the first branch of the charge against Laud: that he had subverted the true religion by the encouragement of Popish superstitions and idolatry.[2] Prynne's first concern is with ceremonial innovations. He points to developments along 'Popish' lines which Laud had encouraged in Lambeth Chapel, the Royal Chapel, Westminster Abbey and the Universities of Oxford and Cambridge.[3] A clear illustration of the way in which a report of the trial could degenerate into a mere polemic was shown by his treatment of Laud's influence upon Cambridge. He said:

> . . . But perchance the Archbishop will object, what are these Innovations in the University of Cambridge unto me, who was neither Chancellor there to councell, or countenance them, nor immediately introduced them . . .

Prynne answers that:

> . . . He must be really guilty of all these Anti-Christian Innovations in both our Universities, whom he thus miserably corrupted to the unspeakable prejudice of Church and State, since from these two Fountaines these Popish superstitions, corruptions, diffused themselves over all our Dominions, like a most contagious Leprosie . . .[4]

Prynne next turns from an outline of the innovations to an account of the persecution of those who would not submit, such as Smart in Durham, Workman in Gloucester, and Burton,

---

[1] Prynne, *Canterburies Doome* . . ., p. 57.    [2] Ibid., pp. 59–408.
[3] Ibid., pp. 59–70.    [4] Ibid., p. 74.

Bastwick and himself.[1] Laud's consecration of churches; his encouragement of the Book of Sports and Wakes to the point of over-ruling the prohibitions by Chief Justice Richardson in Somerset of them; his persecution of Thomas Wilson for refusing to read the Book of Sports: all testified to Popish profanity on the part of one, 'who made but a meere sport of prophaning Gods oune day with sports, and silencing Godly Ministers for not being so prophane in this Kinde as himselfe was'.[2]

When Prynne turned to Laud's subversion of religion through the introduction of doctrinal points of Popery, he supplemented the evidence from material which he had himself used in his earliest pamphlets. A large section of *Canterburies Doome* . . . is taken up with a recapitulation of his arguments against Arminianism.[3] Prynne cites Popish books which had been encouraged by Laud to be published, and attacks Laud's *iure divino* claim for episcopacy in his correspondence with Hall on that question.[4] His conclusion is that:

> By all these Authorized Popish positions, you may easily guesse at this Arch-Prelates Popish intention, to reduce us back to Rome.[5]

Other points which support such a conclusion are: his persecution of godly ministers; his readiness to expunge anti-Papal passages from books; his attack upon the Feoffees for the bringing in of impropriations; his antipathy to the Reformed Churches overseas.[6]

The second part of the first branch of the charge is next considered by Prynne: that Laud had subverted the true religion by the attempt to reconcile the Church of England with Rome.[7] The points which Prynne emphasizes are: that Laud has a Popish reputation; that the projected Spanish Match was a pretext for such a reconciliation; that Laud was on intimate terms with Henrietta Maria; that Laud approved of Mary's reign; that Laud had encouraged Davenport in his scheme for

---

[1] Ibid., pp. 93–113. Prynne, *The Antipathie* . . ., ii, pp. 304–5, had blamed Goodman, not Laud, for the persecution of Workman. Cf. G. I. Soden, *Godfrey Goodman Bishop of Gloucester, 1583–1656* (London, 1953), p. 198, for a criticism of Prynne's inconsistency on this point.

[2] Ibid., pp. 113–28, 128–48, 149–53, 154.  [3] Ibid., pp. 155–240.

[4] Ibid., pp. 186–227, 227–40.  [5] Ibid., p. 242.

[6] Ibid., pp. 349, 245–49, 268–87, 387–90.  [7] Ibid., pp. 409–60.

reconciliation between the Church of England and Rome, and had provided him with money and lodgings at Oxford University; that Laud had discouraged priest-baiting; that Laud had been offered a Cardinal's hat.[1] But Prynne's greatest emphasis is upon the Habernfeld Plot, which he narrated in full in his *Romes Masterpeece*. This was a plot against the lives of the King and Laud by Jesuits working under Con's directions, which had been revealed by one of Con's assistants, Andreas Habernfeld, to the English diplomat, Sir William Boswell, at the Hague. Boswell had despatched the information to Laud in September, 1640, who had then passed it on to the King.[2] Prynne complained that Laud '. . . for all this . . . was so far from crossing this their Jesuiticall designe, that he confederated and joyned with the Jesuits and popish party, in fomenting, maintaining the war against the Scots. . .' The importance which Prynne attached to the Habernfeld Plot in his account of the trial is clear from his description of it there as 'an infallible demonstration, conviction of his guiltinesse'.[3] Prynne claimed that Laud had taken action only when he had thought that it was a Puritan conspiracy; but when he realized that it was a Catholic Plot, implicating among others the Pope's Legate, Con, Toby Matthew, Read and Windebank, he had concealed its existence until Prynne had discovered the relevant papers in his search of Laud's correspondence. The remaining part of *Canterburies Doome* . . . is taken up with Laud's defence against all these charges, and the further replies of the Commons.[4]

*Canterburies Doome* . . . cannot be regarded as a complete record of the case against Laud: Prynne had treated only one aspect of Laudian misrule, which had been given no special emphasis by the men who had drawn up the charges against Laud and which, on Prynne's own analysis, was only the first of four main branches of the general charge against him. Prynne did not pretend that he had published the complete account and he promised to treat the three remaining branches of the charge in a subsequent volume: but this is no answer to criticism of Prynne for distortion. For Prynne said of his account of Laud's trial that the remaining branches 'we shall (God willing)

---

[1] Ibid., pp. 410–15, 415–18, 418, 421, 422–29, 448, 431–2.
[2] Ibid., pp. 421–2, 459–60.     [3] Ibid., pp. 421–2.
[4] Ibid., pp. 462–565.

contract into a lesser volume'.[1] The value of his recognition that the account was incomplete was lessened by his belief that it had, even in its present form, dealt with the major issue; the value of his promise to deal with the other issues was lessened by his subsequent failure to honour that promise.

It could be argued, however, that the actual course of the trial might have taken a different form entirely from that envisaged by the framers of the original charges against Laud; that, under the management of Prynne, the prosecution might have come to lay the main burden of the charge upon evidence of his Popery. If this were so, the emphasis in Prynne's account would be no more than a reflection of the emphasis in the trial itself. Heylyn acknowledged that Laud faced a double charge: 'An endeavour to subvert the Laws of the Land; and a like endeavour to overthrow the true Protestant Religion established by Law.' Mrs. Kirby believed that the weight of emphasis at the trial was upon the first charge:

> By all Puritans the Arch-Bishop was regarded as the incarnation of Thorough in the church, especially of the injustices perpetrated in the Court of High Commission, but in the trial his political offences were stressed.[2]

The comment in news-journal and pamphlets at the time upon the trial supports such an inference;[3] more substantial support comes from the records left by Laud and Browne. In neither of their accounts is the 'Popery' charge against Laud given anything which approaches the attention which it receives from Prynne. The first six days of the trial were taken up almost exclusively with constitutional objections: chronologically, this would have seemed a more obvious starting-point for Prynne.[4] Moreover, the times when the 'Popery' charges are

[1] Ibid., p. 565.

[2] Heylyn, *Cyprianus Anglicus* (London, 1668), p. 534; Kirby, op. cit., p. 71.

[3] E.g. *A Perfect Diurnall* (Numb. 34) 18–25 March 1644; *The Kingdomes Weekly Intelligencer*, 30 April–7 May 1644; *Mercurius Britanicus* (Numb. 29) 25 March–1 April 1644; *A Perfect Diurnall* (Numb. 40), 29 April–6 May 1644; *The Weekly Account* (Numb. 38), 15–22 May 1644; *Mercurius Civicus* (Numb. 77), 11 November 1644; Henry Burton, *The Grand Imposter Unmasked* . . . (London, 1645), pp. 4, 7.

[4] Braye MSS. *Proceedings Against Strafford and Laud* (afterwards cited as: Braye MSS.) f. 1–f. 28; Laud, *Works* . . ., iv, pp. 56–150; 12, 13, 16, 18, 22, 28 March 1644.

brought up are almost always the times when Prynne is seen in a particularly prominent rôle.

The 'Popery' charges brought against Laud at the trial, according to Laud and Browne, were these: that Laud had introduced innovations in chapels; that he had made alterations in the coronation ceremony; that he had consecrated churches; that he had licensed Popish books in doctrinal matters; that he had advanced Papists' careers; that he was under the influence of the Queen; that he had sought to conceal the Habernfeld Plot; that he had encouraged Davenport in schemes for union with Rome.[1]

Laud commented upon repairs which had been made to pictures in chapels: 'Nor was any proof at all offered, that I did it by the pictures in the Mass-book; but only Mr. Pryn testified, that such pictures were there.'[2] Laud claimed that Prynne deliberately concealed, and distorted, evidence about the alteration of the oath in the coronation ceremony of Charles I.[3] When the question was raised about the prayer which Laud had used in consecrating plate at communion, Laud noted that 'here stepped in Mr. Pryn, and said, "This was according to the form in *Missali Parvo*"'.[4] On Laud's consecration of churches in general, Laud observed that 'here Mr. Pryn put Mr. Nicolas in mind to add "that *spargere cinerem* is in the form of consecration used in the Pontifical".'[5] Laud was accused of allowing Popish books to be licensed: 'To this Mr. Pryn (who is the single witness) says "that he tendered a bill to the then Lord Keeper against my chaplain for licensing this book, and that his Lordship refused it".'[6] Laud noted that it was Prynne who sought to exploit his discovery of the works of Mountague, Heylyn and Shelford in Laud's study, and Laud commented upon his alleged Arminian tendencies in doctrine: 'Mr. Pryn says further, "that after this he preached Arminianism at St.

---

[1] Braye MSS., f. 38, f. 42–f. 45, f. 56–7, f. 61, f. 62, f. 63; Laud, *Works* . . . ., iv, pp. 197–208, 211–19, 246–51, 286–91, 292–300, 322–4, 325–6, 326–31.

[2] Laud, *Works* . . ., iv, p. 199.

[3] Ibid., iv, p. 213. Cf. Charles Wordsworth, *The Manner of the Coronation of King Charles the First* . . . (London, 1892), p. xi: 'In spite of what had been said at Laud's trial, Prynne now in 1660 treats the orders for 1603 and 1626 as identical.'

[4] Ibid., iv, p. 203.        [5] Ibid., iv, p. 247.        [6] Ibid., iv, p. 286.

Paul's Cross". Why did not Mr. Pryn come then to me, and acquaint me with it?'[1] Laud noted of the charge that he advanced Papists: 'Here Mr. Pryn came in again, and testified very boldly, "that I gave many benefices, which were in the gift of the Master of the Wards: and all preferments, only to such men as were for ceremonies, Popery and Arminianism." '[2] To the charge that he had worked in collusion with Henrietta Maria, Laud noted that 'the second witness was Mr. Pryn. Who says, "that one Mr. Jones was punished for praying for the Queen".'[3] Upon the Habernfeld Plot, Laud commented: 'Mr. Pryn took all these letters and papers from me, when he searched me at the Tower; and out of them made his book called "Romes Masterpiece": excepting the slanders, which he hath juggled in of his own.'[4] The charge that Laud had encouraged Davenport was weakened by a confusion between two persons, Davenport and St. Giles, who were clearly distinguished in the original framing of the charge.[5] When Brown repeated the charge in summarizing the case for the prosecution, Laud observed: 'Which I much wonder, so able and grave a man as he is, should swallow from Mr. Pryn, who doubtless (being present) was angry to see himself so laid open in the House of Commons.'[6]

On these specific 'Popery' charges, Prynne is revealed to be intervening, advising, explaining, to an extent which is not apparent in the accounts of Browne and Laud of the remaining evidence. These were the charges which Prynne was to bring together, in an expanded form, in his *Canterburies Doome. . .* Did then *Canterburies Doome . . .* represent the form that Prynne would have wished the trial to take? The orthodox constitutional objections had received slighting treatment from Prynne in the period 1626–40; the position had not changed

---

[1] Ibid., iv, pp. 289, 333, 290.    [2] Ibid., iv, p. 297.
[3] Ibid., iv, p. 323.    [4] Ibid., iv, p. 325.
[5] Cf. Prynne, *Canterburies Doome . . .*, p. 39: the seventh Additional Article against Laud clearly distinguishes his encouragement of Davenport's literary activities from his maintenance of St. Giles at Oxford. Cf. Braye MSS. f. 63 and Laud, *Works . . . .*, iv, pp. 326–31 for evidence of failure to maintain this distinction at the trial. Cf. G. I. Soden, *Godfrey Goodman Bishop of Gloucester, 1583–1656* (London, 1953), p. 231, on this question of identity.
[6] Laud, *Works . . . .*, iv, p. 331.

when Prynne wrote his defence of the sovereignty of Parliament in 1643.[1] When Prynne apologized for the delay in publishing *Canterburies Doome* . . . he pointed to the amount of material, the limited time which he could spare from the Committee of Accounts, his other pamphleteering commitments at the time and even 'the coldnesse of this last winters Vacation, when neither pen nor Presse could worke, for sundry weekes together'.[2] These excuses were also valid for failure to complete a second volume, but the real reason for a disinclination to deal with the constitutional objections may lie in this fundamental lack of sympathy with such a point of view. In controversy with Walwyn, Prynne spoke boldly of two volumes against Laud, 'one of them already published and the first part of the other now at Presse, which will render him, the Archest Traiter and underminer of Religion, Laws, Liberties, Parliaments, that ever breathed in England'.[3] But Prynne's failure to provide a second volume of the trial gave an anonymous satirist in 1659 the opportunity to poke fun at him,[4] and gave Peter Heylyn the pretext for a more damaging accusation:

> . . . And he [Laud] is promised to be Painted out in such Lively Colours in the following Branches of his Charge, as should for ever render him as Treasonable and as arch a Malefactor as he was in the other, and in both alike; That promise never being performed in the space of a Dozen years and more so since it first

[1] See Chapter V for a full discussion of this point.

[2] Prynne, *Canterburies Doome* . . ., dedicatory epistle. Cf. Bulstrode Whitelocke, *Memorials of the English Affairs* . . . (Oxford, 1853), i, p. 226, for a reference at this time to 'Busy Mr. Pryn'. Prynne's service on the Committee of Accounts was derided in a hostile news-journal: *Mercurius Pragmaticus* (Numb. 18) 11–18 January 1648: 'Nor is it possible, the Accompts should ever be cleared, as long as Wil Pryn's confused Noddle is ingaged in the businesse.' Prynne apologised for delay in 1656 in somewhat similar terms: Prynne, *The Second Part of a Short Demurrer* . . . (London, 1656), dedicatory epistle: '. . . Extraordinary Coldness and Shortness of the Time I had.'

[3] Prynne, *A Fresh Discovery* . . . (London, 1645), p. 39. Cf. William Walwyn, *A Helpe to the Right Understanding of a Discourse Concerning Independency* . . . (London, 1645), p. 2.

[4] (Anon.) *Paul's Churchyard* . . . (London, 1659), no pagination: 'The Archbishop of Canterburies Triall, writ by William Prinn, declaring all the Archbishop spake or did before he was born, and since his Buriall; being the 9th. Tome of Master Prinns Works.'

was made, in all which time, we hear no news of that performance
for which the Ground could be but Little and the evidence
less . . .[1]

Heylyn thought that it was lack of evidence which had held
back Prynne, but it may well have been a lack of sympathy
with the kind of evidence to be discussed which prevented
Prynne—not necessarily at a conscious level of thinking—from
completing the task which he had set himself.

It is clear from Prynne's handling of the account of the trial
that he believed that 'Popery' was the major charge against
Laud; it is equally clear from the accounts of Browne and Laud
that Prynne was unable to direct the trial along such lines.
This raises important questions as to how far Prynne was a
figure-head, how far the organizer, in the trial of Laud. As
early as 1643 Prynne was gathering material for the trial; it
was Prynne who conducted a minute search of the Archbishop's
papers and diaries and published them in edited form; when
Prynne delivered his speech in the Commons upon the Isle of
Wight negotiations with Charles I, he pointed with pride to his
services in the cases of Laud and Macguire:

> . . . I have brought you off with honor in the cases of Cant. and
> Macg. when you were at a loss in both . . .[2]

Laud would not have thought such a judgment excessive; of
Prynne's part in the trial, Laud said that:

> . . . Mr. Pryn was trusted with the providing of all the evidence,
> and was relater, and prompter, and all, never weary of anything,
> so he might do me mischief . . .[3]

But Laud's consciousness of Prynne's vindictiveness and zeal
in technicalities may have led him to over-estimate Prynne's
part in dictating the general principles along which the trial
was run. An example of how such a misjudgment was possible
is suggested by Laud's reaction to an omission in the ninth

[1] Heylyn, *Cyprianus Anglicus* (London, 1668), p. 525.

[2] B.M.) Sloane MSS. 2035B, f. 12; Laud, *Works* . . ., iv, p. 31; Prynne,
*The Substance of a Speech* . . ., p. 28. On the Macguire case, see Prynne,
*The Whole Trial of Connor Lord Maguire* . . . (London, 1645); for contemporary appreciation of Prynne's handling of the case, see: *The Kingdomes Weekly Intelligencer* (Numb. 89) 24 January 1645.

[3] Laud, *Works* . . ., iv, p. 47.

Additional Article against him. The fifth Article in the original
list of charges attacked the Canons of 1640 as 'contrary to the
King's prerogative, to the fundamental laws and statutes of
this realm, to the right of Parliament, to the propriety and
liberty of the subjects and matters tending to sedition, and of
dangerous consequences'.[1] The ninth Additional Article contained all these charges with one significant exception: no
longer was it claimed that the Canons infringed the King's
prerogative. Laud noted the omission and commented upon it:

> ... I would fain know, if I could, what is the reason of this
> omission in these added Articles. Is it for shame, because there
> was a purpose to charge me (as Sergeant Wild did in his speech
> the first day) that I laboured to advance the king's prerogative
> above the law? To advance it, and yet made contrary Canons
> against it; which is the way to destroy it? What pretty nonsense
> is this? Or is it because the framers of these additionals, (whom I
> conceave were some Committee with the help of Mr. Pryn),
> thought the time was come, or coming in which the King should
> have no more prerogative?[2]

From the tone of Laud's remarks it is clear that his second
explanation is more in the nature of a smearing of his opponents
as anti-monarchical and that his first explanation represents
his considered judgment. Yet it is implausible that Prynne of
all persons should seek to omit the point, that Laud's clericalism
was undermining the royal prerogative, because of its incompatibility with the orthodox constitutional objection to Laudianism. More likely, such an omission represented a defeat, not
a victory, for the point of view which Prynne wished to express.
Similarly, the failure of the trial to concentrate upon the
'Popery' issue argues the view that Prynne's management and
control of the trial was far from absolute.

When Prynne wrote his most exhaustive treatise on magistracy in 1647, he referred back to Laud's trial not for its constitutional, but for its anti-Papal, lessons. Even in 1643 Prynne
had been concerned less with securing the limits of royal
authority than with the right direction of its ends.[3] Laud's
crime, on this view, was his 'Popery': his misdirection of

---

[1] Prynne, *Canterburies Doome* . . ., p. 26; Laud, *Works* . . ., iv, p. 150.
[2] Laud, *Works* . . ., iv, p. 156.
[3] Prynne, *The Soveraigne Power of Parliaments* . . ., *passim*.

monarchy along lines which were contradictory to the imperial
ends for which it had been created. And so Prynne could say
in 1647 that 'the late Archbishops familiarity, correspondence
and confederacy with Priests and Jesuites to introduce Popish
Superstition, and subvert the established Protestant Religion,
was charged against him by the whole House of Commons, as
a Treasonable and Capitall offence'.[1] Prynne's inability to win
most of his contemporaries to the view that this was the basic
issue in Laud's trial has several possible causes. Laud's slighting
treatment of Parliament and Common Law, and exaltation of
monarchy, seemed to many of Prynne's constitutionally-
minded colleagues the basic issue; even Henry Burton, concerned at Laud's 'too much officiousness, and obedience',
defined his treason from this constitutional view-point:

> . . . But this man thought himselfe no Traitor, because not against
> the King: As if Treason against the State of the Kingdome, and
> Common-weale, be not treason also against the King by dividing
> one from the other . . .[2]

Prynne's prestige was enhanced neither by the maladroit
clumsiness of his attempts to discredit Laud at the trial,[3] nor by
the edited versions of Laud's diary which he produced for the
same purpose. Prynne's critics pointed to the failure of Laud's
diary to demonstrate his perfidy. Predictably, a Cavalier
journal sneered at 'that grand Forger William Prynn' and an
Anglican colleague informed Cosin that Laud's diary revealed
the nobility of his aims 'though he owe nothing to that wild brute
who put it out, because for want of naturall logicke hee con-
ceav'd it had made against him'. More damaging were criticisms
of Prynne from opponents of Laud. William Walwyn called it
'the Archbishops Master-peece' and Henry Robinson discerned
in the diary 'which I suppose Mr. Pryn printed not to do him

[1] Prynne, *The Sword of Christian Magistracy* . . . (London, 1647, repub.
1653), p. 68.
[2] Burton, *The Grand Imposter Unmasked* . . ., pp. 4, 7. Cf. Braye MSS.
f. 72: 'The Pope never offered such violacion to the fundamentall Lawes
of this Kingdome as the Archbishop hath done.'
[3] Opponents in 1647 attacked Prynne for his belated concern with legal
niceties by direct reference to his conduct at Laud's trial: (Anon.), *Animadversions Upon a Declaration* . . . (London, 1647), p. 4; (Anon.), *The
Riddles Unridled* . . . (London, 1647), pp. 4-5.

honour . . . Such eminent signes of a morall noble pious
minde, according to such weak principles as hee had beene
bred up in'.[1] Yet the basic cause of Prynne's failure to win his
contemporaries to his point of view is to be found in the dependence of such a position upon belief in the Habernfeld
Plot.

Prynne had hoped to find, in his search of Laud's papers, the
conclusive proof of Laud's complicity in a 'Popish Plot'; his
failure to do so is somewhat naively acknowledged in *Canterburies Doome . . .*:

> That he received no Letters from Priests and Jesuits, is a thing
> not credible; the double proffer of a Cardinalship from Rome, is
> a stronger evidence that he received letters likewise from thence,
> than his own bare word, he received none. It is true we met with
> no such Letters in his Study or Closet.

Prynne pointed out that Laud had had time to dispose of
incriminating evidence:

> . . . though he removed not others thence, wherein he conceived
> least danger, the better to colour his removall and burning of the
> most dangerous . . .[2]

The Habernfeld Plot might have seemed paltry compensation
for the absence of such evidence, but it did not appear in this
light to Prynne. To Prynne, it was 'the infallible demonstration,
conviction of his guiltinesse'.[3] In the news-journals at this time
there is much excited comment on Prynne's forthcoming disclosures, which were expected to seal the case against Laud.
On *Romes Masterpeece . . .*, one journal commented:

> . . . And he that doth not now believe that the Wars against
> Scotland, the Rebellion in Ireland, and this war against the

---

[1] *Mercurius Aulicus*, 5–12 January 1645; *The Correspondence of John
Cosin . . .*, pp. 228–9; William Walwyn, *A Helpe to the Right Understanding
of a Discourse Concerning Independency . . .* (London, 1645), p. 2; Henry
Robinson, *The Falsehood of Mr. William Pryn's Truth Triumphing . . .* (London, 1645), p. 9.

[2] Prynne, *Canterburies Doome . . .*, p. 560. Cf. Laud, *Works . . .*, iv, p. 31;
'. . . mutterings arose, that Mr. Pryn in his search had found great matters
against me. . . .'

[3] Ibid., p. 421.

Parliament, is set on foot by the Jesuits, I thinke that no man will say but God hath given him over to blindnesse of minde . . .[1]

William Starbuck could urge his readers to supplement his criticism of Laud from 'Master Prynnes, *Deeds of Darknesse*, which I heare say is comming forth, if it be not already . . . now he hath or will lay open his hypocrisie'.[2] A news-journal in early 1645 referred to rumours that Prynne had ready for publication sensational disclosures of Jesuit intrigues, which 'will eminently demonstrate by what councells His Majesty is guided, and much conduce to the convincing of any Malignants that have any sparke of reason left in them'.[3] At this same period, *Mercurius Britanicus* could say of Laud:

> . . . But I refer all the world for satisfaction concerning this wretch to what Mr. Prynne hath discovered, and shall discover, by pregnant and undeniable evidences . . .[4]

But the Habernfeld Plot did not really come in the category of 'pregnant and undeniable evidences': these same news-journals preferred to emphasize Laud's constitutional offences at the time of the trial rather than his complicity in that Plot, and they had reason to do so. For the basic inadequacy of the Habernfeld Plot as evidence against Laud sprang from the fact that, although it was a Popish Plot, it was a Popish Plot against Laud. In *Romes Masterpeece* . . ., Prynne tried to explain away the paradox:

> . . . The truth is, the Bishop being very pragmaticall and wilfull in his courses, could not well brooke pragmaticall, peremptory Jesuits, who in Popish Kingdomes are in perpetuall enmity with all other orders, and they with them . . .

But acceptance of the Habernfeld Plot as authentic forced even Prynne to a recognition that Laud was not wholly Papist:

[1] *The Kingdomes Weekly Intelligencer* (Numb. 30) 8–15 August 1643 Cf. Laud, *Works* . . ., iv, p. 28 upon a minister's sermon, in June 1643: '. . . after he had liberally railed on me, he told the auditory, that Mr. Pryn had found a book in my packet which would discover great things: this to inflame the people against me.'

[2] William Starbuck, *A Brief Exposition . . . Upon the Lord of Canterburies Sermon* . . . (London, 1645), pp. 3, 11.

[3] *Mercurius Civicus* (Numb. 85) 2–9 January 1645.

[4] *Mercurius Britanicus* (Numb. 68) 27 January–3 February 1645.

... he was another Cassander, or middle man betweene an absolute Papist and a reall Protestant ... an absolute Papist in all matters of ceremony, pompe, and externall worship ... if not halfe an one at least, in Doctrinall Tenets ...[1]

In the accounts of Laud and Browne, the Habernfeld Plot is given slight attention; that Prynne should depend upon it as a central charge against Laud's 'Popery' in his *Canterburies Doome* ... argues the weakness of his position.

This weakness was seized upon by contemporaries: they expressed scepticism of the Plot. John Owen is one contemporary who did not; he reproached men generally for their ingratitude in face of the menace which they had escaped:

... the strong combination that was thorowout the Papall world for the seducing of this poor Nation ...[2]

He significantly quoted *Romes Masterpeece* ..., and *The Popish Royall Favourite* ..., in the margin. But Owen was silent on Laud's part in this combination: and this was the point of Prynne's disclosures. Laud recognized Prynne's basic dilemma:

... it is one of the greatest evidences that can be of my stead-fastnesse in the protestant Religion, and opposition against Popery, if this plot were reall, and if but counterfeit, then no crime to conceale it ...[3]

There were those, such as Owen, who could accept the authenticity of the Plot without accepting Laud's complicity in it; there were those who could accept neither, such as Prynne's anonymous critic, who said that 'both the Text and the Comment seeme to savour of a Fiction'.[4] More guardedly, Bulstrode Whitelocke referred to Habernfeld's letter 'which Mr. Pryn hath published in print upon trust (as he useth to do) as well as others'.[5] William Walwyn—no friend of Laud—trenchantly condemned Prynne's lack of judgment in publicizing the Habernfeld Plot:

[1] Prynne, *Romes Masterpeece* ... (London, 1644), pp. 28, 29.
[2] John Owen, *A Vision of Unchangeable Free Mercy* (London, 1646), p. 31.
[3] Prynne, *Canterburies Doome* ..., p. 563; cf. Laud, *Works* ..., iv, p. 326; Braye MSS. f. 62, f. 67.
[4] (Anon.), *The Fallacies of Mr. William Prynne* ... (Oxford, 1644), p. 14.
[5] Whitelocke, op. cit., i, p. 95.

... intending, no doubt, to blazon the vilenesse of that Arch
Incendiary to the world; whereas to an advised Reader, it will
be evident, that the first is framed of purpose to lay the designe
of all our troubles upon the Papists; and to make the Archbishop
such an enemy thereunto, as that they plotted to take away his
life; as if Satan were divided against Satan . . .[1]

Peter Heylyn pointed out that even Hamon L'Estrange, who
had accepted the authenticity of the Plot, was sceptical of its
narrator:

... saying expressly, that he inserts it, not on the accompt of
Mr. Prynnes faith, who first made it extant, but because he was
further assured of the truth of it by a more creditable person . . .[2]

An anonymous pamphleteer successfully captured the sceptical
attitude in 1647 to the revealer of the 'Popish Plot' when he
described Prynne as 'a long meager face . . . eares cropt close
to his head, which is stuft with Plots'.[3]

But one writer did come to recognize that 'Popery' was the
treason for which Laud had been condemned: that writer was
Henry Parker. Parker had much sympathy in the earlier period
with Prynne's attack upon the Laudians for the anti-monarchical implications of their break with Elizabethan traditions; yet
he had been too aware of constitutional grievances to allow
this sympathy to blind him to the menace of Laudian exaltation
of monarchy above Parliament and Common Law.[4] In 1645,
however, Laud's trial and execution prompted Parker to a re-
appraisal of his earlier position: he attempted to assess the over-
all significance of Laud's position. Parker now rejected as inade-
quate the view of King and Archbishop working together
consciously to advance the royal prerogative. He saw that the
ultimate aim of Laud and his colleagues was the subordination
of the temporal power to the spiritual; he refused to accept the
view that the King would consciously co-operate in the destruction of his own imperial authority:

... it is not to be imagined that either his Majestie or any other
Christian King, should submit themselves to the bondage of
Popery if they rightly understood what they did . . .[5]

[1] Walwyn, op. cit., p. 2.
[2] Heylyn, *Extraneus Vapulans* . . . (London, 1656), pp. 20–1.
[3] (Anon). *A Speedy Hue and Crie* . . . (London, 1647), p. 6.
[4] See Chapter 1.  [5] Henry Parker, *Ius Regum* . . . (London, 1645), p. 10.

Parker recognized the importance of observing the distinction between the two charges against Laud—his encouragement of Popery and his constitutional excesses—and of giving priority to the 'Popery' charge:

> . . . the designe for altering Religion, and the frame of the Government being two different things, that they were not alike intended by the Designers, but that the designe for altering of Religion was principally intended by them; and that the other designe of introducing an Arbitary Government to the King was but the bait to deceive the King . . .[1]

Parker, from reasoned analysis, was reaching a position which Prynne had almost instinctively grasped from the first: that the immediate exaltation of the Crown had tended to blind men to the ultimate intention behind the bishops' actions, which was the diminution of the royal prerogative. Parker summarized this view:

> For albeit that an Arbitary power in the King hath been made use of in many things, to the great prejudice of the Subject, tending to the manifest destruction of the Subjects liberties, and Priviledges of Parliament; yet when a true account shall be taken, what great benefit hath returned to the Regall Authority by all that hath been done, the totall sum will be found at the end of the Churchmens bill, but none at all at the Kings; where on the contrary, manifest detriment and losse will appeare and that the Kings Prerogative hath been stretched upon the tenters beyond its true byass, to set up and settle an absolute or Independent Prerogative in the Church to Church-men, which is inconsistent with the Prerogative of the Crown.[2]

Laud's encouragement of absolutism in the monarchy may have been the major issue urged against him at his trial, but Parker had come to recognize that Prynne's emphasis was the true one. It was 'not the Kings Prerogative' which was 'a principall motive with them in all their undertakings and designes', but 'this Independent authority of Bishops coveting to be so absolute'.[3]

Parker had been won to a recognition that 'Popery' was Laud's greatest crime, but this recognition was in no way dependent upon belief in the authenticity of the Habernfeld

---

[1] Ibid., p. 26.     [2] Ibid., p. 27.     [3] Ibid., p. 32.

Plot. In another pamphlet he dismissed the Plot with the special contempt which a man of intellect reserved for emotional hysteria:

> . . . His Majestie needs no forraine discovery of Sir William Boswells Letters, to advertise him of dangers, and conspiracies against his sacred Person, the designes of the Jesuites . . . can never end but in the ruine of himselfe, or of the Religion which he professes, there need to be no strange Intelligencer to inform his Majestie of this . . .[1]

Parker did not need to believe in a Popish Plot to be convinced of the existence of the Popish Plot. Prynne, on the other hand, saw the Habernfeld Plot as an essential support for his thesis of Laud's complicity in intrigues with Rome. Parker accepted the thesis but rejected the confirmatory material. To examine Prynne's later development of anti-Papal ideas, and the interest which a later generation took in the Plot, is to be made aware of a reverse process to that noted in Parker's case: belief in the Plot advanced, as belief in the thesis, which it was meant to confirm, receded.

Prynne had believed, up to the time of Laud's execution, that Papist intrigue had mainly been directed within the Church of England. While Prynne had believed that it was only Laud and a few of his colleagues who were subverting the Church of England, he had, in the period 1626–40, defended its traditions in a localized attack upon the minority; but once he had recognized that Laud's principles had won a large acceptance within the Church, he joined the 'root and branch' advocates of 1641.[2] Prynne did not believe that the end of Laudianism marked the end of Popish Plots; what it did mean was that these Plots took a different form. His recognition that the main Papist thrust would no longer be directed towards the Church of England marks the beginning of a period when, despite some serious set-backs, he is gradually weaned from distrust of Anglicanism. In this next phase of Prynne's development, it is in contexts

---

[1] Parker, *The Oath of Pacification* . . . (London, 1643), p. 23. Cf. Hobbes, *English Works* . . ., iv, p. 240, for scepticism about 'Popish Plots' involving Windebank among others.

[2] Cf. Prynne, *Canterburies Doome* . . ., p. 37: '. . . An evill . . . not so much from the personall disposition of the Prelates themselves as from the innate quality and nature of their office. . .'

other than Anglican, for the most part, that Prynne can detect Papist intrigues.

The Habernfeld Plot was a Popish Plot against King and Archbishop: for this reason it was unsatisfactory in the sixteen-forties, when Prynne was concerned to show the Popish sympathies of both. The Habernfeld Plot acquired a new relevance for Prynne, and for a later generation, only when anti-Papal hysteria could be found reconcilable with loyalty to the monarchy and the Church of England. Prynne's hunt for 'Popish Plots' after the death of Laud leads him, almost imperceptibly, to renewal of Foxe's faith in the monarchy and the Church of England as the real enemies of Rome. A vital first step in this process was the belief that the execution of Charles I was a Papist triumph. Prynne eagerly related the rumour that, at the King's execution, 'the Queens own Confessor was present in a Soldiers habit, flourishing his sword when his head was off as well as other Jesuits, Popish Priests, overjoyed with that spectacle'.[1] Davenport acknowledged that such rumours had circulated among the common people ever since the execution, but felt obliged to make public protest on behalf of Catholics when they found acceptance in the writings of Baxter and Prynne in 1659:

> . . . but seeing it lately confirmed by two sober and eminent persons, Mr. Prynne in his *Good Old Cause* and Mr. Backster in his *Key for Catholicks*, I began to suspect the worst . . .[2]

Correspondence has survived between Prynne and Peter du Moulin on this question: Prynne convinced du Moulin that the rumours had their foundations in fact.[3] In addition, Sir William Morice—whose views will be shown later to have an important sympathy with Prynne's on certain issues—wrote to du Moulin to support his belief that 'the irreligion of the Papists was chiefly guilty of the Murther of that Excellent Prince'.[4] Peter

---

[1] Prynne, *A True and Perfect Narrative* . . . (London, 1659), pp. 62–3. This story is repeated by Prynne in his *A Brief Necessary Vindication of the Old and New Secluded Members* . . . (London, 1659), p. 45.

[2] ('Santa Clara') Davenport, *A Cleare Vindication of Roman Catholicke from a Foule Aspersion* . . . (London, 1659), p. 3.

[3] (B.M.) Stowe MSS. 755, f. 14; Prynne: du Moulin, 19th March 1664. Cf. White Kennett, *A Register* . . . (London, 1728), pp. 504, 615.

[4] Peter du Moulin, *A Vindication of the Sincerity of the Protestant Religion* (London, 1671), p. 64.

du Moulin commented on the controversy in a pamphlet in 1671:

> . . . Mr. Prynnes intelligence confirmed mine. He saith that our late excellent King having assented in the Treaty of the Isle of Wight to pass five strict Bills against Popery, the Jesuites in France, at a general meeting there, presently resolved to bring him to Justice and take off his head, by the power of their Friends in the Army . . .[1]

It is important to note that the fourth chapter of du Moulin's work is an historical analysis of the struggles between Pope and Emperor: the necessary explanatory background to the meaning of 1649:

> . . . Indeed Charles the I our holy King and Martyr, suffered for his Religion . . .[2]

For imperial theorists, such as du Moulin and Prynne, it was vital to establish that the King had died at the hands of Papists. The King expiated all his former faults by martyrdom in such a cause; when Prynne had accepted that the King was no longer the *Popish Royall Favourite*, the stage was set for a resumption of his old imperial views.

Prynne believed that the Queen's Confessor had been disguised in the clothes of a soldier: Prynne's fear of Papist infiltration in the Army had supplanted his fear of Papist infiltration in the Church of England, after the death of Laud. The constitutional encroachments by the Army upon the prerogatives of Parliament; the spread of egalitarian concepts within their ranks; their impeachment, and later seclusion, of Members of Parliament; their execution of the King and establishment of a Protectorate: all these actions, to Prynne, were only intelligible upon the recognition that Jesuit control of the Army represented the second phase of the 'Popish Plot'. Prynne, writing in 1649, was careful to express the belief that the majority of the soldiers in the Army were sincere in their desire for justice and freedom, but argued that sincerity was not enough when matched against the 'over-reaching pates and Machiavilian Policies of these cunning Jesuites, who can metamorphose themselves into any shape and invisibly insinuate themselves into their counsels

[1] Ibid., p. 65.    [2] Ibid., p. 116.

and actings, to promote their own interest and our destruction'.[1]
To gather evidence of Jesuit infiltration, Prynne brought together an infinite number of trivialities: the Army apologists'
reliance upon the Jesuit plea of necessity; the presentation of
their Agreement of the People in November, 1647—a month
favoured by Jesuits not only for the Gunpowder Plot but for
the reprinting of Parsons' books; the imprisonment of Prynne
by Cromwell and the Army between 1650 and 1653 while
Jesuits wandered abroad, which was only intelligible on a
desire that 'I could neither write against, nor discover their
Plots against our Church, State, Religion';[2] a declaration by
the Pope to some English gentry of his hope that England would
be reduced to Rome by means of Jesuits and Friars whom he
had smuggled into the Army, which, Prynne said, 'one of them
affirmed lately to a friend of mine'.[3] Such evidence provided
Prynne with the proof of the success of the designs of the Jesuits
which, he said, 'every rationall man must needs acknowledge'.[4]

In a pamphlet which he wrote in 1655, the evolution of his
concept of the 'Popish Plot' is clear. Prynne believed that in
1640 the Jesuits had almost a thousand branches, and that in
England there were fifteen secret societies; a conclave of these
had met in that year under Con's guidance to foment Civil
War and ultimately to destroy the King. Prynne pointed out
that their founder, Ignatius Loyola, had been a soldier and that,
therefore, it was easy for Jesuits to infiltrate into the Army after
the King's defeat. Although Prynne's reference to Con's part
was a deliberate reminder of the Habernfeld Plot, it was a
reminder of the text of the Plot, and not of the disingenuous use
which Prynne had made of it at Laud's trial.[5] For Prynne
quite clearly in 1655 saw the Plot as anti-Anglican: he referred
to the boast made by a Jesuit in 1641 to the effect that 'now at

[1] Prynne, *The Substance of a Speech* . . . (London, 1649), p. 107.
[2] Ibid., pp. 14, 111, 118.
[3] Prynne, *A Gospel Plea* . . . (London, 1653), p. 1.
[4] Prynne, *The Substance of a Speech* . . . p. 99.
[5] Prynne, *A Seasonable, Legal, and Historicall Vindication* . . . (London,
1655), dedicatory epistle. Cf. Prynne, *A Gospel Plea* . . ., p. 1, where he refers
to Jesuits who were intriguing in 1653 in the same manner 'as I long since
by Authority of Parliament discovered in *Romes Masterpiece* (well worth
perusall now)'. But he has tacitly dropped the anti-Laudian inferences
from the Plot.

last, after all their former Plots had miscarried; they had found out a sure way to subvert and ruine the Church of England (which was most formidable to them of all others) by the Independents; who immediately after (by the Jesuites clandestine assistance) infinitely encreased, supplanted the Presbyterians by degrees, got the whole power of the Army (and by it, of the Kingdom) into their hands.'[1] Prynne's recognition that the Church of England was the supreme antagonist of Rome found expression in other ways in this pamphlet: he no longer implicates Bancroft in the Gunpowder Plot; he expresses approval of the anti-Papal sermons of John White, Andrewes, Featley and other Anglicans; his great antipathy is to the sects, in particular the Independents and the Quakers, whom he believed to provide the cloak for Jesuit intrigues.[2]

To arrest the alarming spread of Papists, Prynne suggested a Test Act against Popery in the Army in 1656.[3] In 1659, Prynne referred to the Jesuit plot to set up a Commonwealth, the instigators of which were Parsons and Campanella. Prynne found evidence of such plots in an astrological prognostication by Lilly, and in the relation of a secret conspiracy to him by a 'grave, Protestant Gentleman of the Temple', who had received it from a Popish friend.[4] In 1660, Prynne contributed an introduction to a translation of Campanella's projects for a Spanish hegemony. Prynne agitatedly pointed to the triumph

---

[1] Idem.

[2] Idem. Morice commented upon the Jesuit-Independent identification with obvious reference to Prynne: '. . . for as persons of honor and integrity have undertaken to assure the world, that actually divers Jesuits have passed incontroulably under the mask and notion of Independents, so it is obvious to any that probably it may be so; for Independency is an apt disguise for a Jesuite. . . .': William Morice, *The New-Inclosures Broken Down* . . . (London, 1656), p. 212. Prynne's attack upon the Quakers as the mask for Jesuits was developed in many pamphlets, the most important of which are: *A New Discovery of Some Romish Emissaries* . . . (London, 1656); *The Quakers Unmasked* . . . (London, 1655). A good critique from the Quaker side is: John Audland, 'The School-Master Disciplin'd', *The Memory of the Righteous Revived* . . . (London, 1689). For an attack upon Quakers, which avoids this accusation see: (D.W.L.) Baxter MSS. 59.1, f. 53. For scepticism of the accusation from Anglican sources, see *The Correspondence of Bishop Brian Duppa and Sir Justinian Isham* . . ., p. 186; Isham: Duppa, 27th Aug. 1660.

[3] Prynne, *A New Discovery of Some Romish Emissaries* . . ., p. 28.

[4] Prynne, *A Brief Vindication of the Old and New Secluded Members* . . ., p. 31.

of Campanella's principles: to the fidelity with which the Army leaders had 'punctually pursued Campanella his projects, to advance the Popes and Spaniards Monarchy over our three Kingdoms and the Netherlands, and reduce them under their unsupportable Tyranny both in Civils and Spirituals'[1]. The views of Prynne, and those of Chilmead, the translator, were seriously at variance in their introduction to Campanella's work: while Prynne sought to explain why Campanella's principles had triumphed, Chilmead sought to explain why they had failed. Chilmead's tone was defensive: Campanella might have erred in his main thesis, but his work still contained useful maxims of statecraft. Nearly twenty years later, it was to be the balance of Chilmead, not the hysteria of Prynne, which would seem unrealistic.[2]

The Restoration did not terminate Prynne's search for 'Popish Plots'. On 12 May 1660, Andrew Newport wrote to Sir Richard Leveson that:

> ... Mr. Pryn told the House today that he would discover £200,000 sent hither to the factious party to enable them to keep out the King; and a Committee is appointed to consult about it; 'tis said that the Cardinal sent it and offered further assistance of money and men ...[3]

In 1662, on a less formal plane, Prynne's anti-Papal obsession

[1] Thomas Campanella, *An Italian Friar and Second Machiavel. His Advice to the King of Spain for attaining the Universal Monarchy of the World* ... *Translated into English by Ed. Chilmead* ... *with an admonitive Preface by William Prynne* ... (London, 1660) dedicatory epistle. But in another pamphlet, Prynne had seen France, not Spain, as the instrument of Papal plans and had attributed the Civil War to intrigue by Richelieu and Mazarin: Prynne, *Ius Patronatus* ... (London, 1654), dedicatory epistle.

[2] Idem. *The Harleian Miscellany*, ed. W. Oldys (London, 1808), i, pp. 23–9, has a pamphlet which may have been inspired by Prynne although there is no evidence that he wrote it: (Anon.), *The Plots of Jesuits* ... *Adam Contzen* ... *Thomas Campanella* ... *Robert Parsons* ... *to bring England to the Roman Religion* ... (London, 1653). Oldys notes that it was printed by Sparkes, who printed much of Prynne's works, at a time 'when there was not that public prospect of Popery'; a protest at the reprinting of Parsons' work in 1648 had been made by Prynne in his *The Substance of a Speech* ..., p. 109.

[3] H.M.C. *5th. Report*, p. 207, Cf. (Anon.) *Philanax Protestant* ... (London, 1663), *passim*, which drew extensively upon Prynne's writings, (especially pp. 19–22), to support royal action against Papists.

was noted by Pepys, when he complained of his being seated next to Prynne at a dinner, 'who, in discourse with me, fell upon what records he hath of the lust and wicked lives of the nuns heretofore in England, and showed me out of his pocket one wherein 30 nuns for their lust were ejected out of their house. . . .'[1] The Great Fire intensified Prynne's fears of Papal intrigue; Isaac Basire complained to Joseph Williamson on 4 December 1666, that he:

> . . . Has had a letter from Wm. Prynne, a stranger to him, speaking of fears and jealousies, of plots and designs of Jesuits and Romanists against the Church and Religion, and asking how the English Jesuits at Rome conducted themselves at the late King's murder. Fears this matter, under pretence of indiscreet zeal, will stir up hornets at the present conjecture, witness Scotland . . . thinks of giving Prynne an answer that shall signify little . . .[2]

In 1666 Prynne's zeal to expose 'Popish Plots' was reprehended as 'stirring up hornets'; a decade later it was to be welcomed for that very reason. With justice, John Osborne had pointed in 1659 to the wildness with which Prynne, in his writings, ranged from the matter under discussion: Osborne compared Prynne to an Admiral who 'fetcht his course so far about to gain the winde, that he would never come to strike a blow before the battle was ended'.[3] But in his anti-Papal agitation, Prynne struck his blows before the battle had begun; his interest in the Habernfeld Plot, his belief that the Jesuits had caused the King's death, his attempts to restrict Papist infiltration into the Army: all these had for the generation of Titus Oates a significance in controversy which they had not had, to the same extent, for his own generation.

Professor Abbott has suggested that Titus Oates's story was derived less from generalized anti-Papist sources than from two

---

[1] Samuel Pepys . . . *Diary* . . ., ed. H. B. Wheatley (London, 1904), ii, p. 229.

[2] *Cal. S.P. Dom.*, *Charles II, 1666–7*, p. 318. Prynne feared even that Clarendon's impeachment might have been brought about by Papal intrigue: 'Mr. Prynne . . . Gondomar got Sir Walter Rawleigh's head off. I pray God this be not a foreigner's plot . . .': *The Diary of John Milward, Esq., . . . September, 1666 to May, 1668*, ed. Caroline Robbins (Cambridge, 1938), Appendix II, p. 337.

[3] John Osborne, *An Indictment Against Tythes* . . . (London, 1659), p. 32.

specific accounts: the account of the Gunpowder Plot, and Prynne's account of the Habernfeld Plot. Apart from the stock allegations of conspiracy against the life of the King and a projected change of Government, these three sources have the following details in common: Catholic authorities were aware of, or directed, the Plot; a Catholic in the King's immediate entourage stood ready to kill him; a Catholic rising was to be followed by a Scots' rising and the aid of disaffected Englishmen; the Plot was betrayed by a penitent conspirator to a friend, who communicated it to the government; Lord Arundel of Wardour had a part, through three generations of that name —and three variations of the Plot; there was a list of persons assigned to the leading parts. Moreover, Prynne's pamphlet first used the idea of drawing up information in separate articles, which was to be imitated in the accounts of Oates and Tonge. Professor Abbott has established a strong circumstantial case for Oates's indebtedness to Prynne.[1]

Professor Abbott was not concerned with the use which controversialists made of Prynne's writings at the time of Oates' scare, but this is equally striking. A bridge between Prynne and Oates was provided by a pamphlet of William Denton in 1675. Denton, very much in the Prynne manner, recited examples of Papist treacheries to their sovereign; their masking under the titles of Independents, Quakers, Fifth Monarchy Men, and other extremist sects; their adherence to the tenets of Parsons, Contzen, Watson and Campanella; the joy of the Queen's Confessor at the execution of the King. Denton then said:

> I shall not trouble you with the repetition of many score of the disguised and dark Actings of the Papists against the King and Crown of England, they being already extant in severall treatises . . .

Denton then named the treatises: all works of Prynne.[2] A pamphlet of 1678 recounted the Habernfeld Plot to show that Papists, no less than the sectaries, schemed against the Royal

[1] W. C. Abbott, 'The Origin of Titus Oates' Story,' *English Historical Review XXV* (1910), pp. 126–9.

[2] William Denton, *The Burnt Child Dreads the Fire* . . . (London, 1675), p. 58. Prynne's works were: *Ius Patronatus* . . ., *The Substance of a Speech* . . . *The Quakers Unmasked* . . ., *A Seasonable, Legal, and Historicall Vindication* . . ., *Hidden Workes of Darkness*. . .

Martyr.[1] A pamphlet of 1680 also narrated the Habernfeld Plot and pointed to its basic paradox: that this conspiracy against the King, although known to both King and Archbishop, 'was never divulged till found by Mr. Prynne in 1643'. Prynne's explanation—Laud's perfidy—was not taken up by this pamphlet; instead, it stressed the Papists' cunning in diverting the King's mind from it by fomenting the Scottish troubles. The pamphlet, on all other points, supported Prynne's account; the justness of analogies between the situation in the 'forties and in the 'eighties was stressed:

> ... As for Read, he was an Actor in this Plot, much in the same nature as Coleman was in that lately discovered by Doctor Oates, and others ...

The value of Prynne's testimony as a vindication of Oates was drawn in the same pamphlet:

> ... Whosoever shall compare the before-recited Plot against King Charles the First, of Glorious Memory, with that against His most Sacred Majesty now Reigning, shall find them so like in all the Plots and Circumstances, that never were two Brothers more ... From whence it follows, that there is no such Improbability of the Late discovered PLOT, as the Papists would have us believe ...[2]

Another pamphlet of 1678 drew from the Habernfeld Plot the moral that: 'What has once been done, may be done again.'[3] Bedloe prefaced his account of the Popish Plot with a reference to the question of Catholic complicity in the Great Fire: Prynne was among the Commons' men whom he named as interested in this controversy.[4] John Smith included Prynne's tale of the Queen's Confessor in his narrative, and referred back to the previous Papist attempt to destroy the life of the King: 'See Prynne Discovery of a Popish Plot by Habernfeld.'[5]

---

[1] (Anon.), *The Grand Designs of the Papists* . . . (London, 1678), no pagination.

[2] (Anon.), *A True Narrative of the Popish-Plot* . . . (London, 1680), preface, p. 22.

[3] (Anon.), *The Grand Designs of the Papists* . . ., dedicatory epistle.

[4] William Bedloe, *A Narrative and Impartial Discovery of the Horrid Popish Plot* . . . (London, 1679), p. 4.

[5] John Smith, *The Narrative* . . . (London, 1679), pp. 8, 7.

The greater readiness of a later generation to accept Prynne's thesis of a 'Popish Plot' may only reflect a heightened anti-Papal hysteria in that generation. Superficially, this explanation would seem adequate, yet it must be remembered that the earlier generation were asked not only to believe in the Plot, but in Prynne's interpretation of the Plot. At the time of Laud's trial, Prynne sought to reconcile belief in a Papist Plot against King and Archbishop with belief in Papist influence over King and Archbishop. The latter belief Prynne came gradually to relinquish in the course of his anti-Papal writings after Laud's death; it is notable that the Plot commands widest acceptance in an atmosphere which is certainly anti-Papal, but which is neither anti-monarchical nor anti-episcopalian. The Habernfeld Plot vindicated Foxe's thesis of the antipathy between Roman clericalism and the Tudor imperial concepts of the mission of King and Archbishop. At the time of the publication of the Habernfeld Plot, Prynne could not draw this simple moral, because of his scepticism of Foxe; instead, this moral was drawn out by a later generation, while Prynne sought to wrest the account for a condemnation of Laud. But soon after Laud's death Prynne's own anti-Papal writings show developments which favoured the interpretation of the Plot by the later generation rather than that which he himself offered at Laud's trial: this is particularly true of his more sympathetic approach to monarchy and episcopacy.

Prynne's distrust of the *Popish Royall Favourite* was an important, but ephemeral, phase in Prynne's controversial writings. As Parker had seen, it was difficult to accept the view that the King would consciously will the destruction of his imperial authority. The 'Popish Plot' against the King's life, which triumphed in 1649, restored Prynne's faith in the imperial mission of monarchy. As a pamphleteer pointed out in 1680, it was this faith which made intelligible the 'Popish Plots' against the King's life in both 1640 and 1678:

> . . . because nothing is hoped from him which might seem to promote the Popish Religion . . .[1]

The Habernfeld Plot had relevance for a view of Charles I as the *Royal Martyr*, not as the *Popish Royall Favourite*.

[1] (Anon.), *A True Narrative of the Popish-Plot . . .*, p. 13.

Although Prynne's distrust of Laud had deeper roots, by 1655 he had been won back to the Foxian recognition that the Church of England was the most formidable antagonist of Rome. In 1691 a satire conjured up Prynne's Ghost for his views upon the recent stand of the bishops against Popery. Prynne's Ghost dutifully comments:

> . . . if what you say is really true, it would oblige me to abate a great deal of my old severity and prejudice against them . . .[1]

A great deal of Prynne's old severity against bishops had abated, in point of fact, with the recognition after Laud's death that they were no longer the patronizers of Popery. These fears were temporarily reawakened by the menace of a new Laudianism at the Restoration, but the anti-Papalism of Anglicans such as Tillotson seemed to reassure him during the closing years of his life.[2] It was the honourable anti-Papalism of the bishops which a pamphleteer of 1680 accepted as the explanation for Papist intrigue in 1640, no less than in 1678:

> . . . Yet notwithstanding there remained on the Kings part a Knot hard to be untied, for the Lord Archbishop, by his constancy, interposed himself as a most hard will . . .[3]

The details of the Habernfeld Plot were such that they could command widest sympathy, not simply at the time of greatest anti-Papal feeling, but at the time when that feeling harmonized with respect for monarchy and episcopacy as the embodiment of Tudor imperial ideals. Thus the Bishop of Lincoln, Thomas Barlow, could argue in 1679 that the Popish treachery revealed by Oates was intelligible on the recognition that Popish principles were inimical to the central tenet of Englishmen, 'That England is a Monarchy, the Crown Imperial, and our Kings SUPREME Governors'. Even in Mary's reign, Barlow noted that Popish Parliaments had acknowledged that 'the IMPERIAL CROWN of this Realm, with all its Prerogatives, Jurisdictions etc. was defended by the Queen'. But this view was incompatible with the Popish belief that 'The Pope (by

---

[1] (Anon.), *Novus Reformator Vapulans* . . . (London, 1691), p. 12.
[2] Cf. Thomas Birch, *Remarks Upon the Life of the Most Reverend Dr. John Tillotson* (London, 1754), pp. 7–8.
[3] (Anon.), *A True Narrative of the Popish-Plot* . . ., p. 13.

their Divinity) is *Iure Divino* superior to all Kings and Emperors'. Barlow recited other 'Popish Plots', repeated the story by Prynne and du Moulin of Charles I's death, and laid particular stress upon the significance of the Habernfeld Plot in this context:

> ... And at last it came to this issue, that (other means failing) the King and the Archbishop of Canterbury must be made away ... This Traiterous Conspiracy to murder Charles the First and the Archbishop etc. was discovered (by an honourable person) to the English Ambassador in Holland and, (by him) to the Archbishop, and by him to the King ...[1]

Another respected Anglican figure, White Kennett, Bishop of Peterborough, in a sermon before the Commons nearly sixty years after the King's execution, could still depict it as a Jesuit triumph. He referred directly to Prynne for the story of the Queen's Confessor's joy at the King's death, and to Prynne's *Romes Masterpeece* ... for the evidence which the Habernfeld Plot provided of Jesuit intrigue against the King.[2] The enthusiastic response by a later generation of Anglicans is itself an ironic comment upon the half-success of Prynne's revelations; the Plot was remembered when the purpose, for which Prynne had originally valued it, had long been forgotten.

[1] Thomas Barlow, *Popery: Or, the Principles and Positions Approved by the Church of Rome* ... (London, 1679), pp. 4. 6, 12, 77, 72.

[2] White Kennett, *A Sermon Preached Before the Honourable House of Commons, January 30, 1706* (London, 1706), p. 22. Cf. White Kennett, *A Register* ... (London, 1728), p. 504, on the Habernfeld Plot: 'Mr. Prynne had abundantly proved the Activity of the Papists in the late Confusions.'

# VII

# THE ERASTIAN TRIUMPH

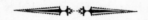

'MR. PRIN and the Erastian lawyers are now our *remora*.'
These are the words that Robert Baillie used, on 5
September 1645, to describe a movement that culminated, on
22 April 1646, in the formal questioning by the Commons of
the *iure divino* claims of the Presbyterian divines in the Westminster Assembly.[1] Clerical ambitions were defeated by other
developments: on a philosophical level, the heightened respect
for the concept of religious toleration; on a political level, the
growing power of the Independents; on a military level, the
weakening of dependence on the Scots. Yet Baillie's representation of events at this time primarily in terms of an Erastian
triumph would find few critics; what would seem more
disputable would be his belief that this triumph was not
inevitable.

In 1641 Baillie had believed in the existence of a powerful
radical feeling that sympathized, but did not necessarily identify
itself, with the Scottish Presbyterians. By 1643, he could look
upon 'root and branch', the summoning of the Westminster
Assembly and the taking of the Solemn League and Covenant
as victories for this radical spirit. Between 1643 and mid-1644
his efforts were directed towards a reconciliation with Independent divines, many of whom he admired personally. But
by June, 1644, he recognized the emergence of a force inimical
to his theocratic hopes: a 'Civilian' group in the Commons
who were anxious that 'Erastus' way would triumph'. On 25
April, 1645, Baillie complained that 'most of the House of

---

[1] Baillie, *Letters and Journals* . . ., ii, p. 315; *Commons Journals*, iv, pp,
517–18.

Commons are downright Erastians: they are likely to create much more woe than all the sectaries of England.' On 17 March 1646, Baillie wrote of the 'great and dangerous combat' that the Erastian lawyers, led by Thomas Coleman, were anxious to promote. Similarly, another Scottish divine, George Gillespie, called Coleman the physician who raised Erastianism up from the gates of death to life.[1]

One historian, W. A. Shaw, believed that the Scottish divines had been indecently hasty to bury Erastianism. Thus Shaw could say of Baillie that, 'in his remarkably interesting letters', he 'often expresses his belief that the triumph of Presbytery was at hand'. Shaw rejected such a belief in the words:

> There is not the slightest doubt that in his ignorance of the English constitution and character, and in his own too sanguine eagerness, he made a great mistake.

Shaw's confidence was based on several points: that Richard Baxter 'represented the constant element of Puritanism as opposed to the mere accident of the Presbyterianism of 1643-7'; that the Covenant was primarily a political *quid pro quo* for Scottish help and that, even so, it represented no slavish surrender to Scottish demands; that the calling of the Westminster Assembly was also a concession dictated by politics which again did not conform to Scottish wishes; that it was only after 1643, under the influence of the Scots, that English Puritans developed more theocratic views, which in itself explains the reaction against them in 1646: 'nothing could be more antagonistic . . . to the whole tradition of English constitutional and ecclesiastical history.'[2]

Only on a superficial reading does this interpretation carry conviction. Baillie was not sanguine: Dr. Jordan could refer to 'the usually gloomy Baillie' and Dr. Yule pointed out that 'the perspicacious Baillie saw in 1640 that the ways of Presbytery were not liked in England'. Baillie's perception of the distance between English and Scottish radicalism led him, if anything, to underrate the achievement of English Puritanism:

[1] Baillie, *Letters and Journals* . . ., i, p. 287; ii, pp. 122, 147, 198, 199, 265, 360; George Gillespie, *Aarons Rod Blossoming* . . . (London, 1646), p. 163.

[2] W. A. Shaw, *A History of the English Church, 1640-60* (London, 1900), i, pp. 101, 7, 316.

for instance, he recognized later that his initial distrust of Burges had been misplaced. If Baillie, nevertheless, believed until 1644 in the possibility of a clericalist solution in England, his views deserve respect; the more so, because in an earlier chapter it had been shown how far English Puritans had moved in 1641 towards acceptance of such a solution. It is true that this solution was at variance with the imperial traditions of English nonconformity, but Dr. Jordan believed that 'the rapid transformation of English Puritanism into Presbyterianism did less violence to the past than has commonly been supposed.' He thought that this process was a reflex response to the clericalist claims of High Church Anglicans—an aspect of English tradition that Shaw had not mentioned:

> Archbishop Laud had endeavoured to establish . . . the *iure divino* character of the episcopacy, thus driving Puritans to an equally inflexible avowal of the divine prescription for government by presbyteries.

To Dr. Jordan, Baxter represented not the 'constant element' of English Puritanism, but an important phase in its development. He associated Baxter with men like Manton and Hodges, who made a 'deliberate attempt to modify and amend Presbyterianism out of all resemblance to the Scottish model'. But this 'very important shift in opposition tactics' did not take place until 1645, in response to the failure of the Westminster Assembly. It must not be ante-dated to the period before the Assembly had been discredited by failure, nor must it be used to explain that failure. J. H. Hexter has made a detailed study of Pym's management of the Commons in the Civil War, and has made it clear that, while Pym and his colleagues could exploit enthusiasm for ecclesiastical radicalism, they did not always control it. The summoning of the Westminster Assembly and the taking of the Covenant might be made palatable by reservations and necessary only by political circumstances, yet to many in the Commons they were welcomed as preliminaries to the establishment of a 'godly discipline':

> By and large, the men who stayed at Westminster when the Civil War broke out were Puritans . . . The first mirage to stir an important faction of Puritans was the Presbyterian Heavenly City, dear to the heart of the old Puritan clergy, wherein all

Englishmen . . . would enjoy the somewhat rigorous delights of the godly discipline . . .[1]

It was not external opposition from the Commons that retarded the progress of the Assembly at first: it was internal politics. The Presbyterian divines, confident of ultimate success, were prepared to make haste slowly in 1643 and early 1644. On 1 January 1644, Baillie said 'that we doubt not to carry all in the assembly and parliament clearly according to our mind; but if we carry not the Independents with us, there will be ground laid for a very troublesome schism.' He had already made clear that the Presbyterian tactics with the Independents were 'not to meddle in haste' and that reconciliation would reward a policy of patient discussion: a belief that was less naive in 1644 than it was to appear to be later. Henderson, in October 1643, wrote to Douglas of a spirit in England that seemed receptive to Scottish ideas, but warned that opposition 'gathereth strenth by delayes'. The letter was prophetic: the opposition to the Assembly increased, as the Assembly became synonymous with procrastination.

Baillie—and others who believed that the Erastian triumph was contingent—connected its rise with the failure of the Assembly to effect moral reform. If Baillie had merely attributed the Assembly's failure to the rise of Erastianism, he would have said nothing remarkable; it was a Presbyterian commonplace that such prejudices traditionally opposed the establishment of a 'godly discipline'. But Baillie argued the reverse: that it was the Assembly's failure that had *caused* the Erastian triumph. In more general terms, *The Scottish Dove* explained the rise of Erastianism as 'an effect of Gods anger, against the nation for non-reformation'.[2] Baillie believed that there were men for whom the mirage of the 'Presbyterian Heavenly City' faded

---

[1] W. K. Jordan, *The Development of Religious Toleration in England* (London, 1938), iii, pp. 94, 268-9, 273, 67; G. Yule, *The Independents in the English Civil War* (Cambridge, 1958), p. 32; Baillie, op. cit., ii, p. 217; i, pp. 302-3; ii, pp. 198-9; J. H. Hexter, *The Reign of King Pym* (Camb., Mass., 1941), pp. 99, 158. Cf (D.W.L.) Baxter MSS. 59.1, f. 251; Baxter: Manton, 1 February 1658. Baxter argued against the summoning of an Assembly from the lesson provided by the failure of the first one: 'they will doe less in a month than one or two men would doe in a day or two'.

[2] Baillie, op. cit., ii, pp. 122, 111; iii, p. 483; ii, p. 298; *The Scottish Dove*, Numb. 130, 15-22 April 1646.

as a result of the slow progress of the Westminster Assembly. Such a belief only becomes intelligible on an examination of the sermons preached by the ministers to the Commons earlier.

In their advocacy of a thorough reformation, a 'root and branch' rejection of episcopacy, and the summoning of a synod of divines, the ministers stressed the importance of a speedy reformation of morals in contrast to the caution which marked the approach of the moderate Anglicans. To Burges a slow building, a 'heavy' Reformation, were characteristic of the unregenerate; when men had made their covenant with God, 'then the work of Reformation and establishment went on merrily, then they prospered'. Burroughs pointed out that reckless speed might have caused Laud's downfall, but would not cause theirs. The difference between the two lay in God's support of one, but not of the other: 'But though mans suddennesse often proves their ruine, yet what God does suddenly, is done strongly and surely; Created things that are properly Gods, are always sudden.' Such reasoning could lead to the conclusion that an Assembly, that failed to carry out a swift reformation of morals, did not represent God's Will. Thus the moral anarchy, that was a natural product of the Civil War, had for Puritans a more sinister interpretation. By 1644 the Presbyterian preachers had come to recognize that their hopes for an easy, speedy reformation of morals had proved illusory, and were driven to defend their position in language that was reminiscent of their opponents of 1641. Thus Hill, in a sermon to the Commons in August 1644, asked:

> Why should any bee offended with delays and difficulties in the present work of Reformation? . . Great works as well as great bodies move but slowly.

But Palmer, speaking on the same day, pointed to the consequences of the Assembly's failure to set up a 'godly discipline':

> . . . and now above all former times, whoredom and adultery doe frequently abound and grow impudent, even Incest is to be found in divers places, and no punishment to be found for it . . .

Palmer thought that this moral breakdown had occurred because 'there is no Government, neither Ecclesiasticall nor Civill, that they think will at all meddle with them how refractory soever they be'. Both preachers recognized that the situation had produced a demand for reform through the civil magistrate: that it had revitalized Erastianism. Thus Palmer asked the Commons not to 'hearken to the suggestion of any that would say, That there is no Discipline or Government of the Church to be found in the Word', while Hill acknowledged that opinions 'of most dangerous consequence begin now to spring among us . . . such who would have nothing *iure divino*, nothing stands by divine right in Church affaires, but resolve all wholly into State power and civill policy'.

An exchange in controversy between the Presbyterian, Ley, and the Independent, Saltmarsh, in 1646 shows how vulnerable were the ministers to taunts at the Assembly's slowness. Ley, like Hill, tried to argue the merits of caution, but let slip a remark against 'the government stuttering upon the lime-twig of deliberation at Westminster, when it should be upon the wing of actuall execution, all over the Kingdome'. Saltmarsh quickly pounced on the slip:

> . . . and will you now mar all, and defile your Argument with a lime-twig, and bewray rather your slow proceeding to have been of constraint than conscience?

The disenchantment with the Assembly is captured in the verse of the time:

> The Synod who dare to controule
> That sit in Sion house,
> The people look't for mountains, but
> They have brought forth a mouse.

In May, 1644, Baillie expressed extreme disgust with the dilatoriness of the Assembly; in December 1644, *The Scottish Dove* contrasted the verbal dissensions within the Assembly with the moral anarchy outside; Nalton spoke of 'a notorious contempt of Ministers and Ministry among us at this day'; *The Moderate* commented wryly that 'he that promises speedily and is long in performance, is but a slack friend'; in October 1644, Calamy acknowledged that there was 'a great deale of talke of reformation, but there is no practice of reformation'; in the same month, Sedgwick described the moral excesses that were reigning unchecked with an outraged precision, while Vines spoke of the increasing number of reformers that 'startled at the name of *ius Divinum*'. John Price, in a pamphlet of 1648,

attacked the earlier sermons of ministers like Calamy and Case
for the disillusionment which they had produced:

> Did not many godly, sober, wise and judicious Presbyterians,
> Parliament men and others, joyne with you, stick unto you, engage
> for you, who now begin to decline you being so greatly mistaken
> in you.[1]

The idea that Erastianism could arise as a protest against
the failure of the Presbyterian ministers to construct a godly
discipline is one that presupposes a greater moral concern in
the Erastians than one normally associates with such men.
That is why critics like Shaw, who believed in the inevitability
of the Erastian triumph, refused to admit the possibility that
men who upheld Erastian principles in 1646 could have been
deflected from them earlier by the chance of a moral reform.
But there is danger in accepting too rigid and simplified an
interpretation of the term: danger that has been well exposed
by J. N. Figgis.

Erastianism is now understood as the claim of the secular
power to control belief; it carries with it pejorative connota-
tions of a cynical indifference to moral questions. The typical
figure that it conjures to mind is a Selden or a Hobbes. Figgis
shows how inaccurately this describes Erastus's position. Erastus
was concerned with the question of how to enforce ecclesiastical discipline in a state that was uniform in its religion: the
limits of the magistrate's coercive authority and the rights of a
persecuted minority to speak the truth were points that were

---

[1] Cornelius Burges, *The First Sermon . . .* (London, 1641), pp. 35, 54;
Jeremiah Burroughs, *Sions Joy . . .* (London, 1641), p. 54; Thomas Hill,
*The Season for England's Selfe-Reflection* (London, 1644), pp. 27, 33, 34;
Herbert Palmer, *The Glasse of Gods Providence* (London, 1644), pp. 35, 51;
John Ley, *The New Querie . . .* (London, 1645), p. 26; John Saltmarsh,
*Some Drops of the Viall . . .* (London, 1646), iii, p. 41; (Anon.), *A Justifica-
tion of the Synod of Sion Colledge against those who say they have sate long, and done
nothing* (London, 1647), no pagination; Baillie, op, cit., ii, pp. 176–7; *The
Scottish Dove*, Numb. 56, 8–15 December 1644; John Nalton, *Delay and
Reformation Provoking Gods Further Indignation . . .* (London, 1646), p. 16;
*The Moderate*, Numb. 32, 13–20 February 1649; Edmund Calamy, *Englands
Antidote Against the Plague of Civil Warre . . .* (London, 1645), p.30; Oba-
diah Sedgwick, *An Arke Against a Deluge* (London, 1644), *passim*; Richard
Vines, *The Posture of David's Spirit . . .* (London, 1644), p. 15; John Price,
*The Pulpit Incendiary . . .* (London, 1648), p. 52.

not germane to his purpose. Erastus' discussion of excommunication was a rejoinder to the theses of George Wither who had proclaimed, in Heidleberg in 1568, a *iure divino* power for the clergy in excommunicating and suspending those whom they judged to be unworthy to join with them. Erastus sought to resist the imposition of the Genevan system on Heidleberg; for him, 'the main object was not to magnify the civil power but to oppose the discipline'. Erastus's opposition was rooted in an ethical concern: 'It seemed to him highly inexpedient to set about excommunicating a population who in reality needed conversion.' Moreover, the clerical claim to judge the sincerity of the penitent offender seemed to Erastus a presumptuous encroachment on God's Prerogative. In arguing against excommunication, Erastus incidentally advanced the proposition that the magistrate was able to implement the ethical reform, at which the clergy professedly aimed. Only in this oblique way did Erastus touch at all upon the authority of the civil magistrate, and even then he did not include within its bounds the power of excommunication or definition of faith: 'he is only considering the case where prince and people are all of the same religion and that the true one.' Figgis points out that Erastus was not blamed in his own day for ascribing too much power to the magistrate: divines such as Bullinger and Beza treated his views with respect; his refusal to serve under a Lutheran magistrate in 1576 is a mark of his distance from the popular concept of an Erastian. And in that pejorative sense, the term only became popular in England in the mid-forties: it was Scottish divines, such as Baillie, Gillespie and Rutherford, that first used the term emotively to discredit the opponents of the Westminster Assembly. Figgis believed that 'the extension of the term Erastian to mean not opponents of excommunication, but upholders of the view that the magistrate could order religion as he liked, and command obedience, was due to this controversy.'[1]

[1] J. N. Figgis, 'Erastus and Erastianism', *Journal of Theological Studies*, ii, 1900, pp. 73, 71, 85, 88, 65, 81. For a typical falsification of Erastus's views on magistacy, see: D. Cawdrey, *Church-Reformation Promoted* . . . (London, 1657), p. 24; Samuel Rutherford, *The Divine Right of Church-Government and Excommunication* . . . (London, 1646), p. 256, showed how this could be done more subtly. He acknowledged that Erastus seemed to be concerned only with opposition to the clerical claim to excommunication,

Paradoxically, the critics who have been sceptical of the Scottish ministers' belief that their aspirations commanded the sympathy of Erastians for a time, have been so, in part at least, because the critics accepted the caricature portrayal of Erastians that the same ministers drew in controversy. The opponents of the Assembly who denied that they were Erastians, were in fact denying this caricature of themselves; and quite rightly, since many of them were true followers of Erastus.

Prynne's quarrel with the Independents early in the Civil War and with the Presbyterians after 1645, was based on Erastus's objections. Prynne had held no doctrinaire attachment to Scottish Presbyterianism in 1641, but he had welcomed it as the agency for ethical reform. He accepted at first the orthodox Presbyterian explanation for delay: the hostility of Independent sects. During 1644 he therefore attacked with fury the Independent 'wandring-blazing-stars'. Against Prynne's 'church-ideal', which emphasised the need to bring the whole nation into outward conformity with godly standards, the Independents stood for the 'sect-ideal', which emphasized the need to preserve the purity of gathered congregations. Prynne thought that their advocacy of toleration and a pure, 'unmixed' communion derived from a common faulty principle: an exclusivist ideal that renounced the attempt to discipline the reprobate majority. His failure to recognize that not all Independents subscribed to the 'sect-ideal' was matched by his failure to recognize that not all Presbyterians subscribed to the 'church-ideal'. By mid-1645, however, he saw, in the emphasis that the Presbyterian ministers were coming to lay upon the necessity to preserve the purity of communion and in their advocacy of a suspending power, the triumph of the 'sect-ideal' within Presbyterianism itself.

Prynne, like Erastus, had become sceptical of the ethical value of a suspending, or excommunicating, power in the hands of ministers. He asked Gillespie, the Presbyterian apologist, why

---

and then gratuitously imputed an additional motive to him. He said that Erastus objected to the claim because 'the Christian Magistrate doth it not'. Against such an idea, Rutherford waxed eloquent: 'But I pray you, doth one Pastor, or the Christian Magistrate know the hearte; but a Presbytery cannot do it, because a Presbytery knoweth not the heart: Is this not too partiall logick?'

he should value the disciplinary power of excommunication, when it was evident that the countries that lacked it had a more effective moral code than those that had it. Gillespie answered readily that the raising of moral standards would be the natural corollary of a Scottish 'sin-searching, sin-discovering and sin-censuring discipline' in England. In the heady atmosphere of 1641, this evasion might have satisfied Prynne; in 1645, he wanted more concrete reassurances.

Prynne not only believed that excommunication was a feeble antidote to the moral breakdown; he believed that it was the cause of what it was supposed to cure. It challenged Prynne's convictions in three ways. Ceremonially, the fallacy behind the claim was a Papist-like exaltation of the sanctity of the Sacrament of the Lord's Supper. Doctrinally, the fallacy behind the claim was a belief in the ministers' powers of selection and rejection which was inconsistent with the Calvinist concept of Grace. Ethically, the fallacy behind the claim was a premature despair of the well-being of the rejected. Presbyterian suspension, Laudian neglect of preaching, and Independent separatism were seen by Prynne as alike in the spiritual deprivation that they inflicted upon those who were rejected; he described them respectively as a 'soul-Murthering tyranny', 'murthering the very soules of thousands of Gods people, by robbing them of their spirituall food', 'a very uncharitable, arrogant, yea unchristian practice'. The terms were almost identical, because the moral anxiety prompted by each was almost identical. In 1630, Prynne had defended Calvinist doctrine with the declaration that the minister can in no way distinguish the Elect from the Reprobate. He pointed then to the ethical consequences of an Arminian belief that the minister had such power:

> If God should cull out his Elect from among the reprobate, making an open division or separation from them here, by preaching the Gospel unto them alone; all Reprobates must needes presently despaire of his grace and runne into some desperate course.

It is to avoid such a breakdown of order that 'Reprobates are intermixed and mingled with the Elect, as the weedes, the tares are with the corne and grasse'. The exclusivist philosophy denies this truth and whether in Laudian, Independent or Presbyterian form destroys the chance of a 'godly discipline'.

Prynne valued the Sacrament of the Lord's Supper as a powerful potential instrument of moral reform, and deplored its frustration by an over-nice rigidity on the part of the ministers. Sadly, he recognized in 1645 that 'in most places else throughout our three Kingdoms . . . there are very few, if any such ministers' as the London radicals, who had excited his imagination in 1641 with their talk of a speedy reformation. This knowledge inspired the anger of his letter to the Standing Committee for Somerset in January 1648, when he pointed to the absurdity of the proceedings against Tanner, a local Swainswick minister, at a time when people 'should want ministers to instruct them, and so fall into atheisme, profanenesse, schisms or heresies'. He now recognized that 'reall speedy reformation in our Church' could not come from that 'strict discipline, which really reforms very few or none'. Prynne pointed to the ethical consequences of the 'strict discipline':

> . . . in the Churches of the Anabaptists and Brownists, both abroad and at home, where excommunication and suspension from the Sacrament are most rigidly and severely exercised, pressed; the sinnes and execrable scandalous crimes . . . doe farre more abound than in many of our English Congregations where there hath been powerfull preaching without the practice of excommunication or suspension from the Sacrament . . .[1]

The violence of his language reflects his bitterness in recognizing that the Presbyterian ministers, by accepting the 'Anabaptisticall and Brownisticall' position on suspension, have a real responsibility for the moral breakdown in England in 1645.

Prynne's opponents occasionally, in the controversies over suspension and excommunication, called him an Erastian in the technically correct sense, that his approach to these issues

[1] Prynne, *A Fresh Discovery of Some Prodigious New Wandring-Blasing-Stars* . . . . (London, 1645); A. S. P. Woodhouse, *Puritanism and Liberty* (London, 1950), p. (36); George Gillespie, *Aarons Rod Blossoming* . . . (London, 1646), p. 587; Prynne, *A Vindication of Four Serious Questions* . . . (London, 1645), p. 45; Prynne, *A Catalogue of Such Testimonies in all Ages* . . . (London 1637), p. 23; Prynne, *Independency Examined* . . . (London, 1644), pp. 8–9; Prynne, *God No Imposter Nor Deluder* . . . (London, 1630), pp. 16–17; Prynne, *A Vindication of Four Serious Questions* . . ., dedicatory epistle, pp. 57, 58; Henry Cary, *Memorials of the Great Civil War in England From 1642 to 1652* (London, 1842), i, p. 374.

had much in common with Erastus. John Collings noted that Prynne borrowed much of his material from Erastus, while Samuel Rutherford could say of Prynne that 'most of all he hath . . . is fully to be seen in Erastus: so that in answering Erastus, I hope, that ingenuous, zealous and learned Divine will acquiesce'. More often, Prynne is called an Erastian in the pejorative sense, that he believed that religion was the plaything of the State. Page, in 1631, had bracketed Prynne with Selden, while Foulis, at the Restoration, had bracketed Prynne with Hobbes:

> . . . did they intend to remove all Religion from its basis of divine right, and fix it as Mr. Hobbs doth, upon humane Constitution?

The view of Prynne as cynical and amoral was expressed in verse in 1648:

> Then lets agree on some way
> It skils not much how true
> Take Pryn and his Clubs, or Say and his tubs,
> Or any sect old or new.

John Lilburne stigmatized Prynne as Turk-like in his servility to the civil power:

> Oh brave Prinn! a fit man indeed to be a Privy-Counsellor to the great Turke, whose will is his Law.

Opponents gave Prynne this label and then accused him of being 'anti-Erastian' in attacking the principle of suspension when it had been conceded by the Commons in their Ordinance of 14 March 1646. Roger Drake criticized Prynne, Humfrey and other opponents of suspension for starting a controversy 'against the votes and judgments of a Parliament'; John Beverley similarly taunted 'Prynne the Erastian' for refusal to 'acuiese' in decisions of Parliament and the Westminster Assembly; Humphrey Saunders pointed out that 'the Authority we live under, did . . . authorize the keeping back of the unfit, and unworthy'. Henry Robinson argued that Prynne's servility to Parliament was dangerous: 'But what if they should ever be for Popery again, Judaisme, or Turcisme?' Prynne, in reply, described this hypothesis as 'destructive to the very fundamentall Power and Being of Parliaments, and as bad or worse than the Popish Gunpowder Plot, to blow up the Sovereign

Ecclesistick, and Civill Authority, of this High Court, in all succeeding Ages.'[1]

It is interesting that Prynne should look on the hypothesis of non-ethical rule as inimical to Parliament's rule in the same way that the Gunpowder Plot had been. For Prynne's surrender of authority to the magistrate had never been unconditional; it had always been dependent on the ability of the magistrate to establish a 'godly discipline'. Prynne looked in turn to the King, the Presbyterian ministers, the Commons, to fulfil this role: he showed great resilience in his readiness to recast his ideas upon their successive failures. His attacks on the King in 1643, the Presbyterian ministers in 1645, and the sovereignty of the Commons after 1647, were in part prompted by a recognition of their failure to wield the sword of the Christian Magistrate. Roger Williams noted as a psychological phenomenon that those who were ready to give most to the magistrate were also most ruthless in their disillusionment.[2]

Robinson's suggestion that Prynne might obey a Parliament that set up Judaism as the State religion was absurdly wide of the mark. The power that Prynne gave to the magistrate was always limited by its subordination to ethical ends. For that reason, Prynne was no 'Byzantinist': the term, which Figgis prefers to 'Erastian', as a description of the Hobbesian attitude to authority. It is a measure of the difference between Prynne and Hobbes that, while both revered Constantine, the first Christian Emperor, Prynne did so for his moral zeal, and Hobbes did so for his amoral interest in order. Prynne rejected the Hobbesian view of authority at the Restoration, when he

---

[1] John Collings, *Responsoria Bipartita* . . . (London, 1655), no pagination. Rutherford, op. cit., p. 646; William Page, *A Treatise* . . . (Oxford, 1631), dedicatory epistle; Oliver Foulis, *Cabala* . . . (London, 1664), p. 52; (Anon.), *The Anarchie* . . . (London, 1648), no pagination; John Lilburne, *Rash Oaths Unwarrantable* . . . (London, 1647), p. 19; Roger Drake, *The Bar Against Free Admission to the Lords Supper* . . . (London, 1656), pp. 31–2; John Beverley, *Unio Reformantium* . . . (London, 1659), pp. 36, 12; Humphrey Saunders, *An Anti-Diatribe* . . . (London, 1655), p. 88; Henry Robinson, *An Answer to Mr. William Pryns Twelve Questions* . . . (London, 1644), p. 2; Prynne, *Truth Triumphing Over Falshood* . . . (London, 1645), p. 2. The Commons had conceded the principle prudentially, but not by divine right; there was no inconsistency, even on this level of argument, while the critics of suspension, like Prynne, limited their attack to the *iure divino* claim.

[2] Roger Williams, *The Bloudy Tenent* . . . (London, 1644), p. 224.

criticized the punishment of men under the Clarendon Code for failure to attend divine service:

> . . . and if it be sayd that their Auncient power to punish absence from divine service will extend to any divine service established by the State, it will follow that (wch God forbid) if the Turkes or the Jewes should overrun England and set up Judaisme or Mahumatamisme, wee have a Court Christian ready, to punish men for not coming to the Divine Service alsoo . . .

Prynne was so far from approving of obedience to a magistrate who set up Judaism that he approved of resistance to a magistrate who did no more than tolerate Jews. He argued—with again that fascinating ambivalence and confusion in his approach to the historical King John—that John's favour to Jews justified the barons' decision 'to take up arms against them for their Laws, Liberties and Properties just defence'.[1]

The idea that Prynne was 'Turk-like' in his servility to the magistrate so caricatures his position that Figgis claimed that the reverse was true: that Prynne was 'a great disciplinarian' and, in the pejorative sense of the term, 'anti-Erastian'. Figgis points out that, against Prynne's argument that men should acquiesce in the discipline supported by the magistrate, John Goodwin could emphasize Prynne's own practice at the time of Laud's rule.[2] But to claim Prynne as 'anti-Erastian', in this sense, is not wholly accurate either. On the question of suspension and excommunication, Prynne, like Erastus, was more concerned with the ethical, than the constitutional, consequences of the discipline, but his great interest in imperial ideas led him to place much more positive emphasis than Erastus did on the powers of the magistrate. From Foxe and Jewel, Prynne had learnt to revere the magistrate as the instrument of anti-Papalism and reform. He was therefore more concerned than Erastus had been to vindicate the magistrate's authority. Prynne showed an awareness of this difference of emphasis when he compared his views in 1645 with those of Erastus. Erastus had denied excommunication to be of divine

---

[1] Prynne, *Histriomastix* . . ., p. 467; Hobbes, *English Works* . . ., iv, p. 393; (B.M.) Add. MSS. 37682, f. 74b; Prynne, *A Short Demurrer* . . . (London, 1656), p. 101.

[2] Figgis, loc. cit., p. 89; John Goodwin, *Certaine Briefe Observations* . . . (London, 1644), p. 5.

institution: a view which Prynne noted as 'seconded by many learned men'. Yet Prynne preferred the view of excommunication as an apostolical institution which had, nevertheless, only been adopted 'for want of Christian Magistrates to restrain and punish scandalous sinners'.[1] The Laudian régime had provoked no crisis of conscience for Prynne the imperialist: John Goodwin was typical of many former sympathizers in his failure to see that Prynne's defiance of Laud was no 'anti-Erastian' defiance of authority, (in the pejorative sense of the word), but rather a defence of the Crown against would-be usurpers. During the Civil War, it is true, Prynne lost faith in the Crown as the traditional instrument of Christian Magistracy. But the failure of other expedients, the King's willingness to negotiate, the King's execution by Papists: all played a part in restoring Prynne's faith in the Crown as the instrument of imperialism by 1649. Therefore, Prynne's opposition to the Protectorate was no 'anti-Erastian' defiance of authority (in the pejorative sense) either; Prynne refused to recognize that loyalty to the legitimate authority of Charles II was compatible with acquiescence in an usurped authority. His crisis of conscience only came after the Restoration, when he was forced to consider how far he could go in defiance of the legitimate authority, which could hardly be claimed to have renounced its imperial mission in the way that Charles I temporarily had. Prynne then chose conformity not martyrdom. For if his consciousness of the need of the sovereign to fulfil his ethical mission acted as a check on the unbridled extent of that authority, and made him contemplate even deposition in the event of failure, it also led him to place great powers in the hands of the sovereign who was the Christian Magistrate. If the one prevented him from being 'Erastian' (in the pejorative sense), the other prevented him from being wholly 'anti-Erastian' (in this same sense).

The powers that Prynne was prepared to concede were outlined in a pamphlet of 1647. From the Old Testament, Prynne derived his concept of a Christian Magistrate, who was to be ruthless in the extirpation of idolaters, apostates, and heretics, and who was not to spare even his nearest relative in the quest of a godly rule. Such a ruler would eliminate the advocates of a free toleration 'without any question or dispute'.

[1] Prynne, *A Vindication of Four Serious Questions* . . ., dedicatory epistle.

To Dell's objection, that the Magistrate's power cannot extend to spiritual things, Prynne answered that this thesis was a 'scandal and reproach upon Magistrates and their Authority . . . as if they were not Gods Ordinance, as well as Ministers of the Word, for the good of men and punishment of all Malefactors . . . as is resolved Romans 13, 1–6': a clear proof of the ethical context in which Prynne set his views on sovereignty. Prynne even cited precedents for 'corporall and capitall punishment inflicted by Christian Princes and Magistrates against Blasphemous, and execrable Cursers and Swearers'. Against such views Prynne noted a common objection: that outward punishments cannot reform the beliefs of men. The Independents had used this argument against the Magistrate's authority; they had stressed the futility of outward compliance. Hobbes had used this argument in favour of the Magistrate's authority; he had stressed the utility of outward compliance. But to Prynne the dichotomy was artificial: 'the very body and outward man infect the created soule infused into it.'[1] It is true that the Magistrate cannot work an inward reformation in all: the Elect, after all, are few in number. But the Magistrate does not know who the Elect are (that is the importance of mixed communion), and even the Elect can fall into scandalous sins, for which they deserve punishment. Above these considerations, the Magistrate has a duty to civilize the reprobate. Prynne's concept of sovereignty is derived ultimately from that pessimistic view of mankind which is Calvin's: a blind obedience in the reprobate majority is the necessary punishment for the original disobedience of mankind. Prynne does not try to answer the objection that his view of magistracy encourages blind obedience, because he does not regard it as an objection. He points out that:

. . . it is most evident, that there alwayes hath been, and ever

[1] Prynne, *The Sword of Christian Magistracy* . . . (London, 1647), pp. 5, 6, 8, 9, 31, 106; William Dell, *Right Reformation* . . . (London, 1646), p. 7; Hobbes, *Leviathan* (Everyman's Library), p. 254. An opponent of Laud in 1638 resorted to Hobbesian tactics: he 'reported that if any question him he shall lose his labour, for that upon appearance he will confess, and then he shall be dismissed; and so he reports that Prynne and Bastwick might have been, if they would have recanted, and thereby he deters every one from prosecuting him'; *Cal. S.P. Dom. Charles I, 1637–38*, p. 296.

will be much blind obedience in the Church of God, arising principally from the Ignorance, Idlenesse, want of love to the truth and inconstancy of men . . .[1]

The date of the pamphlet was 1647, not 1645. In 1647 he was looking to the Commons and to a reformed King to wield these powers. In 1645 he had no such illusions: his aim was to oppose the discipline, not to magnify the civil power. He went beyond Erastus in the power that he gave to the magistrate to establish a 'godly discipline', but his attack on the Presbyterian ministers in 1645, was Erastian, in the literal, not the pejorative, sense. He was not concerned with the constitutional objections to clerical encroachments on the civil power, but with the ethical objections to the effectiveness of the clerical disciplinary powers. There were others who opposed the Westminster Assembly claims after 1644 on grounds that were borrowed from Erastus and shared with Prynne; like Erastus they tended to express views about the functions of magistracy as mere *obiter dicta* in support of the main position. The ministers' claim to effect a reform of morals; the failure of that claim; the connection between that failure and the suspension controversy: these were important issues to men who sympathized with Erastus's views.

When Dr. Jordan discusses the Erastians, these are not the issues that he emphasizes. His main theme—the development of religious toleration in England—leads him to stress the contribution of the amoral laymen who advanced the cause of toleration. He recognizes that 'Erastianism was a sword which could be wielded to cut both ways'—that the magistrate's power could be sought for repression, no less than for toleration—but he comes close in his analysis to an equation of Erastianism with toleration. Shaw went further still, and gave the misleading impression that, after November 1645, the Independents were aware that 'the Erastian lawyers of the House of Commons led by Selden and Prynne were really fighting for them the battle of toleration'. Prynne, in fact, was not a member of the Commons until three years after this date; he was markedly intolerant, particularly towards Independents; and if, in an indirect sense, he may be said to have helped the Independents in their struggle for religious toleration by joining with them in an attack on the Assembly clerics, it was

[1] Prynne, *The Sword of Christian Magistracy . . .*, p. 109.

nevertheless against a belief—the ideal of 'unmixed communion' —that was, to many Independents, more truly an Independent tenet than the concept of religious toleration. Dr. Jordan treats the Erastians as part of one group, 'The Laymen and the Moderates', of whom Bacon, Cotton and Selden are typical figures, and explains the Erastian rejection of the Westminster Assembly claims in terms of a lay rejection of clerical intolerance. The failure of the Erastians to oppose clericalism earlier than 1645 is explained by the military situation in the earlier period, and also by ignorance of the disparity between the Scottish system and 'the historical antecedents of English Puritanism', until the Assembly divines over-reached themselves. On this interpretation, the suspension controversy was the occasion, not the cause, of a dispute that was constitutional, not ethical, in nature; the earlier Erastian acquiescence in clerical plans was the product of deception or self-deception, but not of conviction. The idea, that the ethical plans of the ministers could strike a genuinely sympathetic response from men of Erastian principles, required a more flexible use of the term than Dr. Jordan was prepared to give. Dr. Jordan believed that:

> Something of the hardness, the calculation, and the contemptuous anti-clericalism of Selden and his allies is to be found in the writings of all the Erastian theorists . . . concerned with the fate of the state, they were wholly careless of the fate of the Church . . .[1]

Dr. Jordan's tendency to read Erastianism in the image of Selden makes his analysis of the group unsatisfactory in several ways. First, he ignores Thomas Coleman in his account of the Erastian challenge of 1645. Erastians, such as Robert Bacon and Christopher Cartwright, looked to him as their leader; clericalists, such as Baillie and Gillespie, looked on him as their leading foe. Coleman was an Erastian, in the literal, rather than the pejorative, sense: he followed Erastus in an opposition to the clerical disciplinary powers rather than in an exaltation of the civil magistrate. His great controversy with Gillespie was fought entirely on ethical, not constitutional, grounds. Baxter

[1] Jordan, op. cit., ii, p. 457, 315–491; iii, pp. 73, 80; iv, pp. 268–70; Shaw, op. cit., ii, pp. 46–7; Woodhouse, op. cit., pp. (34), (36); Yule, op. cit., pp. 11, 17, 18.

referred to Coleman as an advocate of a moderate episcopacy; constitutionally, his sympathies should not have been with the ecclesiatical radicals from 1641 to 1644. But ethical aspirations conquered constitutional scruples: he was susceptible to the programme of moral reform outlined by the ministers in their sermons. When he applauded the taking of the Covenant in 1643 as a bond between English and Scottish divines—'they shall have the same Ministery, and Religion'—he referred to the influence on him of clericalists such as White, Nye, Henderson and Gouge:

> Who was not touched with that feeling prayer made by that man of God; that godly exhortation which followed from another; that pithy relation by that man of name; that soule-affecting Thanksgiving, wherewith a godly Doctor closed the day? . .

In another sermon at this time, Coleman argued that it was the moral superiority of the Parliamentary side that justified its cause, and he stressed the influence of the ministers:

> Minde what kinde of Ministers flocke to us, and we receive and provide for; With us are the Priests, the Ministers of the Lord . . . such who have been diligent, and painfull in their callings, zealous for the Lord and his worke . . .

Of episcopacy he said, 'Up with it, up with it to the bottome, root and branch', and he warned of the need to avoid delay: 'Cursed is he that doth the worke of the Lord negligently; The Enemy destroyes a Kingdome by doing, and a friend by not doing.' A theocrat, such as Thomas Case, could refer persons with scruples about the Covenant to Coleman's sermon; Thomas Edwards, the apostle of Presbyterian intolerance, referred to Coleman as an honoured colleague who shared his concern at moral abuses; Daniel Featley, the moderate, bracketed Coleman with the radicals, whose anti-episcopal and pro-Scottish tendencies he deplored.

Thus when Gillespie, in 1645, taunted Coleman with the pejorative label of Erastian for his indifference to the task of establishing a 'Church-refining and sin-censuring government', Coleman heatedly denied that he was a 'Parliament Parasite' and maintained, on the contrary, that his way was 'as active and passive for the Church-refining and sinne-censuring government of Christ as any other'. Thomas Edwards recognized

the concern at moral failure that underlay the writings of
Coleman, and of Prynne, of whom he said:

> ... (an Author whom I greatly love and honour for his former
> sufferings, and for his parts of learning and piety) and this is a
> great Objection in the mindes and mouthes of many, especially
> those who are for the Erastian way ...[1]

Whitelock could speak of 'busy Mr. Pryn', but neither the
pressure of work nor ignorance of the clericalism implicit in
a Presbyterian solution—as Robinson pointed out—could
explain Prynne's failure to speak out for Erastianism until 1645.
When Prynne's opposition to the *iure divino* claims of the
Assembly divines did emerge by that date, it was not because
the divines were significantly more clericalist than they had been
in 1641, but because they had signally failed to establish that
speedy reformation of morals which had alone made tolerable
their earlier clericalism. Dr. Jordan's reluctance to attribute
to Erastians higher ethical aspirations than those of a Selden
or a Hobbes explains his omission of Coleman and misreading
of Prynne. For he treats Prynne's Erastianism, not as a basic
principle in his writings from which he was temporarily deflected in the forties, but as a product of hysteria late in the
Civil War:

> Prynne, in other words, embraced Erastianism because he feared
> the anarchy of sectarianism ... Prynne, fundamentally con-
> servative in politics and in religion, was throughout the revolu-
> tionary era obsessed with an hysterical fear of the changes which
> were rending English society. And fear led Prynne to intoler-
> ance ...[2]

[1] Robert Bacon, *The Spirit of Prelacie* ... (London, 1646), dedicatory
epistle; Christopher Cartwright, *The Magistrates Authority in Matters of
Religion* ... (London, 1647), dedicatory epistle; Baillie, op. cit., ii, p. 360;
George Gillespie, *A Sermon* ... (London, 1645), p. 33, (D.W.L.) Baxter
MSS. 59.3, f. 115; Thomas Coleman, *The Hearts Ingagement* ... (London,
1643), pp. 23, 19; Thomas Coleman, *The Christians Course and Complaint*
... (London, 1643), dedicatory epistle, pp. 24, 68; Thomas Case, *The
Quarrel of the Covenant* ... (London, 1643), p. 53; Thomas Edwards, *Gan-
graena* ... (London, 1646), dedicatory epistle, p. 114; Daniel Featley, *The
League Illegal* (London, 1643), p. 17; Thomas Coleman, *A Brotherly Examina-
tion Re-Examined* ... (London, 1645), pp. 2, 3.

[2] Whitelock, op. cit., i, p. 226; Henry Robinson, *The Falsehood of Mr.
William Pryn's Truth Triumphing* ... (London, 1645), p. 7; Jordan, op. cit.,
iv, p. 227.

This summary is doubly misleading. Prynne did not 'embrace' Erastianism, nor was he 'led' into intolerance, because of fear in 1645. Erastianism and intolerance were principles that were present in his earliest writings: in different ways they both expressed the need to discipline the reprobate majority. In the period from 1641 to 1645 he had been prepared to entrust the Presbyterian ministers with this task, rather than the civil magistrate; he reverted to Erastianism when he became convinced that the Presbyterian divines, by their claim to powers of suspension, were renouncing the task.

Simonds D'Ewes is another Erastian whose ethical ideals are seriously underrated by Dr. Jordan. D'Ewes had joined Selden in attacking the Presbyterian clergy by September 1644, but in the earlier period his sympathies has not been with Selden and the moderates. Dr. Jordan saw D'Ewes as essentially 'an Elizabethan in his political and religious philosophy', but when Charles I had promised an Elizabethan episcopacy in 1641, D'Ewes had commented:

> This speech filled most of us with sad apprehensions of future evills in case his Majestie should be irremoveable fixed to uphold the Bishops in their wealth, pride and tyrannie.

Dr. Jordan pointed out that D'Ewes's moderation was such that he 'found himself unable to lend enthusiastic support to a civil war'. But the point was that he did lend support, and the letter to his brother, Richard, on 21 June 1642, explains why he did. Four days earlier, Richard had invited him to join the King's side. Simonds' reply is one of the most haunting documents of the Civil War in its candour. He had no illusions about the constitutional case for Parliament and admitted that he had often regretted giving his allegiance to it. One thing held him back: the hope of a 'godly discipline'. To achieve this aim, he accepted stoically that brother must fight against brother: 'that soe religion might be established in that power and puritie amongst us, and preaching soe settled in those places where atheism, profaneness and ignorance now raignes'. D'Ewes' sympathy with radical measures was rooted in his ethical values: in his contempt for the 'profane, vicious and atheistical life' of many Anglican clergy. D'Ewes could write to his wife, in December 1640, of his 'most intimate and deare familiaritie with the Arch-Bishop of Armagh', but his admiration for Usher—which he shared with Prynne—did not prevent him from joining Prynne in rejecting compromise schemes associated with Usher in 1641. D'Ewes's radical sympathies were evident in 1643. J. H. Hexter noted that the 'ardent opponent of oaths of association, Sir Simonds D'Ewes, remarked that the Vow and Covenant was both "modest and sober" and took it without a qualm'; D'Ewes referred at this time to the Scots as 'professours of the true Protestant Religion', and spoke darkly of 'a fixed resolution in the popish party utterly to extirpate the true Protestant Religion'. A man of D'Ewes's temperament was simultaneously repelled by clerical claims to jurisdiction and attracted by the moral code that was promised. This ambivalence is clearly expressed in his comment on the New England divines. It had appeared from reports that they had overreached themselves, yet D'Ewes could not find it in his heart to condemn them:

> Vices and sins are so severely punished amongst them, and the godly so countenanced and advanced, as in that respect it seems to be a true type of heaven itself . . .[1]

Nowhere is the ethical craving of Erastians more cogently stated.

John Lightfoot was to be an ally of Selden in a war of erudition against the Assembly divines, but the furious terms in which he denounced Burges's 'captiousness' and 'intolerable impudency' in declining the Covenant in 1643, showed where his sympathies lay at that time. Nathaniel Fiennes attacked the Assembly claims over suspension, although in 1641 he had been a 'root and branch' defender of clerical claims to powers of excommunication: Dr. Jordan includes him in his list of Erastians, but regards his inclusion as something of a paradox.[2]

Henry Parker saw in 1641 that the constitutional objections to a Scottish type of clerical government were valid, and that ethical considerations should not cloud this truth. He stressed

---

[1] Jordan, op. cit., iii, p. 55; iv, p. 20; D'Ewes, *Journal* . . ., i, p. 281; D'Ewes, *Autobiography and Correspondence* . . ., ed. J. O. Halliwell (London, 1845), ii. pp. 292, 114, 252–3, 116; Hexter, op. cit., p. 32; (B.M.) Harleian MSS. 164, f. 400.

[2] John Lightfoot, *Works* . . . (London, 1923), xiii, p. 11; Fiennes, *Speech* . . . *9 February 1641* . . ., p. 8; Jordan, op. cit., iii, p. 83; ii, p. 490.

the need for moderates to return to the Elizabethan concepts of church government and to press for a reformed episcopacy, *iure humano*. Of clerical disputes to the *iure divino* sanction from Anglicans and Presbyterians, Parker said that he 'must neither decree for the Plaintiff, nor the Defendant, but for the King who is in this case a third party'. His quarrel was not with episcopacy, but with the excessive *iure divino* claim. Dr. Jordan thought that Parker was able to argue in such a dispassionate manner, because he was 'an Erastian without . . . real interest in the spiritual problems which tortured England during the early years of the Revolution'.[1] A fairer judgment would be that Parker was an Erastian who did not allow himself to be deflected from constitutional principles by ethical values, which is not the same thing. In his brilliantly sympathetic analysis of 1641, *A Discourse Concerning Puritans*, Parker showed himself sensitive to the demands for moral reform, although Dr. Jordan called him 'completely Erastian, exhibiting little understanding or sympathy for the religious emotion'.[2] Parker thought that the danger in 1641 was not Popery, but Atheism: 'We are not so likely to lose the light of truth as the heat of zeale.' He decried the dangerous tendency to make a virtue out of lukewarmness: the parallel which opponents of the Puritans drew between them and Jesuits was not altogether unflattering, if zeal were the denominator recognized as common to both. If Parker ultimately rejects zeal as his guide to action, it is less because of

---

[1] Henry Parker, *The True Grounds of Ecclesiastical Regiment* . . . (London, 1641), p. 6; W. K. Jordan, *Men of Substance* . . . (Chicago, 1942), p. 68.

[2] W. K. Jordan, *Men of Substance* . . . , p. 93. Perhaps because this pamphlet fails to support his thesis, he dismisses it (p. 69), as of slight importance and even questions Parker's authorship of it. Cf. *Dictionary of Anonymous and Pseudonymous English Literature*, ed. S. Hackett and J. Laing (Edinburgh, 1928), ii, p. 70: 'In Bishop Barlow's copy in the Bodleian the above work is said by Barlow to be "writt by Jo. Ley".' But the pamphlet is not written in Ley's style, nor is its anti-Calvinist position reconcilable with Ley's ideas in 1641: Cf. John Ley, *Defensive Doubts, Hopes and Reasons* . . . (London, 1641). George Thomason—usually a reliable authority—attributed it to Parker. An Anglican accepted this attribution, and referred to him with approval: (Anon.), *Episcopall Inheritance* (Oxford, 1641), p. 23. A Calvinist accepted this attribution, and referred to him with disapproval—'Mr. Parkers discourse about Puritans and his bold censure of Calvin'—: (Anon.) *The Broken Title* . . . (London, 1642), p. 19. M. A. Judson, op. cit., pp. 426–7, accepted this attribution, and argued the importance of the pamphlet.

his 'cold pragmatic and hard lay intelligence' than because he realized the need to keep separate ethical and constitutional objections: to maintain the distinction between 'Puritans in Religion, Puritans in State, and Puritans in Morality'. He acknowledges the impatient feeling of the time against bishops: 'and all our three Kingdomes are growne so sick of their Pride, Injustice and Pragmaticall faction, that scarce any remedy but bloodletting can cure them'. But Parker thought that it would be a mistake to let that impatience determine the attitude to episcopacy. As a corrective to such loose thinking, he pointed to the tenets of those that pressed most zealously for a total ruin of episcopacy. For the Protestants give too much to the Priest, 'not only the Episcopall, but the Presbyteriall side also, not onely Protestant Prelates, but even Master Calvin that great antiprelate also'. Calvin maintains the Papist spiritual-temporal distinction, that Parker fears as 'a way to erect *regnum in regno*'.[1] In 1641 Parker showed an awareness of the constitutional, as opposed to the ethical, consequences of advocacy of a 'godly discipline', that was lacking in men such as D'Ewes, Coleman, Prynne, Lightfoot, Fiennes, Norwood, Mayne and Hussey, until the failure of the ethical promise was apparent.[2]

There is need to recognize that the Erastians, who rebelled against the Assembly divines in 1645, cannot be epitomized by Selden or Hobbes with justice. Thomas Fuller, an intelligent contemporary, recognized the distinction between two different types of men who attacked the clerics in 1645. He referred to Selden's obstructionist tactics against the Assembly, but gave a separate paragraph to the 'Erastians', who followed Erastus in a distrust of clerical disciplinary powers. He singled out, in this group, Coleman and Lightfoot as men who '(for the main) maintained the tenets of Erastus'. He believed that this group were exploited by men in the Commons who 'listened very favourably to their arguments . . . hearing their own power enlarged thereby, and making use of these Erastians for a check

---

[1] Henry Parker, *A Discourse Concerning Puritans* . . . (London, 1641), pp. 59, 52, 13, 38, 30, 33; Jordan, *Men of Substance* . . ., p. 78.

[2] Richard Norwood, *Considerations Tending to Remove the Present Differences* . . . (London, 1646); Jasper Mayne, *The Difference about Church Government Ended* . . . (London, 1646); William Hussey, *A Plea for Christian Magistracie* . . . (London, 1645).

to such who pressed conformity to the Scottish Kirk in all particulars'. A letter to Baxter made a similar distinction:

> . . . first . . Erastus a Phisitian . . . laying open that grand cheat of Ecclesiasticall Jurisdiction and Excommunication, and wch is a greater shame to the holy orders . . . that men ill principled as Grotius and Selden, yea Hobbes as bad as can be should come nearer the truth than many good men, yet God hath raysed good men as I know some in France that witnessed that same truth, and Mr. Coleman, Stillingfleet, Lightfoot were not far from it . . .[1]

The Scottish divines found it useful tactics in controversy to discredit their opponents by grouping them together under one pejorative label that connoted cynicism and servility. But it is clear from their actions, in other ways, that they did not believe their own caricature. They recognized that their claims to a suspending power had revived fears and arguments which Erastus had voiced earlier. They set out to remove these fears and to counter these arguments by a detailed examination of their differences: hence the massive works of scholarship by Gillespie and Rutherford against Coleman, Prynne, and their common ancestor, Erastus.[2] In April, 1645, Baillie complained to Spang that 'it hath been a mighty neglect that no man hath answered Erastus' Reply to Beza'; in August, 1645, he acknowledged that 'Erastus is the book vexes us most'; in April, 1646, he wrote that 'We are longing for Apollonius against Erastus'. Baillie was aware of a generalized lay antipathy to the Assembly from the start that did not rest upon Erastus's treatises; he recognized the intimate connection chronologically between the suspension controversy and the late rise of Erastianism. He had no illusions about Selden: as early as 1641 he had picked him out as an implacable opponent of Presbyterianism.[3]

---

[1] Fuller, op. cit., vi, pp. 286–7; (D.W.L.) Baxter MSS. 59.6, f. 192v. Edward Stillingfleet, *Irenicum* . . . (London, 1662), p. 136, denied that he was an Erastian, but accepted that the term meant antipathy to clerical discipline rather than sympathy for the civil magistrate.

[2] Gillespie, *Aarons Rod Blossoming* . . .; Rutherford, *The Divine Right of Church-Government and Excommunication* . . . Rutherford's work is significantly sub-headed: '*The Arguments of Mr. Pryn, in so far as they side with Erastus, are modestly discussed.*'

[3] Baillie, *Letters and Journals* . . ., ii, pp. 265, 365; i, pp. 302–3, 307.

When Baillie looked back in anger at the Presbyterian ministers'
failure to retain the affection of former sympathizers, he was
not thinking of Selden; another lawyer, however, was probably
in the forefront of his thoughts.[1]

[1] One pamphleteer described the change in Prynne's attitude from his
warmth in 1630 in these dramatic terms: 'Then he pitied the Puritan
Ministers; now with Caligula he wishes surely wee had all but one neck,
and at his mercy': 'S.S.' *Holy Things for Holy Men* . . . (London, 1658), p. 41.

# VIII
# THE INTERREGNUM

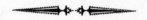

ROGER WILLIAMS had noted that the most ardent apologists
for the power of the civil magistrate were the first to 'cut
off the skirts' when he disappointed their hopes.[1] In the Erastian
controversy in 1645, Prynne had cut off the skirts of the Presbyterian ministers. In the Interregnum, he cut off the skirts of
the House of Commons. He had fought fiercely for both, against
those who disputed their authority, until he recognized the
culpability of both for that breakdown of authority: the
Presbyterian ministers, by their claims to a suspending power;
the apologists of the Commons, by their claims to sovereignty.

Prynne became increasingly agitated during the Civil War
by the growing power of the Army; he clung the more intensely
to the Commons. Yet in June 1647, when the Army attempted
to expel eleven Members of Parliament, a new note can be
detected in Prynne's pamphlets: wrath at the Army is now
linked with impatience with the Commons. Prynne pointed out
that the Army had printed their charges against the Members
of Parliament without the permission of the House; that the
Army's proceedings were dangerously akin to those of Jack
Cade; that such ambiguous charges might become precedents
for future action against Members who opposed the Army's
wishes. He wrote of 'that true-bred Englishman unworthy to
live, who will not die at the Houses feet in maintaining of their
just Freedom, Rights and Liberties, though in some things they
have formerly failed in their duties'.[2] This was not empty

[1] Roger Williams, *The Bloudy Tenent* . . . (London, 1644), p. 224.
[2] Prynne, *Nine Queries Upon the Printed Charge of the Army Against the Eleven
Members* . . . (London, 1647), pp. 3, 4, 6, 12.

rhetoric from Prynne: his words of defiance were to be substantiated in action later. Yet there is reason to claim Prynne's
wry recognition of failure as more meaningful, on a long-term
view, than his outraged protests. For although he resented the
encroachments of the Army on the privileges of the Commons,
he was forced to acknowledge that these privileges in the past
had not secured discipline and order. He was looking beyond
the facile explanation of anarchy: it was not the Army's insubordination that had undermined the constitution; the Army
was insubordinate because the constitution had already been
undermined. In July 1647, Prynne had not reached the conclusion which was to be forced on him by the Commons' seclusion of many of its members, abolition of the Lords, and execution of the King: that it was the claim of the Commons to
sovereignty that had undermined the constitution. Nor had he
yet related the failure of the Commons in the past to an obsessive concern for privilege. But he was aware that the Commons
had failed to wield the sword of the Christian Magistrate. He
was also aware of the growing threat from egalitarian ideas; he
resented the Levellers' attacks on the House of Lords. Was there
a connection between the two? Had disrespect for the Lords
destroyed the constitution?

Prynne had always thought well of the Lords. In verse in
1641 he had expounded his philosophy: that pride was a
characteristic of 'worthlesse upstarts, beggars, peasants vile',
while men of higher birth were distinguished by their humility.
He pointed out that Christ, 'the patterne of Humility', went to
a mountain-top to preach that virtue:

> . . . Showing hereby, that pride more oft doth dwell
> In lowest valleyes, and the meanest Cell;
> Than in the greatest Mounts, Men, Minds . . .[1]

A sermon on humility becomes a vindication of hierarchy: the
conservative Puritan had an unlimited capacity for self-deception. Prynne's regard for the Lords was intensified by Leveller
attacks. Lilburne and Overton justly pointed out that Prynne
had struck at the indispensability of the Lords in his defence of
the sovereignty of Parliament: he had said that the Lords,
representing themselves, were not essential to a full Parliament

---

[1] Prynne, *Mount-Orgueil* . . . (London, 1641), no pagination.

in the way that the Commons were, who represented the whole realm. Lilburne claimed that, in 1641, he had accepted the indispensability of the Lords until he had been weaned from that belief by the advocates of sovereignty in the Commons alone, such as Prynne and Henry Parker:

> . . . And as for Mr. Prynnes *Sovereign Power of Parliaments*, I never read more of that Doctrine . . . that *Gangraena* so much condemnes in me . . . then in that very Book . . .[1]

Prynne had cause to regret the claims that he had made for the Commons in 1643, although it is doubtful if his penitence ever went to the lengths that John Nalson suggested. Nalson said that he had heard 'a Gentleman his familiar averr. That he was so infinitely sensible both of the Folly and Mischief of those Youthful and Passionately Injudicious Essayes of his Unfortunate Pen . . . that he has heard Mr. Prinne say, That if the King had cut off his Head, when he only cropt his Ears, he had done no more than Justice.' An eighteenth-century critic solemnly commented: 'A Confession denoting a noble, generous and forgiving Spirit!'[2]

Robert Filmer provided Prynne with the intellectual justification for his fears and prejudices: he supplanted Coke, in much the same way as Brightman temporarily had supplanted Foxe. In February and March 1648, Prynne wrote two major works of reorientation: *The Levellers Levelled to the Very Ground* and *A Plea for the Lords*. In January 1648, Filmer's work, *The Freeholders Grand Inquest,* had been published: its influence dominated Prynne's pamphlets. In *A Plea for the Lords*, Prynne cited Filmer's work four times and developed his argument against the antiquity of the Commons. A contemporary had written across a copy of Filmer's work: 'in a considerable degree an answer to the exceptionable doctrines in Prynnes *Sovereignty of Parliament*'. In Prynne's willingness to learn from criticism,

---

[1] Richard Overton, *A Defiance of All Arbitary Usurpations or Encroachments, Either of the House of Lords, or Any Other, Upon the Sovereignty of the Supreme House of Commons* (London, 1646), p. 16; John Lilburne, *The Oppressed Mans Oppression Declared* . . . (London, 1646), p. 29; Thomas Edwards, *Gangraena* . . . (London, 1646), iii, p. 196.

[2] John Nalson, *An Impartial Collection of the Great Affairs of State* . . . (London, 1682), i, p. 798; Prynne, *A Memorable New-Year's Gift* . . . (London, 1727), p. xxvi.

he moves from the inflexibility of polemics to the humility of scholarship: he is able later to disagree with Coke's historical judgments without treating him as a moral leper. This development was confined to historical problems. To problems that bore more immediate relevance to politics, Prynne brought a vituperative zeal that did not slacken with the years. 1648 marks the beginning of this dichotomy.

Filmer's work was an examination of election writs to show that the Commons were not historically part of the Common Council; that the Lords were the body summoned to treat with the King; that the King was the initiator in legislation. Filmer denied the antiquity of the Commons. He believed that they did not belong to Parliament until the reign of Henry I and that they were not summoned by writ until 1265: the first extant summons of knights by the sheriff's writ. Filmer pointed out, as Jenkins had done earlier, that Prynne made a clear case for the antiquity of the baronial element in the Common Council:

> ... And if Mr. Pryn could have found so much antiquity, and proof for the Knights, Citizens and Burgesses, being of the Common Council: I make no doubt but we should have heard from him in Capitall characters; but alas! he meets not with so much as these Names in those elder ages ...

Filmer claimed that Prynne had distorted discussion by treating the King as one of the three Estates, whereas even Coke had called the Lords Spiritual and Temporal, and the Commons, the three Estates, which together with the King constituted the High Court of Parliament. He argued that the judicial power exercised by the Lords was derived from the authority outside the Estates: the Crown. He pointed out that the nobility were created by the grace of the King, which was 'contradictory and destructive of that naturall equality and freedome of mankind which many conceive to be the foundation of the Priviledges and Liberties of the House of Commons'. Yet the antithesis between Grace and Nature would have assured eternal discord between the two Houses had they indeed been founded on these bases. From this, Filmer argued that their origins were the same: 'nothing else but the meer and sole grace of Kings'. A large part of Filmer's tract is a refutation of Prynne's claim that the King had no power of veto in the constitution. Ostensibly, the issue was not of the first importance, but Filmer argued the contrary:

> . . . though it gives the King no power to doe any thing; yet it gives him a power to hinder others: though it cannot make Him a King, yet it can help Him to keep others from being Kings . . .

Filmer was implying that Prynne wanted sovereignty for the Commons, not balance. He challenged Prynne on the infallibility of Parliaments; he pointed out that even Coke had recognized their fallibility. To ensure that their laws were just, Prynne was driven to give Parliament the power to judge what was just or unjust; Filmer indicated that this was best secured by the King's discretionary power, given to him by his Coronation Oath, to protect just laws. Filmer concluded with the assertion that writ meant more than privilege in constitutional history: privilege was a gift extracted from the King, often by questionable means, and nebulous in its scope.[1]

Prynne took over Filmer's arguments, but fashioned them to a different end. He accepted that the King and the Lords had antiquity on their side in a way that the Commons had not. He recognized that the writ issued by the King to the Commons conferred on them a status inferior to that of the Lords: the Commons were formally limited to the discussion of matters originated by the King and the Lords. But he subordinated the Commons not, as Filmer did, to the King's will, but to the ancient law of England that required the co-operation of the King and the Lords. In the controversy on the royal veto, Filmer rightly saw that Prynne, in 1643, had been afraid that it would 'keep others from being Kings', but after 1648 Prynne wanted balance, not sovereignty. Dr. Pocock said of Prynne that he 'criticised the antiquity of the Commons in order to bring them not so much under the authority of the sovereign as within the bounds of the ancient constitution'.[2]

In Prynne's first defence of the Lords against the Levellers, he dealt with three common objections to the Lords: that they delayed legislation; that they voted only for themselves, whereas

[1] Sir Robert Filmer, *The Freeholders Grand Inquest Touching Our Soveraigne Lord the King and his Parliament* (London, 1648), pp. 4, 5, 13, 18, 19, 30, 47, 48, 50.

[2] J. G. A. Pocock, *The Ancient Constitution and the Feudal Law* (Cambridge, 1957), pp. 155–6.

the knight and the burgess represented the shire and the borough; that they opposed the people's freedom. Prynne had two answers to the first objection: that Parliamentary actions had recently been too precipitate, notably in the impeachment of the eleven members; that the Lords were more efficient and speedy than the Commons. Prynne's answer to the second objection was to renounce his thesis of 1643:

> . . . many Peers are of greater worth, value, estate and interest in relation to the Kingdom, then many poor Burroughs; and therefore by this reason their voices should be greater then both Burgesses serving for them . . . every Peer votes not onely for himself, but for all the Nobility and whole State and Kingdom whereof he is a member as well and as much as any Commoner . . .

Prynne denied, finally, that the Lords had opposed the people's freedom. He put forward the view of Magna Carta acceptable to Coke, whom he called 'the greatest Lawyer in this latter age', rather than to Foxe: he spoke of the reigns of John, Henry III, Edward II, Richard II and 'other oppressive Princes, against whose innovations of the Kingdomes Lawes and Rights', the Lords 'have ever beene the principall Bulwarkes'. It is notable that the two latter points weaken Filmer's case for the sovereignty of the Crown. Prynne had stressed the right of the Lords, independent of Crown grace, to representation in Parliament, and he had drawn attention to the historic function of the Lords as a check on the excesses of the Crown. Prynne preached constitutionalism, Filmer absolutism, against the Commons' sovereignty that they both deplored.[1]

In *A Plea for the Lords*, Prynne defended the Lords as the stabilizing element that preserved the delicate equilibrium of a balanced polity:

> . . . their Right and Honour, to moderate the Excesses and Encroachments both of King and Commons one upon the other, and keep both of them within their just and ancient bounds . . .

Scholarship and partisanship fused in his plea for the transcribing and publishing of ancient Parliamentary Rolls and Journals: it would preserve them, as historical records, from the threat of fire or war; it would silence 'the Sectaries and

[1] Prynne, *The Levellers Levelled to the Very Ground* . . . (London, 1648), pp. 12, 13, 14, 23, 20.

Levellers ignorant false Allegations against your Honors Parliamentary Jurisdiction and Judicature'. Prynne's rejection of sovereignty in favour of balance was clear in his concern that both Houses should keep within these bounds, 'the exceeding whereof is dangerous, and grievous to the People, except in cases of absolute necessity, for the saving of a Kingdome, whiles that necessity continues and no longer'. He could claim consistency on this point: his defence of the sovereignty of Parliament in 1643 had been very much a temporary expedient to meet an exceptional situation. But Prynne was uncompromising on one point: the supremacy of the Lords in judicial matters. He dealt with the objection, that the absence of a superior authority to override an unjust sentence by the Lords was a serious encroachment on men's liberties. First, he argued that there was no reason to suppose that the Lords would commit a man unjustly. Second, he pointed out that the Lords could be petitioned to review a case. But the Commons were not capable of reversing the findings of the Lords, 'which is paramount to them'. He argued that the Lords, 'being the Superior Authority, and onely Judicatory in Parliament', had the power to reverse the findings of the Commons. The only comfort that Prynne could offer the innocent victim of a censure by the Lords was that he should bear his suffering, with the aid of a good conscience, until his release, 'and not raile, murmur, and play the Bedlam as Lilburne and his Companions'.[1]

Prynne did not confine his defence of the ancient constitution to pamphleteering on behalf of the Lords. In November 1648, he entered the Commons as Member of Parliament for Newport, Cornwall. An anonymous pamphleteer commented savagely on his method of entry; although abusive and partisan, the writer was well-informed and perceptive. His claim that Prynne was one of the Cornish royal borough representatives, who had bought his seat in order to redress the balance of power in the Commons, cannot be dismissed as mere spite.[2] It is clear

---

[1] Prynne, *A Plea for the Lords* . . . (London, 1648), pp. 22, 23, 27, dedicatory epistle, 65, 66.

[2] (Anon.), *A Word to Mr. Wil Pryn* . . . (London, 1649), pp. 7, 13. The writer claimed that Prynne's vituperation was valuable to the King's cause in the latter part of 1648, 'for which reason he bought his membership twentie pounds cheaper than Thomas Temple'.

that Prynne saw his mission to be the reconciliation of King and Commons on the basis of the Isle of Wight negotiations: this was the theme of his speech, on 4 December 1648, in the Commons, which he printed afterwards, 'at the importunate request of divers Members'. He appended to his speech an important letter to his borough, which he wrote in January 1649. He catalogued his labours for peace since entering Parliament as its representative, including his 'indefatigable endeavours' to draw up Bills upon the King's concessions in the negotiations. He appealed to his electors as to whether he had, in any way, violated the trust which they had reposed in him. He acknowledged that, in one sense, such an appeal had no relevance in the English constitutional context:

> . . . I am judically accountable only to the Common House, which knowes the true grounds upon which I went, and can only truly judge of what was there spoken and voted (none being fit to judge, any thing but those who know and hear it too) . . .

Yet, in another sense, there was reason for such an appeal:

> . . . and yet, I hold my selfe in some sort ministerially accomptable unto you for whom I serve, as the properest Judges, without the Houses doores, of what I spake or voted in your behalfe . . .

Prynne's attempted distinction between a ministerial, and a judicial, accountability was important. It represented a *via media* between the total disregard for the people that had vitiated the Royalist cause, and the total dependence on the people that was coming to vitiate the Parliamentary cause.

This same spirit of compromise was evident in the speech itself. Prynne posed the question that, even if the negotiation proposals were acceptable, could Parliament afford to trust the King? In language that betrayed his disillusionment, he developed his philosophy of scepticism, to support his argument that Parliament could no longer afford not to trust the King:

> For my part, I have seen so much experience in the world, that I dare trust none with my own or the Kingdomes safety, but God alone . . . we have seen such strange Mutabilities and perfidiousnesse in men of all sorts since our troubles that we cannot trust neither the King nor Prince, City, nor Countrey, this Generall, nor that Generall; this Army, nor those that went before it, and yet our selves who are jealous one of another, treacherous one to

another, distrustfull of all . . . Let us begin to trust in God alone
in the first place, and then we need not distrust the King for
time to come any more than others, or ourselves . . .

Less spectacularly penitent than in Nalson's anecdote, Prynne
nevertheless comes closer in this statement to a recognition of
misjudgment in the past than in any other writing of his. It is
true that Prynne's disappointment at the failure of the Presbyterian ministers to establish 'the house of the Lord in the top
of the mountain' emerges only by implication. But the tone is
tired and guarded, the defensiveness of the permanently defeated. It contrasts markedly with the trusting spontaneity that
Clarendon noted as characteristic of the younger Prynne.[1]
Prynne's constitutional rethinking is only intelligible against
the background of this change in mood. It says much for the
resilient reserves in his nature that disillusionment did not
cause him to withdraw from political controversy. It led him to
work for compromise in politics, but he was as ready to suffer
in defence of that compromise as he had been ready to suffer
in defence of earlier ideals. Thus Prynne's most clear-sighted
recognition of failure is the prelude, not to retirement from controversy, but to its renewal. A philosophy of scepticism led to
Pendennis Castle.

In an appendix to his speech, Prynne claimed that it had
won over many waverers, although his remark about 'the
Speaker going into the withdrawing Room to refresh himself,
so soon as the Speech was ended' does not, perhaps, support
his point as unambiguously as he supposed. One critic recalled
'how pitifully did you once afflict the House of Commons';
another related how 'Mr. Prin made a Learned simple Speech,
three hours long, setting forth his sufferings by his Majesty
(who had taken all but his eares from him)' and added that 'he
needed not to have been so tedious herein, for he well knew his
Majesties friends were the major part then present'. The critic
claimed that it did not really matter 'whether he had spoken
sense, or non sense'; he was referring to the balance of parties
at that time, yet there was an unintended sense in which his

[1] Prynne, *The Substance of a Speech* . . . (London, 1649), pp. 5, 6, 23, 24,
76; Clarendon, *The History of the Rebellion* . . ., i, pp. 265–6. For evidence
of Prynne's activity on entering Parliament, see: *Common Journals*, v, pp. 73,
75, 77, 78, 79, 81, 83, 86, 87.

comment was also true.[1] For, irrespective of the merits of his speech, only the attitude that it expressed was important: Prynne's prestige, derived from his earlier writings and sufferings, gave his opinions weight in controversy. It became important to sympathizers with the Army to demonstrate that, had he remained faithful to his earlier principles, he would have approved of the deposition and execution of the King. It became equally important to those who wanted a reconciliation between King and Parliament to praise Prynne for dissociating himself from such principles, but this they found difficult to do.

Six articles in the Army's impeachment of the King were 'collected out of *Romes Master-piece* and will be more fully asserted and maintained from the severall Writings and labours of Mr. Wil Pryn, Esquire'. A pamphlet entitled *Mr. Prinns Charge Against the King* was written to scotch rumours in the mouths of 'the over-credulous vulgar' that Prynne had become the King's advocate: from *The Popish Royall Favourite* it quoted Prynne's revelations of Charles I's intrigues with Papists; from *The Soveraigne Power of Parliaments* it quoted Prynne's approval of resistance. Another pamphlet, *Prynne Against Prinn*, also cited from Prynne's writings in 1643 statements to justify the sovereignty of the Commons and the barons' resistance of tyranny. Prynne's partiality for resistance theories was noted by another writer. John Goodwin accused Prynne, in 1648, of seeking to 'melt down' the mountain that he had set up in 1643. A bogus retraction of Prynne's *Histriomastix* contained the apology:

> . . . it is no disparagement for any man to alter his judgment upon better information, besides it was done long ago, and when the King (whose virtues I did not then so perfectly understand) governed without control . . .[2]

[1] Prynne, *The Substance of a Speech* . . ., p. 113; (Anon.), *A Serious Epistle to Mr. William Prynne* . . . (London, 1649), p. 6; *The Moderate*, Numb. 22, 5–12 December 1648; cf. *Parliamentary History of England*, ed. W. Cobbett (London, 1808), iii, p. 1152: 'The person who distinguished himself most upon this occasion, was the famous Mr. Prynne . . . in a set speech of several hours.'

[2] *The Resolution of His Excellency The Lord Generall Fairfax and his Generall Councell of Officers* (London, 1648), p. 3; (Anon.), *Mr. Prinns Charge Against the King* (London, 1648), no pagination; (Anon.), *Prynne Against Prinn* . . . (London, 1648), p. 7; J.L. *Illumination to Sion Colledge* . . . (London, 1649),

The taunts stung Prynne to a vindication of his 'wounded reputation against all imputations of inconstancy, and mutability' in his principles or actions. His Calvinistic regard for constancy was expressed in the words:

> It is Gods owne glory to be unchangeable, unvariable, and without shadow of turning . . . So I trust to manifest my selfe . . to be still the same I was heretofore.

He pointed out that Parliament had professed, in all its legislation, to preserve the Crown; that Jewish Kings, however sinful, had never been judically deposed; that English Kings had only been deposed by 'Popish parliaments in time of ignorance'; that Charles I was a Protestant King 'of a temperate and sober life'.[1] He sheltered in 1648 and 1649 behind the ambiguities in his defence of the sovereignty of Parliament. The basic ambiguity Prynne had never resolved: were the actions of past Parliaments precedents for the present Parliament, or were they more inimical to monarchy and therefore to be rejected as Papist? He now claimed that the second meaning had been intended in 1643: an interpretation that made nonsense of his approbation of such actions in 1643, but that could alone make plausible his claim to consistency in condemning resistance.

It was understandable that Prynne should reply to his opponents in a spirited fashion. It was less understandable that the acquisition of this formidable ally should be treated so sceptically by friends of the King. A Cavalier news-journal asked: 'who would ever have thought, that William should have become a Creature of the contrary Faction?' Another noted that Prynne's criticisms showed that the vices of the 'Saints' were now 'acknowledged by those of their own gang . . . such as have alwayes been privy to their Counsels and the highest of their designes'. Another paid Prynne a doubtful compliment: 'That M. Prin hath a foule mouth wee have experience, but he could not be too invective against this Army Monster.' Even Matthew Rowe, deprecating the Army's proceedings in

---

[1] Prynne, *Prynne The Member Reconciled to Prynne the Barrester* . . . (London, 1649), dedicatory epistle; Prynne, *A Brief Memento to the Present Unparliamentary Junto* . . . (London, 1649), pp. 3, 5, 10, 14, 12.

p. 31; John Goodwin, *Right and Might Well Met* . . . (London, 1649), pp. 4, 8, 9; (Anon.), *Mr. William Prynne His Defence of Stage-Plays* . . . (London, 1649), p. 5.

January 1649, could derive priggish satisfaction from the imprisonment of Prynne: 'So that thus you see, all transgressors must suffer.' The Royalist reserve towards Prynne may be attributed, in part, to the fact that he stood to them as the image of the fanaticism that had precipitated the Civil War; even his services at the Restoration could not, for some of them, expiate his earlier crimes. But in part, too, they minimized the seriousness of the change in Prynne. They accepted their opponents' caricature of him as the constant opponent of all governments, because they failed to understand the relationship between his political activities and his historical revisions. One Royalist understood the significance of Prynne's change of front. At the lowest point in Royalist fortunes, on 11 January 1649, William Sancroft wrote a letter to his father, in which he prophetically read hope for the future in the conversion of Prynne to moderation:

> . . . You see, the army could never ruine the King, till they null'd the Lords and enslav'd the Commons, and soe ruined the Parliament, that lent the first hand to the setting of them up, and pulling downe the King. And what shall wee say if Wm. Prinne (Utter. barr. of Linc. Inne) who was the first incendiary and sowd the first seeds of sedition, suffer at last in the King's quarrell? You will see by the papers I send you, he is engag'd: so you neither know him and his pertinacity, if you thinke he will retreat . . .[1]

Prynne did not retreat. In the controversy over seclusion, he told Ireton to his face that 'Pride's Purge' and the proceedings against the King were treasonous. A news-journal at this time, when grouping the eighteen members arrested by the Army, included Prynne among the 'Assertors who (they suppose) will stand out to the utmost', not among the 'Forlorn hope . . . pillars of the Scottish Interest': possibly the knowledge of Prynne's sympathies in the Erastian controversy lay behind the distinction.[2] Prynne saw the execution of the King as martyrdom for the imperial cause; he was convinced that it was a Jesuit triumph. This belief was valuable in the evolution

---

[1] *Mercurius Pragmaticus*, Numb. 18, 11–18 January 1648; *Mercurius Elencticus*, Numb. 58, 26 December 1648–2 January 1649; *Mercurius Impartialis*, Numb. 1, 5–12 December 1648; H.M.C., *Ormonde Report*, ii, pp. 86–7; (Bodl. Lib.) Tanner MSS., 57, f. 497.

[2] *Mercurius Pragmaticus*, Numb. 39, 19–26 December, 1648.

of his anti-Papal writings, but he was also aware that a constitutional fallacy lay behind the Jesuit triumph. In a pamphlet,
in August 1649, he exposed the fallacy:

> The grosse ignorance of the ancient constitution of our English
> Parliaments; and fanatick dream of A Supreme Parliamentary
> and absolute Legislative Authority in THE HOUSE OF COM-
> MONS ALONE . . . being, in my apprehension, (next to Gods
> wrath for our sins) the principal groundwork of all the late
> unparallel'd, insolent (that I say not monstrous and brutish)
> proceedings, against the late and present King, the House of
> Peers and secluded majority of the late Commons House . . .

His pamphlet was an historical collection of Parliamentary
records in order to educate Englishman in their constitution.
He substantiated Filmer's thesis with records which showed
that, between 673 and 1216, Parliaments were made up exclusively of King and Lords, without Commons, and that it
was 'at least till 49 Henry 3, if not in some ages after' that
knights and burgesses were summoned regularly to Parliament
by writ. He noted that Lilburne and his colleagues were at last
beginning to protest against the theory of Commons' sovereignty
when they understood that, in practice, it meant the rule of
Oliver Cromwell. A critic rebuked Prynne for quoting Lilburne,
as if he were 'a grave veritable authentick Classic author', but
it was his characteristic to borrow arguments from any source,
however tainted—even Jesuit authorities—to support a particular point.[1]

Cromwell's rule provoked no crisis of conscience for Prynne,
because of his conviction that it was rooted in contempt for the
'ancient constitution'. He outlined his objections to the Engagement in December 1649. It disinherited King and Parliament
of their rightful liberties which had been enjoyed not only in
the past, but in a 'great part of King Charles his reign'. This
was an important half-recognition of the royal cause, which was
further vindicated in the words:

> It will really verify and make good all the late King's Declara-
> tions and Remonstrances against the proceedings of the late

[1] Prynne, *The First Part of an Historical Collection of the Ancient Parliaments
of England* . . . (London, 1649), pp. 3, 5, 6, 31; (Anon.), *A Serious Epistle
to Mr. William Prynne* . . . (London, 1649), p. 30.

Houses of Parliament; where Hee prophetically and frequently charged them . . . with a Trayterous RESOLUTION AND DESIGNE . . .

Prynne pointed out that the taking of the Engagement would canonize those who had been slain in the royal cause; that Kings throughout history had been the staunchest upholders of religion—his old imperial faith was evident in his eulogy on Constantine; that Cranmer offered a sad precedent for those who compromised with their consciences to save their lives. Prynne's royalism went further than has commonly been supposed. He was clearly implicated in the examination of Thomas Coke on 25 April 1651, which was reported to the Council of State on 28 May 1651. Coke claimed that at the negotiations at the Isle of Wight for a treaty with Charles I in 1648:

> . . . There was one Clerke, brother-in-law to Mr. Prin, who came thither also to offer his brother's service to the King, if it might bee accepted, which was done accordingly, as the said examinant was told by Sir Edward Waller, to whom hee applyed and who carried him to the King. The same man came afterwards to the King of Scotland upon the same errand to Breda, and had a letter from the said King to Mr. Prin to invite him into Scotland, as the said examinant was told by Secretary Long. The examinant confesseth hee saw the sayd Clerke at the Isle of Wight and allso at Breda, and that hee heard him speaking at Breda what service his brother Prin was both able and willing to doe the King if he might bee employed . . .[1]

Cromwell clearly did believe that Prynne had been 'employed'. Prynne's house was searched, not only for papers written against the Commonwealth, but in 'any way belonging to it': he was looked on as more than a scribbler, perhaps even as a spy.[2] On 30 June 1650, he had been arrested and confined to Dunster Castle; on 12 June 1651, he was transferred to Taunton Castle; on 27 June 1651, he was moved on again to Pendennis Castle. He was offered liberty if he promised not to act against the government. He refused to make any such concession, and

---

[1] Prynne, *Summary Reasons Against the New Oath and Engagement* . . . (London, 1649), pp. 3, 4, 6, 10, 11, 15; H.M.C., *Portland Report*, i, p. 594.

[2] D. M. Stuart, 'Milton and Prynne. Some New Light on the Secret History of the Commonwealth', *New Statesman and Nation*, 28 February 1931, pp. 15–16.

when he was released on 18 February 1653, there were no conditions to it.

Prynne had continually in pamphlets challenged the legality of his imprisonment. In December 1654, he had a face-to-face encounter with Bradshaw, the man responsible for his detention, at Gray's Inn. Unfortunately, we only have Prynne's version of the meeting, which presents Bradshaw in a poor light. Yet Prynne quoted complacently one exchange in which Bradshaw seemed to have outscored his victim. Bradshaw had conceded the illegality of the measures taken against Prynne, but had defended them on those grounds of self-preservation that Prynne had accepted as valid in his defence of the sovereignty of Parliament. Prynne was unimpressed: 'to which I rejoyned; that the similitude suited not with the case in question'. Ostensibly the matter rested there. Yet he was a more flexible and impressionable person than was suggested by the image of himself that he, as much as his critics, was anxious to project. He had grasped the inadequacies of his reasoning of 1643 and a few pages later in the pamphlet he recorded his mature reflections under the heading: 'A Usefull Seasonable Corollary to and from the Premises.' He was appalled at the protestations for liberty from tyrants like Bradshaw and Cromwell. To him they symbolized the frailty of human nature, to which the concept of sovereignty was a dangerous reinforcement. Sovereignty took men from their legal moorings and encouraged them to violate their oaths and obligations. He recognized that magistrates ought to be like Gods and at the same time knew that there was 'a strange corrupting transforming venom . . . in Soveraign powers and dignities'. He summarized under three headings the lessons that recent experiences had taught him. The first was to refuse to censure the actions of Charles I and other Kings, since their excesses had been surpassed by their destroyers. The second was 'not greedily or arbitrarily to seek after Empire, Sovereignty, Power, Magistracy'. The third was to seek in the Christian Magistracy a compassionate integrity above all else; earlier he had asked for the vengeful sword of Jehovah! One might call this Prynne's blueprint for the restoration of Charles II. Prynne rejected the sovereignty of the Commons, not only because it had no warrant in history but because it violated the spirit of compromise. The study of antiquity checked 'New Whimsies'—no wonder Hugh Peter wanted to consign 'all our old Records to a fiery Martyrdom in Smithfield'.

In another pamphlet in 1657 he praised the service of the lawyers in the Commons, who formed the backbone of the constitutional opposition to the early Stuarts: he defended their efforts at compromise; he noted their antipathy to Laud and Strafford; he praised their resolute determination to preserve individual liberties and their proceedings against the Court divine, Mainwaring.[1] Yet Prynne, as the 'royal' pamphleteer between 1626 and 1640, had shown little sympathy with their case and had not even mentioned Mainwaring in his pamphlets. Why was it that Prynne should be most appreciative of the orthodox constitutional case against the Crown at the very time when he was working for its restoration? The paradox can be resolved. Prynne's main efforts before the Civil War had been to preserve the sovereignty of the Crown from the encroachments of the Church, not the balance of the Constitution from the sovereignty of the Crown. In the Interregnum, his efforts, although on behalf of the Crown, were directed to the restoration, not of its sovereignty, but of the balance of the Constitution.

By the spring of 1659 Prynne saw that the balance was threatened, no longer by a revived Richard III in Cromwell, but by the 'good old cause'. Mr. Woolrych has discussed in detail the steps by which this shibboleth came to represent the political aspirations of different groups; he has shown the need to look beyond the personal ambitions of individual Army officers to the pressure from below that shaped the course of these ambitions. The Army's agitation for the recall of the Rump was in response to propaganda from Republicans and sectaries: Mr. Woolrych praises Prynne's perspicacity in grasping this immediately. Prynne was able to exploit the 'passionate nostalgia for the earlier years of the revolution and an acute sense of present betrayal' that underlay the campaign—its counterpart in ecclesiastical controversies at this time was the

---

[1] Prynne, *A New Discovery of Free-State Tyranny* . . . (London, 1655), pp. 53, 59, 66, 70, 73, 75; Prynne, *The Second Part of a Short Demurrer* . . . (London, 1656), pp. 136, 138, 141; Prynne, *Demophilos. Or The Assertor of the Peoples Liberty* . . . (London, 1657), pp. 2, 7, 25.

appeal from different groups to the principles of 'old non-conformity'—to argue from Long Parliament pronouncements in the Civil War that the 'good old cause' was to be found between 1641 and 1648, not between 1649 and 1653. His pamphleteering on behalf of the secluded members of the Long Parliament was a valuable corrective to the myth of the 'good old cause', and was praised as such at the Restoration.[1]

As early as November, 1658, the beginnings of what Prynne called 'the confederated Triumvirate of Republicans, Sectaries and Soldiers' were apparent; in that month, he offered as the only solution, 'a Free Parliament duly summoned and rightly constituted'. It was significant of Prynne's regard for the Lords that he should suggest that the calling of Parliament according to the provisions of the Triennial Act should be preceded by a conference between those in present power and '12 or more of the ablest well-affected antient Peers of the Realm (the Hereditary Great Council of the Nation, in all times of Difficulty, danger, or Interregnum) and other Gentlemen of estates, interest, quality, who had a chief hand in passing this Act'. In another pamphlet, at the end of April, 1659, Prynne compared the Army's enthusiasm for the government that it had destroyed six years earlier with the Jesuit mock-reverence for antiquity. Prynne sought to show how the early actions of Parliament in the Civil War embodied the principles of the true 'good old cause'. His defence was weakened in some respects by his own later repudiation of sovereignty for the Commons and his recognition of the substance behind the fears expressed in the King's Declarations. By concentrating on the Parliamentary professions in favour of balance rather than those in favour of sovereignty, Prynne achieved some consistency, yet it was not easy for him to read back for himself and the Commons into the earlier period a sympathy for the Crown and the Lords that was more recent in origin.

On 8 May 1659, Prynne succeeded in entering the House, where he voiced doubts as to whether the Long Parliament had not come to an end with the death of the King. His presence was challenged by Haselrig and Vane, and after dining at Lincoln's Inn he found himself debarred from re-entering. An

[1] A. H. Woolrych, 'The Good Old Cause and the Fall of the Protectorate', *Cambridge Historical Journal*, xiii, 2 (1957), pp. 133–61.

Army officer accused Prynne of apostasy from the 'good old cause'. He answered that the 'true good cause for which they were first raised, was only to defend the King's person, Kingdom, Parliament, all its Members, Priviledges'. When the officer admitted that they now pursued another cause, Prynne replied 'that they were real Back sliders therein'.[1] But another pamphleteer claimed that Prynne was the backslider; he exploited Prynne's lack of concern for the ancient constitution, or for the importance of balance, in his writings in the early part of the Civil War. Prynne had come to believe that the constitution was immemorial, although the Commons were not. The critic used the new scepticism about the origins of the Commons to discredit constitutionalism itself:

> . . . This Form of Government (By Kings, Lords and Commons) being laid in the thick of Popery by King Henry I (for the Popes Interest as well as his own, Mr. Prin cannot deny) which merits the denomination of his Good Old Cause . . .

The pamphleteer argued that the 'good old cause' was the concept of liberty that existed long before King, Lords and Commons.[2]

Another pamphleteer noted in November 1659, that Prynne's efforts were directed towards the restoration of the nobility, but argued that 'without the King, such a Government will be but an Utopian Idea, formed by Mr. Prinn's operative fantasie'. The writer was clever to grasp that Prynne loved the Lords more than the Crown, but he failed to realize that Prynne had no time for Utopias in his sober mood of compromise. And Prynne knew that the restoration of monarchy took precedence over other ideas: in the latter part of 1659 and the early part of 1660 he became obsessed with the defence of kingship.[3] In June, 1659, a Royalist noted that Prynne 'hath

---

[1] Prynne, *The Republicans and Other Spurious Good Old Cause* . . . (London, 1659), p. 1; Prynne, *A Probable Expedient for Present and Future Publique Settlement* . . . (London, 1658), pp. 1, 4; Prynne, *The True Good Old Cause Rightly Stated, and the False Uncased* . . . (London, 1659), pp. 1, 8; Prynne, *Loyalty Banished* . . . (London, 1659), pp. 3, 5, 7, 8; *The Nicholas Papers* . . ., iv, pp. 134–5.

[2] (Anon.), *Mr. Pryns Good Old Cause Stated and Stunted* . . . (London, 1659), pp. 5, 8, 10.

[3] (Anon.), *A Reply to Mr. William Prinne* . . . (London, 1659), p. 3; Prynne, *A Brief Necessary Vindication of the Old and New Secluded Members* . . . (London,

made full satisfaction to the presse for former erratas', and a month later another Royalist commented that 'Mr. Prynn is still imployeinge the presse, and is loath that the nation should owne the unsavoury Rumpe'. In June, Prynne had made another effort to secure admission to the House. A hostile news-journal, while sneering at Prynne's belief that 'there is no Government like unto King, Lords, and Commons', could not withhold admiration for his courage:

> ... neither will I trace the steps of this invincible Lawyer any longer; for certainly, mighty is the mans Courage, and great his Prowess, who dares attempt to notifie such things in the Face of Authority ...

In Clarendon's extant correspondence, the importance of Prynne's pamphleteering on behalf of the secluded members is repeatedly stressed in December 1659. In January 1660, Lord Mordaunt reported to Charles II that he had sent arguments from Prynne on behalf of a free Parliament out to the counties. On 21 February 1660, Prynne marched in at the head of the re-admitted members of the Long Parliament, with sword at his side. This was a dramatic moment, representing the climax to an arduous campaign of lobbying and pamphleteering on behalf of the secluded members, but it was tinged with that element of farce which rarely escaped Prynne's actions for long. Pepys recorded that 'his long sword got between Sir William Waller's short legs and threw him down, which caused laughter'.[1]

Prynne became more actively Royalist on re-entering Parliament. On 24 February, Major-General Massey praised Prynne's work to Clarendon, and in the following month Prynne performed one of his most vital services for the Royalist cause. On 12 March, Ludlow noted how essential it was to the safety of

---

[1] *The Nicholas Papers* . . ., iv, pp. 157, 171; Baillie, *Letters and Journals* . . ., iii, p. 427; *The Faithfull Scout*, Numb. 6, 27 May–3 June 1659; *Cal. Clar. S.P.*, iv, pp. 483, 484, 499, 502, 432; *The Letter-Book of John Viscount Mordaunt 1658–60*, ed. M. Coate (Camden Society, Third Series, lxix), p. 177; (B.M.) Add. MSS. 19526, f. 46; Pepys, *Diary* . . ., ed. H. B. Wheatley (London, 1904), i, p. 60.

---

1659), pp. 47–60; Prynne, *A Plea for Sir George Booth* . . . (London, 1660), *passim*; Prynne, *The Signal Loyalty and Devotion of Gods True Saints* . . . (London, 1660), preface.

the secluded members to ensure that the control of the militia passed out of the hands of their opponents. Monk, acting on pressure from some of the officers, wrote a letter instructing Parliament to execute no Act to that effect. Ludlow reported that it caused agitation among some of the secluded members when it was read to the House:

> But others understood him well enough; and, therefore, notwithstanding his letter Mr. Prynn went to the printer, and procured the Act to be immediately made publick, knowing it to be the desire of Monk that it should be so.

Ludlow was an enemy to Prynne, yet the extant correspondence on the Royalist side confirms his belief that Prynne was an intimate to their designs. Possibly Morice acted as an intermediary between Prynne and Monk; certainly he had to exercise a restraining influence on Prynne's impetuosity in the interests of Royalist tactics.[1] Nevertheless, Professor Davies has shown that Prynne's services to the Restoration must not be underrated. On 8 March 1660, in the debate on a bill to call a Parliament on 25 April, Prynne again emphasized that Parliament had been dissolved on the death of Charles I and that, even if not, the Commons could do nothing without the King and the Lords. Professor Davies regards the proviso added to the bill as a triumph for Prynne.[2] His insistence—noted by Pepys—that writs for the new Parliament should be issued in the name of Charles II before the decision to recall him had formally been taken, together with his plea for the necessity of the King and the Lords in a balanced constitution, were the

---

[1] *Cal. Clar. S.P.* iv., pp. 573, 616; Ludlow, *Memoirs . . .*, ed. C. Firth (Oxford, 1894), ii, pp. 248–9; John Price, *The Mystery and Method of His Majesties Happy Restoration* (London, 1680), p. 131: 'Mr. Prin spake it openly, That if the King must come in it was safest for them that he should come in by their Votes who had made the War against his Father. Whereupon Prin was sent for, and admonished to be quiet: and it was the business of Mr. Morice to keep this expiring Session of Parliament steddy, and clear from intermedling with the change of the Government.'

[2] Godfrey Davies, *The Restoration of Charles II, 1658–60* (Oxford, 1955), pp. 304–5. The proviso read: 'That the single Actings of this House, enforced by the pressing necessities of the present times, are not intended to infringe, much less take away, that Ancient Nature Right which the House of Peers . . . had and have to be a part of the Parliament of England.'

translations of Filmer's thesis into political action.[1] Royalist appreciation is evident in the correspondence in Clarendon's papers: 'Mr. Prinnes speech in plain terms for the restitution of King, Lords, and Commons'; 'Prynne's speech for the dissolution of this and the calling of a lawful Parliament'; 'Assertion of the Kings rights by Mr. Prinne'; 'Pryn, Sir Edward Partridge and blind Steevens have been bold champions, speaking plain English'; 'Mr. Prinn is now the great champion for Monarchy'; 'Pryn has exceedingly asserted the King's right.' Charles II wrote effusively to Prynne:

> I have not only received particular information of your great services and indefatigable endeavours to awaken my people of England from that deplorable condition they have run themselves into, but have had the perusall of some of your labours myself; And I must believe that the efficacy of your pen has been so prevalent in the discovery of such dark designes that it has and will facilitate my restoration . . .[2]

The words were prophetic: Prynne's pen did facilitate his restoration to the throne. Yet the very boldness of Prynne's refusal to consider any rule other than the Stuarts as legitimate had created problems in his attitude to Church matters in the Interregnum.

The difference between theory and practice was the major cause of the Presbyterian decline after the Restoration: the Presbyterians clung to their ideal of a National Church when, in practice, they had to conform more and more to a sectarian position.[3] This inconsistency was a source of anxiety to Presbyterians as early as the Interregnum, and it expressed itself in the controversy over suspension. The Presbyterian dilemma sprang from the passivity, rather than the hostility, of Cromwellian rule in the Church. Dr. Bosher had described Cromwell's policy in ecclesiastical matters as 'Erastianism with a

---

[1] Pepys, *Diary* . . ., i, p. 72. Pocock, op. cit., p. 159, noted this action as practical evidence of Prynne's concern for the importance of the writ as the expression of royal power. Cf. Holdsworth, op. cit., i, p. 366, for a similar appreciation.

[2] *Cal. Clar. S.P.*, iv, pp. 591–2, 593, 603, 606, 615; *The Letter-Book of John Viscount Mordaunt* . . ., p. 126.

[3] C. E. Whiting, *Studies in English Puritanism from the Restoration to the Revolution, 1660–88* (London, 1931), p. 46.

twist': the authority of the State was exercised, not for the regulation of religious doctrine and practice, but for the prevention of such regulation. Dr. Bosher has shown how this position stimulated controversy between those Anglicans who were grateful for the opportunity to work at parish-level at the risk of loss of personal identity, and those Anglicans who remained unassimilable at the risk of persecution. The unheroic found their apologist in Robert Sanderson. Sanderson argued that disobedience to the *de facto* ruler was a failure in duty: 'And surely it argueth a most perverse mind, to be willing to live under the protection of his Government, whom you are unwilling to obey'. No study comparable to that by Dr. Bosher exists for the Presbyterian position in the Interregnum. Yet the Presbyterians' dilemma was equally acute. When John Wilson wrote to Richard Baxter on 28 February 1659, explaining his doubts about giving support to Booth's rising, his scruples only partly came from fears of a Cavalier Restoration. He was haunted by the precepts of Bucer, Calvin and Pareus against active resistance to 'even a meer possessory power'.[1] Prynne had no patience with such hesitations: he derided the time-serving acquiescence of men such as Durie, Peter and John Goodwin. Yet the effects of the contrary policy on Presbyterian principles were not what Prynne had desired.

In 1645, Samuel Hudson had quoted Prynne on the need for a 'National Church'; in 1668, in a debate in the Commons, Colonel Birch observed that 'the Church will be stronger the fewer it has'.[2] The one expressed the 'church-ideal'; the other, the 'sect-ideal'. In the middle-forties, Prynne had been a vigorous opponent of the clerical claims to a power to suspend scandalous persons from the Sacrament of the Lord's Supper. To Prynne they represented the triumph of the 'sect-ideal', which he noted with alarm in Presbyterian, no less than Independent, thought. Between 1647 and 1649, Prynne was more concerned with the threat of the Army than the threat of the Kirk to the balanced constitution. Yet the issue had not been

---

[1] R. E. Bosher, *The Making of the Restoration Settlement* (Westminster, 1951), pp. 13–18; Robert Sanderson, *Several Cases of Conscience Discussed* ... (London, 1660), p. 170; (D.W.L.) Baxter MSS. 59.1, f. 261.

[2] Samuel Hudson, *The Essence and Unitie of the Church* ... (London, 1645), p. 22; Anchitel Grey, *Debates of the House of Commons* (London, 1769), p. 127.

resolved: it was only natural that Prynne should resume his attack upon the supporters of suspension in the Interregnum. But there was an important difference in the Interregnum. In the forties, Prynne could legitimately invoke the 'church-ideal' against the clerical claim to suspension, because the civil power was then the ally of the Presbyterians: hence Prynne's wrath at those ministers who wished to encroach upon, rather than to work with, the civil power. In the Interregnum the support of the civil power was withdrawn; more than that, Prynne sought actively to dissuade subjects from working with the civil power. This position strengthened the hands of those who wanted suspension. Prynne himself, in 1645, had distinguished Erastus's opposition to excommunication from his own belief that it was 'but a temporary Ordinance, taken up by Christians out of meer necessity, for want of Christian Magistrates to restrain and punish scandalous sinners'.[1] In the Interregnum, for want of such coercive power by the Christian Magistrate, a breakdown of order was threatened: the Presbyterian ministers' claim for more stringent disciplinary powers, to fill the vacuum left by the withdrawal of the support of the civil magistrate, carried a plausibility that such a claim had lacked in the forties. And indeed it was not only Scottish theocrats, but moderate English Presbyterians such as Baxter, Manton and Vines, who regarded a rigorous scrutiny of candidates for the Sacrament of the Lord's Supper as an essential disciplinary measure in the chaos of ecclesiastical life in the Interregnum. Yet there were other English Presbyterians, besides Prynne, who viewed with alarm the growing sectarian character of Presbyterianism in the Interregnum. The controversy over suspension helped to shape the future character of Presbyterianism.

Richard Baxter stated the case for suspension. He was hostile to separatism, yet he could not accept mixed communion either:

[1] Prynne, *A Vindication of Four Serious Questions* . . . (London, 1645), dedicatory epistle. Lewis du Moulin, *The Power of the Christian Magistrate in Sacred Things* . . . (London, 1650), pp. 84–5, rejected the idea that the ministers had the right to extra powers because a new Richard III was on the throne. But even Prynne recognized that the withdrawal of support by the *de facto* ruler had created for Presbyterians an intolerable problem of discipline: Prynne, *A Legal Resolution of two Important Queries* . . . (London, 1656), p. 16.

it was identical with the renunciation of discipline, which was the attempt to distinguish the clean from the unclean. Although Baxter was sincere in his efforts at unity in the Interregnum, he could never throw his weight unreservedly, either behind the Presbyterians who wanted union with the separatist Independents on the basis of an unmixed communion, or behind the Presbyterians who wanted union with the moderate Anglicans on the basis of a mixed communion. The Worcestershire Association reflected this confusion. In 1654, he had felt confident that he stood for the middle way in the controversy; by 1658, however, parties had hardened and Baxter was forced to recognize that he had failed to find 'a middle way'.[1] He believed in the communicant's need to profess a saving faith and in the ineffectiveness of the Sacrament as a converting instrument. He vigorously attacked Prynne. Prynne had argued that the duty of the receivers to demand the Sacrament obliged the minister to admit them to it. Baxter—with a shrewd thrust at Prynne's position in the Interregnum—argued that the duty of the Government to secure Prynne's allegiance did not oblige him to give it. Baxter claimed that 'Commanding and Obeying are as much Relates, as Demanding and Delivering are'. Baxter cleverly exploited Prynne's central dilemma, when he pointed out that Prynne had urged that coercive action should be taken against those who refused their parishioners admission to the Sacrament, and had yet maintained elsewhere that 'no Ordinance can be made without the consent of King, Lords and Commons and that the Ordinances wanting these are meer Nullities in Law'. Prynne was torn by his conflicting aspirations for Church and State: he wanted the Presbyterians to play their historic rôle of working through the State, rather than drifting

---

[1] (D.W.L.) Baxter MSS. 59.1, f. 198–f. 204. Baxter's ambivalence made him suspect to the extreme Presbyterians: Baillie, *Letters and Journals* . . ., iii, p. 307. The practical difficulties of a 'middle way' were illustrated by John Bryan's query to Baxter whether the minister should continue to withhold the Sacrament from his parishioners in Shrewsbury. He pointed out that it was a large parish, with many ignorant persons, and that ministers in country districts were generally more exacting than in the towns. Although Baxter abhorred the neglect of the Sacrament, he could not disapprove of the minister's search for 'order and decencye'; his reply illustrates the Presbyterian difficulty in establishing a discipline that did not rest on the classical organization: (D.W.L.) Baxter MSS. 59.1, f. 253.

into sectarianism; but he also wanted the Presbyterians to defy the State. Baxter criticized Prynne's desire for punitive measures against the 'rigid' ministers and regretted that 'such a spirit of violence should be found in so good a man, that hath tasted of so much persecution himself'. He recognized that Prynne was probably moved by concern at the deprivation from good men of their spiritual food, but deplored his violence:

> . . . and herein I see what one bad opinion or principall in practicals will doe, even in the best and most experienced men; and what actions must be expected from the best man, if his Judgment bee mistaken: And I see also whither the Doctrine of Common Admission leadeth . . .[1]

Baxter was unfair to identify the opposition to suspension with the particular violence that characterized Prynne's writings, most particularly in *The Sword of Christian Magistracy*. His readiness to do so pointed to the bitterness of party divisions.

Prynne's case against the supporters of suspension was that they deprived thousands of the comfort of the Sacrament through fear that it should be polluted by the presence of the unworthy. He asked 'these Sacrilegious, Novellizing Ministers' to read the 'incomparably learned, most judicious, pious Bishop Jewel'. From 1626 to 1640, Prynne had defended the Jewel traditions against the Laudian Anglicans; after 1645 Prynne defended the Jewel traditions against Presbyterian clericalists.[2] He asked how it was that men who professed themselves holy and devout could dismiss the supporters of more frequent communion as 'Erastian Hereticks'. Their requirement of visible worthiness in the communicant was the counterpart of Papist 'merited Grace'; their reluctance to admit people to the comforts of the Sacrament was the counterpart of Papist reluctance to admit people to the comforts of Scripture. Presbyterians like Rutherford, Gillespie and Collings, by their fatal surrender to sectarian objections, had caused 'the total subversion, and unexpected sudden frustration of their intended platform and elevated hopes'. Their surrender had four

---

[1] Richard Baxter, *Certain Disputations of Right to Sacraments* . . . (London, 1658), pp. 121, 426–30, 432, 433, 434.

[2] Prynne, *A Seasonable Vindication of Free-Admission* . . . (London, 1656), p. 5.

dangerous results. It had swollen the ranks of Independents and Anabaptists; the Presbyterians had accepted their principles, and were only applying them less logically and completely. It had caused many to become Quakers, Ranters or Atheists: men who reviled all ordinances. It had caused many 'to resort to old Episcopal Clergy-men, and those who will freely admit them to the Lord's Table': the prospect did not seem to darken Prynne's spirits unduly. It had caused a shocking decline in the moral standards of the people and in their respect for the ministry; the people's reluctance to pay tithes to their ministers was a reflection of how the ministers had become 'generally odious, contemptible, opprobius throughout the whole Nation; as themselves experimentally feel, complain of, and all intelligent men observe'. It was a short step from an appreciation of the reluctance of the people to pay tithes, to an exhortation of them not to: this is the step that leads Prynne from former principles.[1]

Prynne had supported tithes for several reasons. Theologically, he accepted that they were of divine warrant: he quoted Carleton and Mountague on their Scriptural validity. Historically, he accepted that they were legally binding: he quoted Selden on their ratification by English Kings, both before and after the Conquest. Socially, he accepted that 'Nine parts of Ten of the present eager Petitioners against our Ministers Tithes' were 'poore mecanical persons': his hostility to Quakerism as a social menace sprang from the Quakers' refusal to pay tithes. Philosophically, he accepted that the corrupt nature of the people justified tithing, rather than reliance on 'the meer arbitary uncoercive Benevolence of the people (who being generally profane, covetous, vicious, and enemies to all godly Ministers, will not voluntarily contribute one farthing towards them)'. He was expressing his ideal of a Presbyterianism that was neither wholly neglectful of, nor wholly dependent on, the reprobate majority, but which sought to discipline it into virtue. Politically, he accepted that tithes were a necessary mark of respect to the clergy. His case against the voluntary principle was that it struck at the exalted position of the clergy:

Therefore to force our Ministers to become Mechanickes and

[1] Ibid., pp. 24, 30, 33, 36, 43, 44, 57, 59, 60.

give themselves wholly to worldly callings or imployments incompatible with their professions, must needs be an irrationall,
unchristian project . . .

Of all the arguments which shaped Prynne's support for tithes,
his political conviction—that the clergy deserved to be honoured—seemed to offer least encouragement to the voluntary
position. Miss James has emphasized the strong radical feeling
in 1653 that ministers should be dependent on the voluntary
contributions of their flocks, and should support themselves in
addition with manual work. Prynne was horrified at the suggestion and found it necessary to deny that Christ and St. Paul had
ever laboured with their hands. Yet, paradoxically, Prynne's
acceptance of the political argument in favour of tithes led him
to an acceptance of the voluntary principle. For he had argued
that the tribute which the people paid to their ministers, in the
form of tithes, was a small return for what they received from
the ministers:

> For the things the people enjoy by Ministers are spirituall, which
> concern their souls, spirits . . . farre excelling Gold, Silver,
> Tithes, and all earthly Treasures . . .

Yet he was forced to recognize that this situation was becoming
increasingly less true in the Interregnum: the ministers were
refusing to fulfil their spiritual duties by their reluctance to
preach, or to adminster the Sacrament of the Lord's Supper.
By their captious rules for admission to the Sacrament, the
ministers were losing the respect and honour of the people:

> . . . they have by divine retaliating Justice or Providence at least
> (and I desire them to observe it) sodeinly, unexpectedly, beyond
> all humane probability, by an unparalleld sacrilege, lost most of
> their Church revenues, Tithes, Duties, either seised, or detained
> from them by their people from whom they detain this Sacra-
> ment . . .

Prynne's tone was carefully neutral: he had not necessarily
given his approval to a process that involved 'unparalleld
sacrilege'. But he had seen in this development the hand of
'divine retaliating Justice or Providence'; it was with the voice
of Thomas Beard, not of Carleton, Mountague or even Selden,
that he discussed the people's refusal to pay tithes to negligent

ministers. Opponents could claim that the observation of God's judgments on sinners was as much an oblique plea for human action as his earlier descriptions of the evils that had happened to rulers who had approved of plays. The difference now was that Prynne gave this Beard-like didacticism a legal expression. He sought for some means of redress which the parishioner could claim from the minister who refused to administer the Sacrament. He recognized that, in the situation in the Interregnum, there was no disciplinary ecclesiastical court. In these exceptional circumstances he suggested that the people should refuse to pay tithes to the minister, 'who disclaims to own them as his proper Flocke and Cure, owning only his Segregated Congregations for such, in opposition and contradistinction to his Parish.'[1]

Prynne returned to this stratagem in other pamphlets, calling it in one a 'Theme not formerly handled by any of my profession, generally unversed in such Law-points'.[2] Its significance must not be underrated. It is true that even Carleton had conceded that the minister earned his tithes by preaching, but he had carefully avoided any suggestion of a *quid pro quo* arrangement. He had argued that more generous payment was the answer to indifferent preaching, whereas opponents had claimed to be ready to pay more when they got better preachers. Prynne had borrowed from the opponents of tithes the emphasis on the minister's obligation to his people rather than his right to a privilege. Baxter grasped the significance of the change. He pointed out to Prynne the direct consequence of his counsel to withhold tithes from unsatisfactory ministers:

> . . . That the Quakers, who are now crying down Tithes should bee so much furthered in their design, as to have the people taught to detain them by Law; and they that were crying down the Ministry, should bee so far directed to eject them . . .[3]

---

[1] Prynne, *A Gospel Plea* . . . (London, 1653), pp. 9, 34, 39, 12; Prynne, *Ten Considerable Questions Concerning Tithes* . . . (London, 1659), p. 3; Prynne, *A Seasonable Vindication of Free-Admission* . . ., p. 60; Prynne, *A Legal Resolution of Two Important Quaeries* . . ., p. 17.

[2] Prynne, *A Seasonable Vindication of Free-Admission* . . ., p. 2; Prynne, *The Lords Supper Briefly Vindicated* . . . (London, 1658), p. 59; Prynne, *A New Discovery of Some Romish Emissaries* . . . (London, 1656), p. 51.

[3] Baxter, *Certain Disputations of Right to Sacraments* . . ., pp. 432, 433.

Prynne was no ally of the Quakers, but he profoundly disagreed with Baxter's analysis. To him the Quakers were Jesuits
in disguise. They attacked tithes. The ministers, who infre-
quently administered the Sacrament, undermined their status
and ultimately the right to receive tithes. Therefore, consciously
or unconsciously, the ministers were instruments of Jesuit
intrigue.

William Morice supported tithes and pointed out that opponents frequently justified their refusal on the grounds that the
minister refused the Sacrament to them. Morice explained that
he tried to persuade them to pay, with the promise that he
would try to secure their re-admission. Morice acknowledged
the logic of the grievance, but not the logic of the action;
Prynne acknowledged the logic of both. When the full weight
of the Protectorate was thrown against the opposition to tithes,
the Lord Protector's Proclamation of 25 November 1658
could be read as a condemnation of Prynne's position:

> ... the practices of some, not onely in withholding from them
> the Tithes and other Duties, which by the Laws of this Common-
> wealth are belonging to them as publique preachers; but prose-
> cuting them by indictments for not using the Common-Prayer
> Book, not administering Sacraments unto all their parishioners
> and the like omissions, and considering how apt the evil example
> and suggests of some few persons is . . .[1]

There was rich irony in a situation where Prynne could be
tacitly rebuked for principles shared with Levellers, Quakers
and Fifth Monarchy Men. Miss James has shown the importance of tithes as an index to the social programme of the
Protectorate. Both she and Mr. Hill portray Prynne as a person
to whom the preservation of tithes was an essential conservative measure for social order. Miss James quotes the observation
of Culmer that 'landlords rent and tithe rent will stand or fall
together'. Prynne showed a similar social awareness when he
called tithes in 1653 'a charge, debt, duty, as well as their
Landlords Rents'. As late as June 1659, Prynne was still defending tithes against radical criticism, and the vigour of that
defence owed much to his conservative prejudices in social

---

[1] William Morice, *The New-Inclosures Broken Down* . . . (London, 1656),
preface; *A Proclamation* . . . (London, 1658).

matters.[1] In discussing Prynne's adoption of the voluntary principle in the tithes controversy we are therefore not discussing a complete reversal of policy—as in 1641 and 1645—but a significant tactical surrender. What Mr. Hill interprets as an essential radical principle—the Covenant: the ministers should have no claim on the community for services rendered incompetently—was borrowed by Prynne as a weapon in the conservative game. He was prepared to qualify his support for tithes by a concession to the voluntary principle: perhaps the 'Covenant Theology' taught by Preston had bitten deeper into Prynne's soul than an examination of Prynne's doctrinal writings alone would suggest.

More probably it testifies to the importance that Prynne attached to the Presbyterian ministers' neglect of the Sacrament. To ensure its frequent administration, he had repudiated ecclesiastical radicalism in the forties. To achieve the same aim in the fifties, Prynne was prepared, in effect, to risk 'his Mannour of Swainscomb or Swainswick; of which he writes himself Esquire'.[2]

[1] Margaret James, 'The Political Importance of the Tithes Controversy in the English Revolution, 1640–60', *History*, xxvi (June, 1941), pp. 13, 6; Christopher Hill, *Economic Problems of the Church from Archbishop Whitgift to the Long Parliament* (Oxford, 1956), pp. 144, 155, 160, 221; Prynne, *A Gospel Plea* . . ., p. 3. John Canne recognized that the inalienability of tithes was a *sine qua non* of Presbyterian thought. Although he was writing against Prynne, he did not bring out Prynne's deviation from orthodoxy on this point: John Osborne, *An Indictment Against Tythes* . . . (London, 1659), preface (by John Canne).

[2] D.L., *Israel's Condition and Cause Pleaded* (London, 1656), p. 70: the pamphlet brilliantly links Prynne's anti-Semitism with his reactionary social views.

# THE RESTORATION AND AFTER

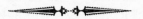

In the early part of the nineteenth century, Ephraim Hard-castle wrote a novel on the Restoration. William Prynne occupied a leading rôle in the novel as 'one of the triumvirate of fanatics, who were the chief instruments in undermining the established religion of the country'. He stood as a symbol of the puritanical zeal that the Restoration repudiated. In Hard-castle's novel, he presided over a committee which fined an inn-keeper for retaining a sign depicting the Devil. In revenge, Cavaliers seized Prynne, pinioned him to a chair, 'although he struggled and fought most manfully'—this was an authentic touch—and bore him in triumph on their shoulders. After taking him through Ludgate and Templegate, they deposited him in the inn with the offending sign and 'landed the Christian hero in the bar of the tavern, safe and sound'.[1] Although fictitious, the episode is illuminating: the author had captured Prynne's alienation from the mood of the period. Anthony Wood saw Prynne as a quaint hangover from the Jacobean period.[2] The principles that Prynne had imbibed from an earlier period led him, one of the architects of the Restoration, to oppose its chief beneficiaries. The Christian hero was safe and sound at the Restoration, but found himself in the bar of a tavern.

In the early months of the Restoration, Prynne was promi-nent as a staunch Royalist. John Aubrey recognized that Prynne was '(really) very instrumentall in his restauracion': a sentiment

---

[1] Ephraim Hardcastle, *The Twenty-Ninth of May: Rare Doings at the Restoration* (London, 1825), i, pp. 2, 6, 246-51.

[2] Anthony Wood, *The Life and Times* . . ., ed. A. Clark (Oxford, 1891), ii, pp. 110-11.

handsomely underwritten by Charles II in his appointment of Prynne as Keeper of the Records of the Tower of London. No post could have been happier for 'Marginal Prynne'; he recognized that it was 'most suitable to my Genius'. He left an unforgettable picture of the work in a letter to Sir Harbottle Grimston:

> . . . whilst you are sucking in the fresh country air, I have been almost choked with the dust of neglected records (interred in their own rubbish for sundry years) in the White Tower; their rust eating out the tops of my gloves with their touch, and their dust rendering me, twice a day, as black as a chimney sweeper . . .

Maitland had this vision in mind when he called Prynne 'an heroic figure'.[1] Prynne's antiquarian leanings could reinforce his Royalism; he urged that Judge Thorpe should suffer in the same way as had 'one Thorpe, that was a Judge in Edw. 2nd's time, who, for taking bribes and other misdemeanours, was punished'.[2] Prynne had no mercy for regicides. On 17 August 1660, an important debate took place on the Indemnity Bill. The Commons had voted in favour of a Proclamation to encourage past offenders to give themselves up; the Lords, however, exempted the King's judges from the pardon and refused mercy to those who had surrendered on the strength of the Proclamation. In the debate in the Commons, Colonel Birch argued that it was a point of military honour to abide by the Proclamation: 'if he should give Articles to a garrison, he should think himself very unworthy to break them'. Similarly, Swinfen claimed that the Proclamation was morally binding 'though there was no positive promise in it; yet it was as much security as that house could give; and that it would discourage all for the future from trusting to any such thing'. On the opposite side, Sir Harry North argued that the Commons were not bound by their vote, because it was contingent upon the agreement of the Lords. This was the point of view that Prynne supported:

[1] John Aubrey, *Brief Lives* . . ., ed. A. Clark (Oxford, 1898), ii, p. 175; R. E. M. Peach, *History of Swainswick* (Bath, 1890), p. 61; Prynne, *Brevia Parliamentaria Rediviva* (London, 1662), dedicatory epistle; H.M.C., *Verulam Report*, p. 58; W. Holdsworth, *A History of English Law* (London, 1955), v, p. 407.

[2] W. Cobbett, *Parliamentary History of England* (London, 1808), iv, p. 75.

Mr. Prynne argued, That he was for excepting all at first, and was so still; and if they were not all so, they themselves must be guilty of the King's blood, those being such horrid traitors as never yet were known: that our oaths bound us much more than our votes, which we alter daily: what would the world say of us, adds he, but call us regicides. And said, they were bound, in conscience and honour, to agree with the Lords.

Prynne was untypically ranging himself against the advocates of constancy and honour. That he should do so, out of deference to the Lords and desire for revenge upon the regicides, testifies to the dominance that these two impulses had upon his behaviour after the Restoration. Ludlow thought that Prynne was 'singularly remarkable' in his vindictiveness, even compared to those who appeared to be 'the most basely subservient to these exorbitances of the Court'. In May 1660, he expressed relief at not being included in Prynne's intended list of victims. He noted Prynne's 'more than ordinary zeal for disbanding the army' as another facet of his loyalism. The last regiment was disbanded on Tower Hill in February 1661. Five companies were drawn in a circle around Prynne and Colonel Birch, who made short speeches. With a touch of showmanship—reminiscent of his long sword that tripped up poor little Waller when the Long Parliament was recalled— Prynne ordered the four companies that he had disbanded 'to lay down their Armes at his feet in testimony of their disbanding, and then to take them up again as entertained by his Majesty in service'. Yet when Prynne came to report to the House upon the disbanding of the militia, Ludlow noted that his enthusiasm had given way to a more cynical outlook, and that he urged the House:

. . . that they would be mindful not to do those things that might bring them together again. Upon which the adverse party fell upon him with that fury, that if the House had not risen immediately in great disorder, he had been obliged to explain himself at the bar.[1]

What developments after the Restoration had soured Prynne's judgment and estranged his affections? Highly regarded by the King, Member of Parliament for Bath, Keeper of the Records of the Tower of London, once more Recorder for

[1] Ibid., iv, pp. 100–2; Ludlow, *Memoirs* . . ., ii, pp. 277, 272, 326; *The Kingdomes Intelligencer*, Numb. 8, 18–25 February 1661.

Bath, Prynne seemed certain, in 1661, to die in the odour of sanctity. But Hardcastle was right: the Cavaliers soon regarded him with suspicion. Sir Thomas Bridges wrote to Secretary Nicholas, on 20 March 1661, to suggest that, at all costs, Prynne must be prevented from resuming his seat in the Cavalier Parliament; a fascinating record that has survived of a dispute over local elections in Bath, in which Prynne became involved, reflected the strength of this antagonism.[1] At the funeral of Archbishop Juxon in 1663, Robert South seized the opportunity to deliver a biting harangue against Prynne, 'that furious and scurrilous *municipium*'. This hostility is partly to be explained by the Cavalier unwillingness to forgive the past. As late as 18 March 1668, in a debate in the Commons, Prynne urged that a certain person should be exempted from the royal pardon. Even the Presbyterian, Sir Thomas Littleton, could not resist a favourite Anglican sneer that 'if Prynne had not his, he might have been in the same predicament'. Characteristic of the Anglican attitude to him in 1661 was a pamphlet that discussed analogies between ancient and modern fanatics. Although the author described him as 'the only person in this unhappy parallel, who has given large testimonies of his reconcilement to loyalty and reason', Prynne's name was retained among the 'Saints and Martyrs' from whom the author begged deliverance.[2] The hostility also sprang from the incongruity of his ethical desires in the society of that time. Yet mainly the hostility derives from Prynne's obvious dissatisfaction with the Restoration: the Cavaliers saw in him a dangerous disruptive force.

The popular explanation of Prynne's discontent is facile: that he was against all governments. Contemporaries would have liked to dismiss him as nineteenth-century critics dismissed the Anarchist, Bakunin: 'What a man! The first day of the revolution he is a perfect treasure; but on the next day he ought to be shot.'[3] Yet Prynne's joy at the Restoration had been

[1] *Cal. S.P. Dom. Charles II 1660–61*, p. 564; Bath, Victoria Art Gallery and Municipal Library: Council Minutes, Numb. 2, f. 68. See Appendix B.

[2] Wood, op. cit., i, p. 481; Anchitel Grey, *Debates of the House of Commons from the Year 1667 to the Year 1694* (London, 1769), p. 118; *Harleian Miscellany* . . ., vii, pp. 406–7.

[3] Edmund Wilson, *To The Finland Station* (Fontana Library, 1960), p. 271.

unfeigned: the return to government by King, Lords and Commons, even by bishops, was consistent with the ideals that he had propagated in the Interregnum. They were, however, only the outline of his desires and the details were equally important. Prynne had wanted the restoration of monarchy, but he wanted it to fulfil its historic imperial rôle. He had wanted the restoration of the Lords, but he wanted it to be recognized as the senior partner in the balanced constitution. He had wanted the restoration of the Commons, but he wanted it to abandon the claim to sovereignty through privilege. He had even wanted the restoration of episcopacy, but he wanted the bishops to recognize their *iure divino* equality with presbyters, to claim only an *iure humano* superiority by the grace of the King, and to work for a moral reformation by frequent preaching and administration of the Sacrament of the Lord's Supper. When Prynne saw these details dishonoured by the Restoration, he felt betrayed; he could not feel satisfied with a settlement that represented the shadow, not the substance, of his ideals. This did not necessarily stamp him as a Bakunin. The complaint of a nineteenth-century antiquarian, Jerom Murch, against Prynne was not on his failure to conceal his disillusionment, but on his success. Murch pointed to the discrepancy between the Restoration settlement and Prynne's hopes:

> ... after the Restoration, among all his multitude of books there is not one on the vices of the Court. Why was the author of *Histrio-mastix* silent on this subject through so many years ... when Episcopacy revived in full vigour, when the two thousand conscientious clergymen were ejected from their livings: when those Test and Corporation Acts were passed, which for a century and a half inflicted so much cruel injustice?[1]

Prynne was less passive than Murch had supposed: this was one reason for Cavalier hostility. But it is true that he was less active than Murch had hoped: the reason for this is to be found in events of July 1661.

Prynne had reverted to the moderate Anglican ideals of his

[1] Jerom Murch, *William Prynne* (Bath, 1878), pp. 31–2. Prynne's ethical concern was still marked after the Restoration. He reprinted *Healthes Sicknesse* and attacked duels, taverns, and the drinking of healths: Prynne, *The Second Part of the Signal Loyalty* ... (London, 1660), dedicatory epistle; Prynne, *Letters and Proposals* ... (London, 1660), *passim*.

pamphleteering before the Civil War. He could rightly reprint in 1660 a pamphlet of 1636, as representative of the principles that he respected at the Restoration. His disingenuousness lay in the pretence that he had always respected these principles; he was anxious to conceal the extent to which he had been deflected from them by the 'root and branch' ministers in 1641. He was sincere in reaffirming his earlier professions of faith in moderate episcopacy, but his reasons for doing so had changed. Prynne in 1660 was not the same person as Prynne in 1636. In 1636 his moderate Anglicanism had been very much dependent upon a belief in the worth of the 'good bishops'; in 1660 he was disillusioned on that point and he reaffirmed his faith for other reasons: irritation with the sectarian tendencies in Presbyterianism; sympathy with Anglican sufferings in the Interregnum; the abandonment of his campaign against Laud. If Prynne had merely republished the earlier work as it stood, the difference in motive might not have emerged so clearly, but to the earlier work he added slight marginal notes in 1660. They reveal his disillusionment with 'good bishops'; he could revert to the earlier position, but not to the beliefs that had once made it tenable.[1]

Prynne was ready to welcome Anglicanism in 1660, but not Laudianism. Along with Morice and Humfrey, he had been an uncompromising opponent of the Presbyterian ministers' rigidity in the suspension controversy in the Interregnum. But in their generosity to moderate Anglicanism, they had not intended to condone the triumph of militant Anglicanism; after the Act of Uniformity, Humfrey tore up his letters of orders as a priest and became a nonconformist, and Morice and Prynne opposed the persecuting Anglicanism of Gunning.[2] It was one thing to approve of Archbishop Usher; another, to approve of Archbishop Sheldon. Looking back on events in December 1663, Prynne believed that something like a revival of Laudianism had taken place under Sheldon's guidance. Against the bishops' claim to impose oaths, he cited Foxe and the Petition of Right. He noted that the effect of their action

---

[1] Prynne, *The Unbishoping of Timothy and Titus* . . . (London, 1636; repr. 1660), pp. 1, 4, 8, 79, 123, for marginal sneers at Downame, White, Hall and even Usher.

[2] Whiting, op. cit., p. 53; H.M.C. *5th Report*, p. 160.

was the 'derogation of the Kings Royall Crowne and Dignity'. Essential to his philosophy was the belief that the Cavalier Parliament had revived 'only the Bishops Antient and Legall Jurisdiction Authorized by or Lawes, but noo former illegal usurpations upon the Kings prerogatives and subjects Libertyes': his language was deliberately that of his anti-Laudian writings of the thirties. Prynne stressed the importance of writs going out in the King's name: this was a legal manifestation of the authority of the 'Imperiall Crowne', which bishops must honour. He attacked the punishment of men who refused to acknowledge the Book of Common Prayer; he exposed the illogicality of the claim that it was implicit in the ancient punishment of men for refusing to attend divine service. He was aware of the threat to liberty in the branding of nonconformist meetings as illegal conventicles, and he seized upon verbal ambiguities in the recent Act against Quakers to demonstrate the confusions that existed in men's minds about the nature of conventicles. Thus he showed a greater concern at repression than Murch had credited him with. Nor was this wisdom retrospective only. Throughout 1660 and 1661, his speeches and pamphlets had drawn attention to the dangers of a revival of the Laudian spirit.[1]

As early as May 1660, Pepys suggested that a Bill for the restitution of bishops to the Lords had been speeded up 'to despite Mr. Prin, who is every day so bitter against them in his discourse in the House'. Prynne's mistrust of clericalism—Anglican or Presbyterian—was evident in his motion, on 9 July, that resolutions by a synod must be confirmed by King and Parliament. On 16 July, he expressed his desire for a *iure humano* episcopacy:

> Mr. Prynne said, He could not be for bishops, unless they would derive their power from the King, and not vaunt themselves to be *iure divino*.

On 30 July, in a debate on the confirmation of ministers in their livings, Sir Heneage Finch moved against those who refused the Oath of Allegiance and those who had been presented against the wishes of their legitimate patron. He was supported by Sir John Masham, one of the persecuting squirearchy, who

[1] (B.M.) Add. MSS. 37682, f. 71–f. 76.

was to have several important verbal duels with Prynne. Although Prynne was in favour of the ministers' taking their oaths, he argued 'for their presentation to be good throughout, though not by the right patrons, in times of trouble'. His determination to defeat the new Anglicanism was clear in the debate on the King's Declaration of October 1660.

The King's Declaration was a classic plea for moderation in ecclesiastical matters. Baxter called the terms 'such as any sober honest ministers might submit to', but he feared that it was but a temporary, insincere expedient. The uncertain legal status of a Proclamation justified such fears. The Presbyterians called the Anglican bluff by a brilliant tactical move: they proposed the enactment of the Declaration into law. The Anglicans were then left with the dilemma of either impugning the King's good faith or of assenting to a settlement alien to their hopes. The debate in the Commons on this issue was crucial. It is important to see what part Prynne played in the controversy. On 6 November, Sir Anthony Irby moved that an Act should be passed confirming the Declaration. Sir John Masham argued that this should not be considered. At this point, Prynne intervened to move that the matter should be referred to a committee. Prynne's behaviour during the debates confirms this impression of alertness. On 28 November, before the crucial debate on the King's Declaration, there was one on the Lord's Day Bill. The aim of the Bill was to prevent the profanation of the Sabbath. Sir John Masham said that he was not sure which day was the Lord's Day, that ought to be respected more than the rest, which brought Prynne to his feet, 'alledging several reasons, and vouching divers authorities for the antiquity of the custom'. The two opponents clashed again in the debate on the King's Declaration:

> Sir John Masham said, They had before them an excellent Declaration metamorphosed into a very ugly bill; that the King's intention was for a settlement of Religion amongst us, which surely this bill did thwart; and moved to throw it out. Mr. Prynne answered the last speaker and said, The Declaration was to settle peace in the Kingdom only . . . what a wonder would it be, after they had given the King thanks, to throw out the bill . . .[1]

[1] Pepys, op. cit., ii, p. 43; Cobbett, op. cit., iv, pp. 80, 82, 95, 141, 142, 152, 154; Richard Baxter, *Autobiography* . . . (Everyman's Library), pp. 155-6.

The defeat of the Bill was the proof of Anglican treachery to Prynne. Thomas Smith wrote to Joseph Williamson to complain that Prynne was writing once more against bishops, and expressed sorrow that he 'should thus blemish his late services'. Ludlow attributed Prynne's disenchantment to that debate: released from fear of the Army, 'the Court began to take off the mask and all the hopes of the Presbyterians vanished'.[1] In a pamphlet in 1662, Prynne asked for an indulgence to tender consciences to permit them not to bow at the name of Jesus nor to kneel in the act of receiving the Sacrament of the Lord's Supper. He stressed that such had been the intention of the King's Declaration; to thwart his Declaration was to deny the Royal Supremacy. Prynne had published a defence of the Royal Supremacy in the same month as the debate on the King's Declaration. Bishop Barlow criticized Prynne, not for the material in the pamphlet, but for its timing. He argued that a vindication of Kingship had a relevance in the forties that it lacked in the sixties. He recognized that Prynne, in the Interregnum, had 'vindicated the King's Supremacy in our worst times and that with the hazzard of his head'. To continue to do so after the Restoration was, however, to reduce a meaningful conflict to shadow-boxing. For what Anglican bishops denied the Supremacy? Barlow's question was not rhetorical to Prynne in 1660. He saw in the actions of Anglicans, not least in their rejection of the King's Declaration, the same anti-imperial spirit that had vitiated the Laudian episcopate.[2]

Thus, in another pamphlet of 1660, Prynne reiterated the imperial sentiments of his writings before 1641: he referred proudly to the fact that, in Lucius, England had her first Christian Emperor; he quoted Jewel, Foxe and Usher for their imperial theories: he quoted Bilson for the approval of prayers for even persecuting Emperors; he showed, from the writings of White, Abbott, Davenant and others, how the imperial tradition dominated Anglican thought. In Laudian times, the *iure divino* claim for episcopacy had been the challenge to imperialism: in the sermons of Sancroft, Allestree and Clark,

---

[1] *Cal. S.P. Dom. Charles II 1660–61*, p. 308; Ludlow, op. cit., ii, p. 326.

[2] Prynne, *A Moderate, Seasonable Apology* . . . (London, 1662), dedicatory epistle; Prynne, *A Seasonable Vindication* . . . (London, 1660); Coll. Reg. Oxon. MSS. 340, f. 13–f. 95.

Prynne saw the reincarnation of Laudianism.[1] Even in the Interregnum, he had not allowed his sympathy with moderate Anglicanism to blind him to the existence of more extreme views. In 1648 he had accused Cromwell of negotiating with 'Dr. Hammond, Dr. Sheldon and other disperate Malignants': he had shrewdly seized upon the two key figures of militant Anglicanism in the Interregnum. In 1661, he wrote a pamphlet that stressed the discrepancy between the ideals of a persecuting Anglicanism and the aims of the King's Declaration. He asked for the abolition of the superfluous ceremonies prescribed by the Prayer Book which had caused schism in the Church from 1549 to the present day: a remark that suggested a closer affinity with earlier critics of the Church than was always the case. He also asked for the free admission of all godly ministers who had been ordained by Presbyters during the Interregnum and who had not submitted to reordination by bishops. He pointed out that he had never been a separatist, nor had doubted the value of 'Common Prayer Sacramental Admin-strations' inasmuch as they were not prescribed as essentials but recognized simply as 'convenient, for the well-being and unity of a National Church'. The essential tasks of minister and bishop were the constant preaching of the Gospel and administration of the Sacraments: he noted that they were now as negligent in these tasks as his 'rigid' Presbyterian opponents had been in the Interregnum. Prynne noted the *iure divino* claims in the sermons of Sancroft and Allestree. He condemned them alongside Hall and Downame, who had been two of the key figures that he had revered before 1641. Although Prynne reverted after the Restoration to moderate Anglicanism, he no longer held illusions about his former idols. Downame and Hall might have disagreed with Laud on doctrine, but this did not mean that they were immune from Laudian vices. Laud was dead, and Sheldon had not been his friend; this did not mean that a significant revival of some of Laud's policies was not taking place under Sheldon's direction. Prynne's attack upon High Church Anglicanism in the sixties had a maturity that it

---

[1] Prynne, *The Second Part of the Signal Loyalty and Devotion* . . ., pp. 2, 3, 71, 8, 9; William Sancroft, *A Sermon* . . . (London, 1661), pp. 2, 9–11; Richard Allestree, *A Sermon* . . . (London, 1661), p. 13; Samuel Clark, *Ministers Dues and Peoples Duty* . . . (London, 1661), pp. 3, 8, 24, 25, 26.

had lacked in the thirties: no longer did it seek to isolate the evils in one compact, easily identifiable group that were Jesuits in disguise. By 1641, he had recognized that the evils had contaminated the supposedly good bishops; by the Interregnum, he had also identified them in Presbyterian ministers. Prynne had formerly respected the Jacobean bishops, but in 1661 he was comparing the 1603 Canons with the 'Canons and Constitutions of our Popish Archbishops'. He could still look back with nostalgia to the Tudor Age as the time when bishops honoured the imperial traditions, without believing the corollary to it of the thirties: that only Laud, and a small clique about him, were undermining the traditions. The Church of England had been debased, not by false persons, but by a false principle. Its downfall had been caused by the continual pressing of trivialities on tender consciences; this was as evident in 'the Bishops obstinacy, potency and pride' at the Hampton Court Conference as in the activities in the Laudians. History may repeat itself: he pointed out that the recent actions of bishops against the principles of the King's Declaration may 'end in their second subversion and future suppression'.[1]

Prynne was not alone in these warnings. A writer of 1661 argued that Charles I's fatal mistake had been to renounce the Royal Supremacy in favour of *iure divino* bishops, and urged Charles II 'if he will have Bishops again, he may so provide, that they swallow not up His Royall Prerogative of Supremacy'. Zachary Crofton called his opponents 'the *Laudenses* of our Age' and advised them to read the arguments by which Prynne unbishoped Timothy and Titus. He noted also that Prynne, 'that profound Lawyer', had denounced as illegal the bishops' claims for the necessity of reordination; it manifested the same proud spirit that had produced the *iure divino* claim for episcopacy. Robert Baillie viewed with alarm the militancy of Anglicans like Hammond, Thorndyke and Heylyn, and suggested that either Prynne or Reynolds should compose a reply 'for the crushing of that high, proud, malicious and now very active and dangerous party'. Nor was Prynne's opposition confined to pamphleteering. On 30 May 1661, Andrew Newport wrote

[1] Prynne, *The Machavilian Cromwellist* . . . (London, 1648), p. 10; Prynne, *A Short Sober Pacific Examination* . . . (London, 1661), dedicatory epistle, pp. 1–4, 63–5.

that Prynne had refused to receive Communion kneeling in St. Margaret's Church, and that Prynne and Morice had refused to support a vote of thanks to Gunning for an aggressive High Church sermon: 'in waggery', some desired that those two opposers should be the persons to carry the vote of thanks to the preacher, but this was over-ruled. According to another version Prynne had received the Sacrament seated. The minister who gave the bread refused it to Prynne: the minister who gave the wine allowed it to Prynne in the mistaken belief that he had received the bread: 'so that Prynne received but the wine'.[1] His opposition to the new Laudianism culminated in his appearance before the House two months later, to answer for his denunciation of the Corporations Act.

His later ecclesiastical activities are not so well documented as those of the first few months of the Restoration. Nevertheless, it is possible to see a decline in anti-episcopal zeal. His next major contribution in Church matters after the denunciation of the Corporations Act was to strengthen, rather than to weaken, punitive Anglicanism. On 22 September 1666, he introduced a bill to debar Papist and sectarian from residing within ten miles of the City, but it was laid aside. On 15 October 1666, he proposed that a shilling fine should be paid to the poor by Members of Parliament who absented themselves from prayers in the House. On 7 November 1666, he introduced a Bill against pluralism, which stipulated that offenders would be fined £200; the money would be used for the building of churches in London. On 11 March 1668, an important debate took place on the King's Speech. Sir Thomas Littleton seized the opportunity to advocate Calvinism. He pointed out that, during the rule of James I and of Archbishop Abbott, it had been the dominant theology in England. This was a favourite hobby-horse of Prynne; would it lure him back to controversy? In the heated debate that followed on toleration, Prynne's contribution was monumentally uncontroversial:

> Mr. Prynne said that he was for taking away the causes of separation, and the vacancy of many churches was a main cause, for some churches not having any ministers, the people took a liberty

[1] (Anon.), *The Humble Petition* (London, 1661), p. 9; Zachary Crofton, *A Serious Review of Presbyters Reordination by Bishops* (London, 1661); Baillie, *Letters and Journals* . . ., iii, p. 400; H.M.C. *5th Report*, pp. 160, 171.

to go where they had a fancy, and therefore moved that painful ministers might be put into such churches . . .[1]

'*Etiam es tu Prynne*': thus a critic had exploded in 1658, and had gone on to regret the spectacle of 'a petty-Martyr, an old Professor and a learned one, even a Mr. Prynne to fall from his own steadfastness'.[2] The sneer had more point in 1668. Although throughout his career he had put practical morality before party dogma—he was that rarity: a fanatical empiricist —it had never before triumphed to the extent of obliterating totally questions of theology and discipline. Again, on 18 March 1668, a debate on a poll tax produced a fresh controversy in which Prynne took no decisive part. Suggestions about taxing clergy always incited fierce discussion, and John Milward noted that the motion 'took very much in the House, especially with the nonconformists'. Milward said that Sir Thomas Littleton offended many people by falling 'foul and unmannerly upon the bishops'. Many others spoke in a similar vein against the bishops 'as having raised great sums of money and were wanting in charitable works'. Although Milward reported Prynne's speech on the motion, nothing of this anti-episcopal bitterness emerges. Prynne was wholly taken up with peripheral matters. He suggested that persons who fought duels should have their estates confiscated: he had in mind the recent duel between the Duke of Buckingham and the Earl of Shrewsbury. This was a cause near to his heart, but, from the point of view of the Presbyterian partisan, to be concerned about duelling in a debate about bishops was to be irrelevant to the point of unfriendliness. To Littleton it naturally seemed a side-issue, which prompted his angry taunt that Prynne had needed the royal pardon no less than had the duellists.[3]

Prynne's inability to identify himself with the Presbyterians sprang directly from his experiences in the Civil War and the

[1] John Milward, *Diary* . . ., ed. Caroline Robbins (Cambridge, 1938), pp. 4, 23, 117, 219–22. Typical of Prynne's co-operation with the Established Church in 1666 to ensure moral discipline are his appointments to committees against profanity and swearing, Popish recusancy, and neglect of the Sacrament by Members of Parliament: *Commons Journals*, viii, pp. 630, 638, 663.

[2] S.S. *Holy Things for Holy Men* . . . (London, 1658), dedicatory epistle.

[3] Milward, op. cit., pp. 230–1; Grey, op. cit., p. 118; *Commons Journals*, viii, p. 633.

Interregnum. The suspension controversy had shattered for him the equation of the advancement of Presbyterian discipline with a strict moral code. His writings immediately after the Restoration were a reproach to intolerant Anglicanism, not a plea for Presbyterianism. It is true that, as late as 1663, he had misgivings about the restored bishops, and that the paucity of evidence directly bearing on Prynne's attitude between 1663 and 1666 forbids the assumption that silence meant assent. Between 1666 and 1668 the situation is different. The period is adequately covered in Milward's diary. Now Milward was markedly hostile to the Presbyterian 'gang', as he termed them. Had Prynne been significantly hostile to bishops, Milward would have made it clear. He had no love for the persecutor of Laud. Yet it is clear from Milward's observations that Prynne had no marked bias against Anglicanism in this period. The tremendous drop in fervour about theological niceties, in preference for working at a lower level of practical morality, was characteristic of the older Prynne. It was also characteristic of the Latitudinarian school that was emerging within Anglicanism at this time.

John Tillotson may provide the link between these two developments. On 26 November 1663, he had been elected preacher at Lincoln's Inn. What would be his influence there upon Prynne? Tillotson was strongly sympathetic to nonconformist scruples. Birch wrote of his indifference as to whether Anglicanism or Presbyterianism were established at the Restoration, and described his congregation as 'half-converts' to episcopacy: 'such as rather bore with it, than loved it, because he preach'd and persuaded them to it, as a tolerable, but not as a laudable and excellent Constitution'. Hickes and Burnet agreed that Tillotson tried to avoid bowing at the name of Jesus, and that he gave communion in Lincoln's Inn Chapel to persons who remained seated. He was markedly anti-Papist and wrote pamphlets on the disciplinary value of frequent administration of the Sacrament of the Lord's Supper. It was said of Tillotson that he converted the pulpit at Lincoln's Inn from the mouthpiece of Puritanism, that it had been under Preston, to 'a powerful agency for weaning men from Puritan ideas'. Intolerant of Papists and sectarians, respectful of the traditions of old nonconformity, Tillotson was a preacher such that Prynne could revere. The proof of Prynne's high regard is to be found in his will, where he bequeathed to 'Doctor Tillotson one of each of my three tomes of my *Exact Chronologicall Vindication*'.[1] There is reason to think that Tillotson was a formative influence in reconciling Prynne to the moderate Anglican principles of his earliest writings. In defence of moderate Anglicanism, Prynne could appeal to Jewel against Laud in the thirties; to Tillotson against Sheldon in the sixties.

Another clue to Prynne's abandonment of the militant campaign against bishops may be found in the reaction to his opposition to the Corporations Bill in July 1661. Yet the significance of his position then must be appreciated against the background of his constitutional, as well as his ecclesiastical, rethinking after the Restoration.

In the Interregnum his constitutional rethinking had been marked by respect for the Lords. At times it had seemed less important than his attachment to the Crown: this was only because the restoration of King, Lords and Commons was then the issue, not the relationship between them. After the Restoration, the primacy of his concern for the Lords becomes more apparent. In 1659 he had complained of the failure of men to grasp the significance of his researches, and he threatened to withdraw into antiquarianism in retaliation. The threat was half-fulfilled. After the Restoration, Prynne wrote most of his important antiquarian works. They have an intrinsic value that lies outside the consideration of this study, but they generally served some controversial theme as well: the sovereign authority of Kings, perhaps, or the judicial supremacy of the Lords. In the same pamphlet in which he threatened to retire from controversy, he ridiculed Coke's belief that the *Modus Tenendi Parliamenti* had been written in the time of Edward the Confessor. He showed, therefore, how misleading it was to think that the Commons existed before the Conquest. 1265 was

---

[1] Thomas Birch, *Remarks Upon the Life of the Most Reverend Dr. John Tillotson* (London, 1754), pp. 7–8; L. G. Locke, *Tillotson: A Study in Seventeenth Century Literature* (Copenhagen, 1954), p. 23; John Tillotson, *A Persuasive to Frequent Communion* . . . (London, 1683), pp. 3, 4, 16; *Documents Relating to Proceedings Against William Prynne* . . ., p. 98. Prynne was referring to his *An Exact Chronologicall History* . . . (London, 1666–70), which appeared in three volumes; there is a unique copy of a fourth volume—probably the Introduction—in Lincoln's Inn Library.

the earliest date that the evidence of writs would argue. From this, Prynne drew a very practical conclusion: excesses by the Commons in the future would justify the existence of Parliaments consisting 'only of a House of Lords and Great men of the Realme without any Knights, Citizens, Burgesses, Barons of Forts, or House of Commons'. Prynne was harshly critical of Coke's credulity, but it was the language of Round on Freeman rather than of Bastwick on Laud. He preferred an accurate scholar like Sir Henry Spelman to Coke, who simply had not the leisure to study the original sources.[1]

When Prynne extended the pamphlet in 1662, he argued against a universal claim by freemen to the franchise. He defended his own election by the Mayor, Aldermen and Common Council to Bath as legitimate and indeed desirable. It avoided elections which were 'mercenary, arbitrary, tumultuous, disputable, as they usually prove when they are popular by all the Freemen'. More important, it avoided the enshrinement of the principle of the sovereignty of the people, to which Prynne attributed all the recent ills that had beset England. A narrow franchise was more likely to yield representatives of 'that venerable Gravity, Order, Silence, Attention, in such Robes, Vestments, Postures, as became the Majesty, Wisdom, Seriosity' of the Commons, instead of the 'noyse, clamour, talking, skipping up and down from place to place, with drawing to smoke Tobacco'. His perception of the distance between his aspirations for the Commons and the commonplace realities strengthened his regard for the Lords.[2]

When Prynne extended the pamphlet still further in 1664, he also extended its scope, so that it became one of the most searching criticisms of Coke's history and the use that he made of it. Prynne waxed eloquent against the concept of the Committee of Twenty-five in the *Modus Tenendi Parliamenti*, which strengthened his belief that it was 'contrived, compiled by some Leveller or creature of Richard, Duke of York . . . from 7, till 33, H.6'; he noted that it was a pleasing idea for Levellers of his own time, and no doubt for their time too. He was not

---

[1] Prynne, *The First Part of a Brief Register* . . . (London, 1659), dedicatory epistle, pp. 422, 440, 446. Prynne, *Aurum Reginae* . . . (London, 1668), dedicatory epistle.

[2] Prynne, *Brevia Parliamentaria Rediviva* (London, 1662), pp. 323, 324, 381.

only using historical disciplines to challenge the dating of authorities; he was drawing attention to the historical context in which the authority was set. Both destroyed the magic of Coke's precedents. And Prynne saw that the claims to privilege, through shaky precedents, had ruined the Commons. He argued that every Parliament was a new court, petitioned for by the Speaker, and granted by the King with reservations. These reservations limited the extent of the privileges which members of the Commons could claim, and privileges began and ended with their convening and dissolution. Both in the pamphlet, and in debates in the Commons, Prynne rejected the idea that privileges extended for twenty days before and after sessions. He argued that it was from the grace and indulgence of the King that 'all the other Members Parliamentary priviledges only flow'. It followed, therefore, that the King, not the Commons, was the proper interpreter of privilege:

> . . . *tunc eius est interpretare, cuius est concedere:* Therefore the King being the sole Granter of these Priviledges, must be the only proper interpreter and judge of them . . .

The Commons based their false claim to sovereignty on the right to judge privilege—not only the Rump, but even the opposition to Charles I. He dealt with specific claims of privilege, made by the Commons in Charles I's reign, under the spell of Coke. He showed that there was no warrant for Coke to serve in Parliament while he was Sheriff of Buckingham; equally, there were no grounds for Sir Simon Steward's evasion of Star Chamber by a plea of privileged status. In the first case, Coke's practice ran contrary to custom and to the wording of the writ of summons; in the second case, the House voted itself judge of any offence done by its members, 'upon Sir Edward Cookes assertion of it', against the evidence of Parliamentary records. Prynne described Ferrers' case as:

> . . . The very first and onely President I can yet discover, wherein the House of Commons assayed by their own sole authority (like a distinct court, as Sir Edward Cooke styles it, without any ground, Record or Antient Record to warrant it) to demand and enlarge any of their Members out of prison or out of execution . . .

Prynne extolled to students at Lincoln's Inn, after the Restoration, the glories of the Petition of Right, yet in striking at Coke he was also striking at the legal case of the opposition in Charles I's reign. He seemed aware of this danger, for after drawing attention to other misrepresentations by Coke, he claimed the right to withhold further criticism:

> . . . As for some other Commons late votes, presidents in the Parliaments of King James, King Charles the I and 2nd concerning priviledges of the Members and their menial servants, I conceive it fitter silently to pretermit, than by any recital of them to expose them to the examination or censure of posterity . . .[1]

This self-denying ordinance was too austere for Prynne: in various political crises he used his historical researches to support the case of the Lords against the Commons—the impeachment of Lord Mordaunt, the impeachment of Clarendon, the dispute between Skinner and the East India Company.[2] On the other hand, he was no court lackey: he opposed the grant of an Excise on beer and ale to the Crown, and on Clarendon's impeachment he said flatly that the King 'cannot do it; it is against his Coronation Oath and Magna Charta'.[3]

Prynne resented very keenly the impeachment of Clarendon. He admired Clarendon: both wished to see 'Gravity' and 'Seriosity' in the Commons; both looked to the period before the Civil War for the standards of uprightness and decency that the Restoration flouted. The regard was never mutual. Prynne dedicated one of his works to Clarendon in 1664 as 'a visible Expression of my real Gratitude, for the many Noble Favors, Civilities I have received upon all Occasions from your Lordship'. He referred to the encouragement he had received from Clarendon to write a history of the struggle between Papal ambitions and Parliamentary resolutions. This work had not

---

[1] Prynne, *The Fourth Part of a Brief Register* . . . (London, 1664), pp. 604–6, 625, 640, 696, 840, 850. Prynne was so sceptical of the Commons' claims to privilege that, on 17 December 1660, he even opposed a proposal that Members' letters should have free postage: Cobbett, op. cit., iv, p. 163; (B.M.) Stowe MSS. 302, f. 48v–f. 49; Prynne, *Brief Animadversions On* . . . *The Fourth Part of the Institutes* . . . (London, 1669), dedicatory epistle, deplored the uncritical reliance on Coke, 'yea by many Members of Parliament in their Debates, Conferences, without the least examination of their originals'.

[2] Cobbett, op. cit., iv, pp. 356–8; Grey, op. cit., pp. 151–3; Milward, op. cit., pp. 288–9, 336.

[3] Cobbett, op. cit., iv, pp. 148–51; Milward, op. cit., p. 337.

been completed by 1664, and in its place he published an attack on the sovereignty of the Commons, based on a study of past records. From such a study, he hoped for two beneficial results: briefer and more efficient sessions; less straining of privilege. He hoped that Clarendon would be able 'to reduce the Grand Abuses of Excommunication, imposing new illegal Oathes, Articles, without authority of King and Parliament, and other extravagant usurpations upon the Kings Prerogative and Subjects Liberties, lately revived, exercised by some indiscreet Ecclesiastical Courts, Officers'.[1] This was one of Prynne's strongest criticisms of the Clarendon Code, and he dissociated Clarendon from the criticisms. He looked on Clarendon as a natural ally against the twin menace of unbridled clericalism and an over-reaching Commons. The proceedings of the Commons against Clarendon were, to Prynne, the logical climax to this conflict. He fought them item-by-item in their attempt to impeach Clarendon; he clashed with Vaughan on the question of the Lords' superior judicatory powers. He gave his customary squadron of precedents to support the Lords' refusal to commit Clarendon. On 13 December 1667, a Bill was introduced in the Commons to banish Clarendon. It is interesting that Prynne abandoned the academic approach when he saw that it no longer carried weight. For the first time, his remarks carried a personal tone, as he defended the honour of Clarendon with impassioned eloquence. In part, anti-Papal hysteria underlay his eloquence; he remembered that Gondomar 'got Sir Walter Rawleigh's head off', and he cried: 'I pray God this be not a foreigner's plot.' Yet probably his respect for the *gravitas* and integrity of Clarendon counted most with Prynne; it was the ancient Roman virtues that he evoked in his concluding image:

> Cicero was banished without cause, and to his honour, not to that of the Romans who banished him[2]

Prynne's opposition to the Corporations Bill must be assessed against the background of his perfervid championship of the

[1] Prynne, *The Fourth Part of a Brief Register* . . ., dedicatory epistle. The work to which Prynne referred was: *An Exact Chronological History* . . . (London, 1666–70).

[2] Grey, op. cit., pp. 52, 55, 65; Milward, op. cit., pp. 148, 151, 337; (B.M.) Egerton MSS. 2543, f. 196.

Lords, as well as his mistrust of Laudianism. On 27 June 1661, Prynne attempted to add a proviso to the Corporations Bill, which was defeated. On 5 July, Prynne was a teller for the Noes upon the third reading of the Bill, which was carried. Thwarted from expression of opposition to the Bill in Parliament, Prynne turned to pamphleteering. On 12 July, a Committee was appointed by the Commons to investigate the authorship of a paper entitled, *Summary Reasons, Humbly Tendered to the Most Honourable House of Peeres*, which was described as seditious. On 15 July, the Committee reported that Prynne had confessed to the authorship of the pamphlet, and the House proceeded to a consideration of his offence.[1]

When Shaftesbury wrote his warning against the new Laudianism in 1675, he seized on the Corporations Act as the first step in the 'State Master-Piece'.[2] What was striking about Prynne's attack on it was his failure to see it in the context of punitive Anglicanism. He saw it primarily as an affront to the Lords by the Commons: the pamphlet was addressed to the Lords. He deplored the retributive measures against members of corporations, and emphasized the powers given to the Commissioners by the Act:

> It gives the numerous Commissioners named in the Bill, or any five of them (who are all Commoners) an absolute arbitary power over the greatest Peers of the Realm . . . to remove and displace them at their pleasure and discretion, without any legal tryal, contrary to Magna Charta, their Peerage and privilege of Parliament . . .

He deplored, above all, the fact that beyond the Commissioners there was no higher appeal to Justices of the Peace, King's Courts or the House of Lords.[3]

The Commons ruled that the pamphlet was 'illegal, false,

---

[1] *Commons Journals*, viii, pp. 282, 291, 299, 302; H.M.C. *12th Report*, ix, p. 50; *Mercurius Publicus*, Numb. 28, 11–18 July 1661: 'Mr. Prynne was unable to conceal it any longer, for 'twas proved that he had sent that Paper to the Printing-house, that he had corrected the Proof-Sheet, and also the Revise with his own hand, and as soon as the House rose (on Friday last) he flew to the Printing-House and commanded them to distribute the Form, for they would be searched.'

[2] Shaftesbury, *A Letter From A Person of Quality* (London, 1675), pp. 1–2.

[3] Prynne, *Summary Reasons Humbly Tendered to the Most Honourable House of Peeres* . . . (London, 1661), single sheet.

scandalous and seditious'. The Speaker gave Prynne 'a grave and severe reprehension'. He told Prynne that he deserved to suffer again his former punishments, but that his services to the Restoration would earn him a pardon if he showed true penitence. The sequel was as dramatic as it was unexpected. Prynne made a full recantation. According to one news-journal, 'he spake with a great sense of his own offence and the Houses goodness, not offering to justifie the least line of his Paper, which his conscience told him he could not'.[1] The House was satisfied with his statement. The Cavalier pleasure at Prynne's degradation was evident in many comments, but comes out most stridently in Lord Herbert's account to his wife:

> Mr. Prinne, contrary to what everybody expected from his temper, very humbly and penitently begg'd pardon of the House, owned the judgment they had given to be just and that he did concurre with us in it, and shoulde receave the pardon hee askt from us as a meere mercy and not at all bee pretended to by any merit of his. This we esteeme I assure you a conquest worthy to be bragged of, and therefore I cannot forbeare letting you know it . . .[2]

Was Lord Herbert right to regard Prynne's submission as a 'conquest?' To see the episode in perspective, certain qualifications must be made to that judgment. First, it cannot be assumed that Prynne's campaign against the new Laudianism was halted by the submission. Prynne continued to attack manifestations of the persecuting spirit after 1661 in speeches and in pamphlets, although there was less reason to do so near the close of his life, when the counsels of men such as Tillotson were winning acceptance in Anglican circles. Moreover, the issue was not primarily ecclesiastical, but constitutional. Prynne had offended the Commons, less by attacking the bishops, than by appealing to the Lords. The episode should properly be seen in the perspective of the quarrels between the Commons and the Lords after the Restoration. Second, from this constitutional viewpoint, the episode seems even less momentous. Prynne's regard for the Lords was to lead him into further trouble with the Commons after 1661.[3] He was to be censured

---

[1] *Commons Journals*, viii, p. 302; *Mercurius Publicus*, Numb. 28, 11–18 July 1661; *Cal. S.P. Ven. Charles II*, xxxii, p. 26.

[2] H.M.C., *12th Report*, ix, pp. 50–1.     [3] Milward, op. cit., p. 293.

again by the Commons for breach of privilege after 1661.[1] It does not appear even that his prestige was damaged as an immediate consequence of the episode. For, on 29 July—a fortnight after his disgrace—he was ordered, with Sir John Birkenhead, Finch and Waller, to manage a Conference with the Lords. The subject of the Conference was a Bill from the Commons for restraining unlicensed and disorderly printing. The Lords were pleading, on grounds of privilege, to be exempt from scrutiny. In the report that Finch drew up, it was agreed that there ought to be no sanctuary for seditious literature; that every possible outlet for books, which tended to the overthrow of religion, ought to be sealed; that 'All Houses as well of Commons as Peers, are equally the Castles and Proprieties of the Owners'. The Commons went out of the way to praise the services of the persons who managed the Conference. There are three curiosities about this matter: he was one of a select group, who had been appointed to discuss a delicate point that touched on the question of seditious pamphlets, for which he had himself only recently been disgraced; he was appointed in order to defeat an attempt by the Lords to claim special privileges; he was working with Birkenhead, who had been on the original Committee that had investigated Prynne's pamphlet, and of whom it was said that he and Prynne 'were allwayes antagonists in the Parliament House'. One would have expected Prynne's *parti pris* on the first two points to disqualify him. Yet the evidence suggests that the House's confidence in him had not been shaken seriously by his disgrace.[2]

Lord Herbert was wrong to think of Prynne's submission as a

[1] On 13 May 1664, Prynne was once more in trouble: 'Mr. Prynne, having taken the liberty to alter the draught of a Bill relating to Public-Houses, having urged in his excuse, "That he did not do it out of any ill intent, but to rectify some matters mistaken in it, and to make the Bill agree with the sense of the house", the house ordered him to withdraw, and after debate, being again called in, the Speaker acquainted him, "That the house was very sensible of this great mistake in so ancient and knowing a member as he was, to break so material and essential an order of the house, as to alter, amend or interline a bill after commitment: but the house had considered of his Answer and Submission, and were content at this time, in respect thereof, to remit the offence" ': Cobbett, op. cit., iv, p. 293; *Commons Journals*, viii, p. 563.

[2] *Commons Journals*, viii, pp. 315–16; Aubrey, op. cit., ii, p. 173; Milward, op. cit., p. xlvii.

'conquest'; his later ecclesiastical and constitutional activities
give the lie to such a judgment. But, from Prynne's point of
view, his recantation was a 'conquest': in this sense, Lord
Herbert was right. It was this sense that Lord Herbert tried to
convey to his wife in describing Prynne's humiliation:

> . . . Mr. Prinne . . . did that to us hee never could be brought to
> do before to any persons breathing by any meanes imaginable.
> Hee owned himself very submissively to have committed an
> offence and askt our pardon with teares in his eyes . . .[1]

There was pathos in this scene which the Cavalier, in his
jubilation, could not quite obscure. The recantation was a
defeat for Prynne in nothing, except on a personal level; but
on that level, the defeat was real and painful. It shattered the
image of himself that had sustained him in exile and suffering:
of a proud rectitude that would not yield to force. 'The more I
am beat down, the more am I lift up', was Prynne's answer to
the executioner in 1637. He had been offered martyrdom in
1661 and refused it: the Speaker had 'reproacht him with all
hee had already suffered, his imprisonments, his being in the
pillory and stigmatized', and threatened him with their renewal unless he repented.[2] Why did he allow the Lord Herberts
of the world their triumph?

In February 1661, Prynne described himself as 'quite tyred
out'.[3] Was loss of stamina the key to his acquiescence? Prynne
was not always honest in self-analysis; once before, he had pro-
nounced a *nunc dimittis* upon his controversial career:

> . . . Mr. Prynne having thus fully, faithfully, sincerely discharged
> his own dutie, and satisfied his own conscience, is resolved to lie
> down quietly, to take his rest, and hope for the salvation of his
> God . . .[4]

The date was 1659 and the pronouncement was premature: the
next few months were among the most active periods of pamphleteering in his life. As a critic had noted years earlier, writing
was as necessary to him as 'meat and drink, a thing without
which, he cannot live'.[5] After 1661, his outpouring of writings

[1] H.M.C., *12th Report*, ix, pp. 50–1.
[2] Idem; Prynne, *A New Discovery* . . . (London, 1641), no pagination.
[3] Prynne, *Brevia Parliamentaria Rediviva* . . ., p. 315.
[4] Prynne, *Ten Considerable Questions Concerning Tithes* . . ., p. 98.
[5] (Anon.), *A Word to Mr. Wil Prynn* . . . (London, 1649), pp. 5–6.

was as formidable as ever, but his preference for antiquarian to polemical works might be interpreted as signs of a mellowing spirit. In a debate on the alimony for wives living apart from their husbands, a Bill was introduced in November 1660, to forbid wives, separated from their husbands, from having alimony or their debts paid. The Parliamentary diarist noted that:

> Mr. Knightley moved to lay the bill aside; but Mr. Prynne humourously saying, That if they did, those that had ill wives would call for it again within a day or two, the question was put.

A few days later, Prynne supported a Bill against women who refused to cohabit with their husbands, 'though he never had a good or bad wife in his life'.[1] These flashes of self-mocking humour make a welcome contrast to the hysterical, sex-ridden repressions of *Histriomastix*. Too much, however, should not be made of Prynne's mellowing after the Restoration; to regicides, Papists, Jews and Quakers he was as unrelentingly vindictive as in his earlier years.

A news-journal noted that, in his recantation, Prynne 'spake largely, setting forth what service he had done for the King formerly, how kind and civil the King had been to him etc.': these words provide the most probable explanation of his acquiescence.[2] Imperialism had been the dominant theme in his writings: he believed that the King had his powers from God, and he attacked the clergy when he thought that they were opposing these powers. As an imperial theorist, Prynne put the rights of the magistrate very high. He had defended, not defied, the Crown in his opposition to Laud. Similarly, he had not defied the magistrate in his opposition to Cromwell; the legitimate magistrate was Charles II in exile. For a period in the Civil War, his faith in the Crown as the instrument of imperialism had waned; it was then that he had flirted with deposition theories in his abhorrence of *The Popish Royall Favourite*. Charles I's martyrdom at the hands of Papists ended this atypical phase in his thought. Stephen Charlton noted, in May 1661, that 'Parliament have voted it to be a *Premunire* to say that His Majesty is popishly affected':[3] it was impossible

---

[1] Cobbett, op. cit., iv, pp. 143, 145.
[2] *Mercurius Publicus*, Numb. 28, 11–18 July 1661.
[3] H.M.C., *5th Report*, p. 170.

for Prynne to regard Charles II in that light then. He could see in Charles II only the legitimate ruler, whose claims to obedience were formidable. Prynne was no Byzantinist, as he showed by his opposition to Excise and to the impeachment of Clarendon, but he was an imperialist. To the claims upon his loyalty which such principles exacted were added the less obvious, but equally important, claims of affection. Prynne was not merely grateful to Charles II for giving him the post of Keeper of the Records; the feelings of a dependant to a patron are usually ambivalent. Oddly enough, Prynne saw the roles in reverse: he saw himself as the patron who had supported Charles II at his lowest point and had assured his return to the throne. He valued his appointment, but as the tangible symbol of this relationship: he felt towards Charles II something of that deep indebtedness that a patron feels towards his successful protégé.[1] Episcopacy, in 1661, could not inspire him with the same terror that the activities of Laud had done in the thirties; Presbyterianism, in 1661, could not inspire him with the hopes that were destroyed in the suspension controversies of the forties and fifties. In September 1661, Prynne wrote of his work among the records that 'it was so filthy and unpleasant that Mr. Riley and others would not soil their hands, nor indanger their healthes to assist me in it'.[2] Prynne had domesticated his craving for martyrdom.

One pamphleteer expressed sorrow that Prynne had not died in 1637 and saved his reputation.[3] Had he died then, he would have been accepted as a martyr to Laud's cruelty, whereas the most popular explanation of his subsequent actions was that he was the perverse opponent of all governments. This was less than fair to Prynne. For most of his life he attempted to reconcile respect for the Crown and the Church of England with pamphleteering on behalf of moral reform and against Popery. Only in the period between 1641 and 1644 did the two appear to him as antitheses; they were never more closely synthesized

---

[1] In his will, Prynne referred to the post with pride: 'freely given mee by his Majesty King Charles the Second of his own meere motion, for my services and sufferings for him under the late usurpers, and strenuous endeavours, by printing and otherwise, to restore His Majestie to the actuall possession of his royal government and kingdome without opposicion or effusion of blood': Peach, op. cit., p. 61.

[2] H.M.C., *Verulam Report*, p. 58.

[3] 'S.S.', *Holy Things for Holy Men* . . . (London, 1658), p. 22.

than in the last years of his life. Yet it is worth remembering that only three years separated Prynne's death in 1669 from the Declaration of Indulgence: the bishops opposed the Crown's attempted generosity to Papists. There can be little doubt but that Prynne also would have opposed the Crown. Resistance of a monarch who betrayed his imperial mission was justified: he had argued this point in 1643, and it was on similar grounds that James II was to be resisted when he, too, attempted to exercise his suspending power. The bishops' action then would have drawn Prynne still closer to the Church of England. In 1691, informed of the bishops' stand against Popery, Prynne's Ghost was credited with the statement that 'if what you say is really true, it would oblige me to abate a great deal of my old Severity and prejudices against them'.[1] Before his death, Prynne had come to recognize, in Anglicanism, the safest defence of imperial ideals; by his death, he was spared disillusionment about the sympathies of the Crown.

In his lifetime Prynne wrote more than two hundred pamphlets. Among the motives that prevent a man from writing, there is a point at which diffidence and vanity fuse: a man's genuine mistrust in his powers links with a secret dread of being worsted in competition. The Puritan was protected from such scruples. In an analysis of the Putney debates, Dr. Woodhouse remarks that:

> ... the Puritan temper is in general active rather than contemplative. Though its official creed repudiates works as a means of salvation, it emphasises them as a sign, and the Puritan has an overwhelming sense of one's responsibility to use every effort for advancing the Kingdom of God ...

Baxter said: 'It is action that God is most served and honoured by.'[2] Prynne's massive outpourings represented his action, his effort to advance the Kingdom of God; he never questioned their value. He had that lack of self-criticism which could only come from an acute and agonizing search for assurance of Grace. One opponent thought that his confidence was the key to his success.[3]

If Prynne did not question the value of his writings, there

[1] (Anon.), *Novus Reformator Vapulans* .. . (London, 1691), p. 12.
[2] Woodhouse, op. cit., p. [44.]
[3] (Anon.), *The Fallacies of Mr. William Prynne* ... (Oxford, 1644), p. 2.

were many critics, both then and later, who did. This study of Prynne has been offered in the conviction that his controversial writings have value for the light that they throw upon problems of his time. One contemporary went further and claimed for Prynne's works an intrinsic value comparable to that of Jewel or Foxe.[1] In terms of literary achievement, the comparison grossly flatters Prynne, who wrote at times with power but rarely with charm or real distinction. In terms of literary conception, however, the comparison has a validity that Prynne's detractors failed to recognize. Like Foxe and Jewel, Prynne wrote his works on a grand scale, with the aim of bringing Man closer to God. The means that he adopted were bigoted and often destructive of the end in view; yet there is much to admire about a dedication to fearless writing on such a scale throughout his life, and an integrity that rejected even his admired Foxe and Jewel in pursuit of that vision.

At Prynne's first trial in 1634, his counsel compared him to a learned astronomer who looked so fixedly upon the stars that he forgot himself and fell into a ditch.[2] His critics, who dismissed him so flippantly, saw only the figure in the ditch; perhaps from their safe position on the ground, however, they were deprived of his view of the stars. Prynne was less polished, less balanced, less subtle than almost all his critics, but perhaps he had intimations which they would never share.

[1] (Anon.), *A New and True Eccho from Old and Bold Authors* . . . (London, 1648), p. 3.
[2] (Bodl. Lib.) Douce MSS. 173, f. 2.

# APPENDIX A
# PROBLEMS OF SOURCE
# MATERIAL FOR BIOGRAPHY

THIS study was not intended as a biography of Prynne;
the manuscript material, which has proved helpful for
an understanding of his controversial writings, is described in
the Bibliography. Yet the paucity of material, relating to
Prynne's personal life, was a handicap in attempting to analyse
his pamphleteering, even if to a far less extent than if a straightforward biography had been planned. Descriptions of Prynne's
birth and background are to be found in the works of Warner,
Peach, Mrs. Kirby, Murch and Bruce: the sum total of our
knowledge remains disappointingly meagre.[1] For instance, we
know that Prynne was the grandson, on his mother's side, of
William Sherston, the first Mayor of Bath under Elizabeth's
charter; we do not know what part the Sherston connection
played in Prynne's career. We can still see engraved in the
parish church at Upper Swainswick, almost directly opposite
the house in which Prynne was born, the name of Prynne's
father; we do not know how far Prynne's convictions were
shaped by those of his father. We know that Prynne went to
Oriel College, Oxford and to Lincoln's Inn; we do not know how
formative were the relationships which he entered into there.[2]

[1] Richard Warner, *The History of Bath* (Bath, 1801), pp. 204–7; R. E. M.
Peach, *History of Swainswick* (Bath, 1890), pp. 58–61; E. W. Kirby, *William
Prynne . . .*, passim; Jerom Murch, *Biographical Sketches of Bath Celebrities,
Ancient and Modern* (Bath, 1893), pp. 54–9; *Documents Relating to Proceedings
Against William Prynne* (Camden Society, 1877, ed. S. R. Gardiner), passim.

[2] Cf. M. A. Judson, *The Crisis of the Constitution . . .*, p. 314, upon the need
for a detailed study of University connections at this time.

The answer to at least some of these questions and to other crucial points relating to his later career might be provided by the discovery of Prynne's personal papers. It seems implausible that all Prynne's energies in writing should have been directed to public controversy, and yet no private correspondence of magnitude has been discovered at Bath or at Lincoln's Inn. The correspondence between two antiquarians—who wished to obtain access to Prynne's papers in the interests of scholarship—throws some light upon the fate of these papers. On 15 February, 1670, Sir William Dugdale wrote to Anthony Wood, complaining that:

> ... As to the search of Mr. Prynne's Study, though the Executors did promise that we should have leave so to do, for the finding out of those papers wch were by him taken from that most reverend and renowned Prelate Arch-B Laud (whose memory ought to be highly honoured by all good men) yet, when it came to the poynt they had no minde to trust us, but tooke upon them the labour themselves; and delivered to us all those papers wch they could finde (as they sayd) and having so done, one of them (to have the credit thereof) went with the Dean of Pauls and myselfe to the Arch-Bpp of Canterbury and presented them to his Hands ... now I feare it is too late, his study and lodgings being all cleared; and what is not sold, conveyed as I thinke into survey, unto his brother, who is one of the Executors ...

On 19 February, Anthony Wood resigned himself to their loss, in his reply to Dugdale:

> ... that forasmuch as tis too late to obtaine those pap's from Mr. Prin's study, I must rest contented ...[1]

An unpublished manuscript in the Bodleian Library throws confirmatory light upon Dugdale's account. From this letter from Jonas Moore to Archbishop Sheldon in October, 1669, immediately after Prynne's death, it is clear that Sheldon was anxious to obtain Prynne's papers relating to Laud's trial, and that George Clarke, Prynne's brother-in-law, who had been his contact with Charles II once in the Interregnum,[2] was the middle man in the transaction:

---

[1] *The Life, Diary and Correspondence of Sir William Dugdale*, ed. W. Hamper (London, 1827), pp. 390–1.

[2] H.M.C. *13th Report*, i, p. 594.

... I dined with Matr. Clark yesterday, he is as willing as you or any one can be to desire, to have the least skripp that any way shall relate to that business of my late Ld. Arbp., and has given strict direction—all M. Prinns papers may by putt into cheste and trunks that any whom my lorde hereto shall appoint may peruse them first of all. Matr. Brookes the bookseller has the Inventories of his bookes and I send him with this that he may take directions from you if he can shew you being an honest man. Matr. Clark lyves att the Goat near the Pump in Chauntry Lane and will goe to Lambeth whensoever it pleases yourself or Mr. Dugdale should call of him . . .[1]

What is not clear from the letter is how much of Prynne's private papers, independent of the Laud connection, found their way into Sheldon's hands. Although the present writer has been unable to find any of Prynne's papers among Sheldon's manuscripts, this remains a possible line of enquiry.

There remains one other manuscript source which has not been fully tapped by previous biographers of Prynne: the Council Minute Books at Bath. They throw a fascinating light upon Prynne's services in local politics as Recorder of Bath. On 4 April, 1664, the Council formally thanked Prynne for his 'readiness to promote the advantages of this Citty'.[2] This is an unusual side of Prynne, which has never been stressed, but the pages of the Minute Books give meaning to this tribute.[3]

---

[1] (Bodl. Lib.), Tanner MSS 44, f. 157.
[2] Bath Council Minutes, Numb. 2, f. 89.
[3] Ibid., f. 67–127.

# APPENDIX B

# PRYNNE, BATH, AND A
# RESTORATION ELECTION

THE Council Minutes at Bath contain interesting information about Prynne's part in thwarting a Cavalier intrigue
in local politics in September, 1661. Sir Thomas Bridges had
written to Sir Edward Nicholas, on 20 March, 1661, of the need
to curb Prynne's influence:

Had not a misfortune I met with last nighte comeing to the towne
p'vented mee, I had waited on you myself, but being disabled by
that accident wch keepes me yet in my beede, I have sent my
brother to acquainte you with my indeavours in the country for
promoting his Matys. interest by the election of loyall and able
gentlemen to serve in the approaching Parlement, but failing of
the success I aymed at by the opposition of the Maior of Bath
(whose character I have sent you in these few articles) I am bolde
to desire some instructions from yr experience, how to proceed
in the affaire, for the preventing of the election of Mr. Prynne
and Mr. Popham at Bathe, persons notorious enough for their
actions in the late rebellions, and that still courte the populacy
for their applause by their p'tended supporting of their libertyes;
it was in my thoughts to move the Lds. of the Counsell upon
these articles, for an order to sumon him up before them, and to
invest alderman Henry Chapman (a person whose loyalty is
unquestionable, nor blemished by the least failing under his
great sufferings) wth his authority during his absence; if this
course finds the approbation of yr judgment I shall humbly
desire the favr of you to promote it in the Counsell, by exhibiting

the articles to their Lops. in the next Counsell, for the business requires dispatche . . .[1]

On 19 September, 1661, this antagonism came to the surface. Henry Chapman decided upon a daring coup to ensure his election as Mayor: he kidnapped members of the Corporation whom he considered to be opposed to his election. When Prynne arrived that morning to keep the Quarter Sessions in the City, he found that nine of the Aldermen and Councillors had been seized and carried away to Ilchester Gaol. On the same day, Prynne penned a dignified protest to Sir Hugh Smith, a Deputy Lieutenant of Somerset:

Coming this morning to the City of Bath to keepe the general quarter-sessions on his Majties who on wednesday Sennight was acquainted therewith and wished me a good journey thither to discharge that service, Sone after my arrivall there a party of Sir William Bassetts troope, by your order, Seized nine of the Aldermen and Comon Councell of the Citty, the one a Justice of the peace, another a Constable, whereby the peace of the Citty was much disturbed, and the quarter Sessions interrupted, Soe that I was forced to adjourne the Same till this Sennight. The orders to Sir William Bassett to seize and send them away forthwith this very morning, neare fourty miles of to the Sheriff to secure them in the Marshalsey there to remain till further order without any Cause expressed, or previous examination before your Selfe, being soe near a neighbour unto them without proof or Conviction of any offences that might demerrit such severe proceedings, against all rules of law and Justice, is generally interpreted by the Citty and Countrey, to be a designe (at least in the informers, who engaged you in these unpresidented proceedings) to interrupt the quarter-Sessions of the Citty this day and the Election of the Maior and all-other officers for this Citty on Monday next for the year ensuing (wherein nine of them ought to have their voices) and to put an affront upon my selfe their newly elected and sworne Recorder: who being by my oath obliged to maintaine their just rights and liberties to my power and meeting with this high violation of them beyond expectation I thought it my duty to acquaint you therewith and to advise you as your friend and neighbour speedily to release them, that they may attend the election on monday next to prevent Complaints thereof to his Majesty and his honourable Council by the next post, and unto

[1] R. E. M. Peach, *History of Swainswick* (Bath, 1890), pp. 44–5.

their Parliament at their next meeting who how ill they are like to resent such irregular proceedings, I leave to your oune Judgment to Consider . . .[1]

Before Prynne could fulfil his threat, further developments took place. On 22 September, Chapman and his confederates met at the Sun Inn, (which stood on the site of the present Guildhall, Bath), and counted the possible votes which would be cast for him the next day. The majority still seemed uncertain, and so, on 23 September, Chapman again arrested under a warrant two more of the City Council and sent them to Keynsham where they were imprisoned in the stables of Sir Thomas Bridges. The depleted Council then elected Chapman to the office of Mayor.

Prynne was swift in his counter-attack. On 27 September, the Privy Council received two petitions: one from the 'Rump' Council excusing their action; one from Prynne, Recorder of Bath, protesting against 'this unparalleled disturbance'. In his petition, Prynne complained of the lack of respect which Chapman had shown to his arguments from history:

> . . . the King by the Statute of the 3 of Edw. the first Cap 5 commandeth upon greivous forfeiture that no great man or other by force of arms or menaces should disturbe any to make ffree elections. That this disturbance now made by Capt. Champmans procurement was the highest breach of their Charter and priviledge and of their ffreedome of Elections that was ever acted in this Realme and of dangerous consequences and very prejudiciall to his Maties service. Whereupon the said Chapman told him he was a seditious person and deserved to lose his head when he lost some thing else, and that he was a publique enemy to the King and Kingdome and the first that moved in the house of Commons to sett up excise, with many other reproachfull speeches which was a most notorious falsity . . .[2]

---

[1] Bath Council Minutes, Numb. 2, f. 68. Prynne's sense of outrage against Bassett may have been heightened by the knowledge that he had performed a service for Bassett in 1646: *Calendar of the Proceedings of the Committee for Compounding of Cases 1643–46*, p. 1181. It was Bassett whom Marvell cited as 'always drunk when he can get money': Andrew Marvell, *A Seasonable Argument to Persuade All the Grand Juries in England to Petition For a New Parliament* (Amsterdam, 1677) [reproduced in: *Parliamentary History of England*, ed. W. Cobbett, iv, Appendix iii, p. xxix.]

[2] Bath Council Minutes, Numb. 2, f. 68.

The Privy Council, on that same day, ordered the release of the prisoners, and summoned them, together with Sir Hugh Smith and Sir Thomas Bridges, to appear before them on 14 October.[1] Prynne called a further election on 30 September and the return of the prisoners ensured a victory for Alderman John Parker, who was elected in Chapman's place. The Privy Council's decision, communicated by Morice on 25 October, represented a victory for Prynne:

> . . . both parties being called in and heard his Matie was displeased that his Militia should be any way Imployed to strengthen a faction. And to disturbe the Civill Govt. It is ordered by his Maty that Alderman John Parker who is chosen Mayor of the said Cittie be (and hereby is) directed and commanded to Continew in the said office for the next year ensueing, the said Chapman being left to take his remedy by Course of Law if he so think fitt. And to the end, that all Enmity might cease, and all Animositye be so quieted that no seedes of Division might remayne amongst them. It is also further ordered that the right Honible the Duke of Ormond do forth with recall his Comission granted to Capte Henry Chapman. And that the said Chapman doe not no longer thereby. And also that his Grace doe take care that the Comande of the Trayned band of that Citty and hundred of Bathforum be conferred upon some wortheir and fitt person liveing in or neare the said Citty . . .[2]

Prynne's triumph in this local skirmish was underlined by the appointment, as Chapman's successor, of his own brother-in-law, George Clarke.[3]

[1] Peach, op. cit., pp. 43–4.
[2] Bath Council Minutes, Numb. 2, f. 71.
[3] Peach, op. cit., p. 44.

# BIBLIOGRAPHY

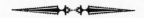

### I. UNPRINTED SOURCES

Although this study was an analysis of printed works, the following unprinted sources provided useful help.

(A) *Bath*
    Council Minutes, No. 2 (Prynne's interest in local affairs)

(B) *Bodleian Library*
    Cherry MSS 2 (Prynne and John Williams)
    Douce MSS 173 (Prynne's trial)
    Laud Misc. MSS 760 (Laud on Prynne)
    Tanner MSS 44 (Prynne's papers)
    Tanner MSS 57 (Sancroft on Prynne)
    Tanner MSS 69 (Prynne's gift of Foxe to Swainswick)
    Wood MSS D22 (Wood on Prynne's works)

(C) *British Museum*
    Additional MSS 985 (Petition of Prynne, Bastwick, Burton)
    Additional MSS 5, 994 (Prynne's letter to Laud)
    Additional MSS 8, 127 (Prynne's letter of 1652)
    Additional MSS 11, 308 (Proceedings against Prynne, Bastwick, Burton)
    Additional MSS 11, 764 (Prynne's trial)
    Additional MSS 19, 526 (Prynne against the Rump)
    Additional MSS 37, 682 (Prynne against the bishops)
    Egerton MSS 2, 182 (Goodman on Prynne)
    Egerton MSS 2, 543 (Prynne on Clarendon's impeachment)
    Harleian MSS 164 (D'Ewes's journal)
    Harleian MSS 664 (Reynolds against stage plays)
    Harleian MSS 980 (Gossip about Prynne 1629)
    Harleian MSS 1,026 (Prynne and stage plays)
    Lansdowne MSS 228 (Prynne's works)

# BIBLIOGRAPHY

Sloane MSS 2035B (Prynne on Laud)
Stowe MSS 159 (Proceedings against Prynne)
180 ⎫
182 ⎬ (Dering's correspondence)
184 ⎭
302 (Prynne on the Petition of Right)
743 ⎫
744 ⎬ (Dering's correspondence)
755 (Prynne's letter to du Moulin)
1,056–7 (Notes on Prynne's works)

(D) *Doctor William's Library*
Baxter MSS 59 (Correspondence of Richard Baxter)

(E) *House of Lords' Record Office*
Braye MSS Proceedings Against Stafford and Laud
Braye MSS 110/91 (Browne's notes on Prynne)

(F) *Public Record Office*
State Papers 16/377 (Prynne's works listed)
State Papers 16/424 (Nathaniel Wickens' petition, 1639)
State Papers 16/503 (Godfrey's letter to Prynne)
State Papers 16/534 (The prosecution of Prynne, 1634)

(G) *Queen's College, Oxford*
Coll. Reg. MSS 340 (Barlow on Prynne)

## II. PRINTED SOURCES

(A) *Primary*

It would be a work of supererogation to list the pamphlets consulted in the study. There are comprehensive lists in:

Pollard, A. W., and Redgrave, C. R., *Short-Title Catalogue of Books Printed . . . 1475–1640* (London, 1926)

Wing, D., *Short-Title Catalogue of Books Printed . . . 1641–1700* (New York, 1945)

Prynne's pamphlets are quoted with full references in the text of the study. The best bibliography of his writings is contained in:

Fry, Mary Isabel, and Davies, Godfrey, 'Notes and Documents', *Huntington Library Quarterly*, XX,1 (1956) pp. 55–93

Other useful lists will be found in:

(i) the lists drawn up by Prynne's publisher, Michael Sparke, in 1643 and 1660 respectively of his works, *A Catalogue of Printed Books . . .*, and *An Exact Catalogue . . .*

(ii) Wood, Anthony, *Athenae Oxonienses . . .*, ed. Bliss, W. (Oxford, 1817), pp. 844–877

(iii) Green, E., *Bibliotheca Somersetiensis* (Taunton, 1902) iii, pp. 160–187

(iv) Camden Society, New Series, xviii, *Documents Relating to the Proceedings Against William Prynne* . . ., ed. S. R. Gardiner, pp. 101–118

In addition to pamphlet material, the following printed works were of particular use:

Aubrey, John, *Brief Lives* . . ., ed. A. Clark (Oxford, 1898)

Baillie, Robert, *Letters and Journals* . . ., ed. D. Laing (Edinburgh, 1841–1842)

Bale, John, *Select Works* (Cambridge, 1849)

Ball, Thomas, *The Life of the Renowned Doctor Preston* . . ., ed. D. W. Harcourt (Cambridge, 1885)

Barnard, John, *Theologo-Historicus* . . . (London, 1683)

Baxter, Richard, *Reliquiae Baxterianae* . . ., ed. M. Sylvester (London, 1696)

Birch, Thomas, *Remarks Upon the Life of the Most Reverend Dr. John Tillotson* (London, 1754)

*Calendar of Claredon State Papers*

*Calendar of State Papers Domestic*

*Calendar of State Papers Venetian*

*Camden Society*

First Series, XXXII, *The Autobiography of Sir John Bramston*

First Series, LXXX, *Proceedings* . . . *in Kent* . . . *in 1640*

New Series, XVIII, *Documents Relating to the Proceedings Against William Prynne*

Third Series, XXVIII, *The Autobiography of Thomas Raymond*

Third Series, XXXI, iv, *The Nicholas Papers*

Third Series, LXIX, *The Letter Book of John Viscount Mordaunt, 1658–60*

Cary, Henry, *Memorials of the Great Civil War* . . . (London, 1842)

Clarendon, *The History of the Rebellion* . . ., ed. W. Macray (Oxford, 1888)

*Commons Journals*

D'Ewes, Simonds, *Autobiography and Correspondence* . . ., ed. J. O. Halliwell (London, 1845)

—— *Journal* . . ., ed. W. Notestein (London, 1925)

Dugdale, William, *Life, Diary and Correspondence* . . ., ed. W. Hamper (London, 1827)

*The Correspondence of Bishop Brian Duppa and Sir Justinian Isham, 1650–60*, ed. G. Isham (Publications of the Northamptonshire Record Society, XVII, 1950–1)

Evelyn, John, *Diary* . . ., ed. E. S. De Beer (Oxford, 1955)

Foxe, John, *The Acts and Monuments* . . ., ed. J. R. Catley (London, 1837–41)

Fuller, Thomas, *The Church History of Britain* . . ., ed. J. Brewer (Oxford, 1845)

Grey, Anchitel, *Debates of the House of Commons* (London, 1769)

Hacket, John, *Scrinia Reserata* . . . (London, 1692)

Hanbury, Benjamin, *Historical Memorials* . . . (London, 1844)

Hardcastle, Ephraim, *The Twenty-Ninth of May: Rare Doings at the Restoration* (London, 1825)

Heylyn, Peter, *Cyprianus Anglicus* . . . (London, 1671)

Historical Manuscript Commission: Reports 4, 5, 9, 10, 12, 13, 14
  Ormonde MSS
  Portland MSS
  Verulam MSS

Hobbes, Thomas, *English Works* . . ., ed. W. Moleworth (London, 1839–45)

Jewel, John, *Works* (Cambridge, 1849)

White, Kennett, *A Register* . . . (London, 1728)

Laud, William, *Works* . . . (Oxford, 1847–60)

Lightfoot, John, *Works* (London, 1823–4)

*Lords Journals*

Ludlow, Edmund, *Memoirs* . . ., ed. C. H. Firth (Oxford, 1894)

*Mercurius Aulicus*

*Mercurius Britanicus*

*Mercurius Civicus*

*Mercurius Democritus*

*Mercurius Elencticus*

*Mercurius Impartialis*

*Mercurius Melancholicus*

*Mercurius Pragmaticus*

*Mercurius Publicus*

Milward, John, *Diary* . . ., ed. Caroline Robbins (Cambridge, 1939)

*Minutes of the Sessions of the Westminster Assembly of Divines* . . ., ed. Mitchell and Struthers (Edinburgh, 1874)

Nalson, John, *An Impartial Collection of the Great Affairs of State* . . . (London, 1682)

*Parliamentary History of England*, ed. W. Cobbett (London, 1808)

*Parliamentary Intelligencer*

Pepys, Samuel, *Diary* . . ., ed. H. B. Wheatley (London, 1904)

Price, John, *The Mystery and Method of His Majesty's Happy Restauration* . . . (London, 1680)

*The Records of the Honourable Society of Lincolns Inn, The Black Books* (London, 1898)

Selden, John, . . . *Table Talk* . . ., ed. F. Pollock (London, 1927)

Strafford, *Letters and Dispatches* . . ., ed. W. Knowler (London, 1739)

Surtees Society, LII, *The Correspondence of John Cosin . . .*, ed. G. Ormsby
*The Faithfull Scout*
*The Kingdomes Intelligencer*
*The Moderate*
*The Moderate Intelligencer*
*The Perfect Weekly Account*
*The Scottish Dove*
*The Weekly Account*
*The Weekly Intelligencer*
*The Weekly Post*
*Memoirs of the Verney Family During the Seventeenth Century . . .*, ed. M. Verney (London, 1907)
Whitelocke, Bulstrode, *Memorials of the English Affairs . . .* (Oxford, 1853)
Wood, Anthony, *Athenae Oxonienses . . .*, ed. W. Bliss (Oxford, 1817)
Wood, Anthony, *The Life and Times . . .*, ed. A. Clark (Oxford, 1891)

*(B) Secondary*
Abbott, W. C., 'The Origin of Titus Oates' Story', *English Historical Review*, XXV (1910)
Albion, G., *Charles I and the Court of Rome* (London, 1935)
Allen, J. W., *English Political Thought, 1603–40* (London, 1938)
Ashley, M., *The Greatness of Oliver Cromwell* (London, 1958)
Bosher, R. S., *The Making of the Restoration Settlement* (London, 1951)
Brown, L. F., 'Idea of Representation from Elizabeth to Charles II', *Journal of Modern History*, XI (1936)
Church, W. F., *Constitutional Thought in Sixteen Century France: A Study in the Evolution of Ideas* (Camb. Mass., 1941)
Cowell, H. J., *The Four Chained Books* (London, 1938)
Davies, E. T., *Episcopacy and the Royal Supremacy* (Oxford, 1950)
Davies, G., 'English Political Sermons', *Huntington Library Quarterly*, III (1939)
—— *The Early Stuarts* (Oxford, 1937)
—— *The Restoration of Charles II, 1658–60* (Oxford, 1955)
Figgis, J. N., 'Erastus and Erastianism', *Journal of Theological Studies*, II (1900)
Gardiner, S. R., *History of the Great Civil War* (London, 1901)
Haller, W., 'John Foxe and the Puritan Revolution', *The Seventeenth Century*, ed. R. F. Jones (Stanford, 1951)
—— *Liberty and Reformation in the Puritan Revolution* (New York, 1955)
—— *The Rise of Puritanism* (New York, 1938)
—— *Tracts on Liberty in the Puritan Revolution, 1638–47* (New York, 1934)

## BIBLIOGRAPHY

Harris, J. W., 'John Bale', *Illinois Studies in Language and Literature*, XXV, 4 (Urbana, 1940)

Hexter, J. H., *The Reign of King Pym* (Harvard, 1941)

—— 'The Problem of the Presbyterian Independents', *American Historical Review*, XLIV (1938–9)

Hill, C., *Economic Problems of the Church from Archbishop Whitgift to the Long Parliament* (Oxford, 1956)

—— *Puritanism and Revolution* (London, 1958)

James, M., 'The Political Importance of the Tithes Controversy in the English Revolution, 1640–60', *History*, XXVI (1940)

Jordan, W. K., *Men of Substance* . . . (Chicago, 1942)

—— *The Development of Religious Toleration in England* . . . (London, 1938)

Judson, M. A., *The Crisis of the Constitution* . . . (New Brunswick, 1949)

Keeler, M. F., *The Long Parliament, 1640–1* (Philadelphia, 1954)

Kinloch, T. F., *Life and Works of Joseph Hall* (London, 1951)

Kirby, E. W., 'Sermons Before the Commons, 1640–2', *American Historical Review*, XLIV (1938–9)

—— *William Prynne* (Camb. Mass., 1931)

Locke, L. G., *Tillotson: A Study in Seventeenth Century Literature* (Copenhagen, 1954)

Miller, P., *The New England Mind: The Seventeenth Century* (New York, 1939)

Mitchell, W. F., *English Pulpit Oratory from Andrewes to Tillotson* (London, 1932)

Morgan, I., *Prince Charles's Puritan Chaplain* (London, 1957)

Murch, J., *William Prynne* (Bath, 1878)

Nobbs, D., 'Philip Nye on Church and State', *Cambridge Historical Journal*, V (1935)

Peach, R. E. M., *History of Swainswick* (Bath, 1890)

Pearl, Valerie, *London and the Outbreak of the Puritan Revolution* (Oxford, 1961)

Pocock, J. G. A., *The Ancient Constitution and the Feudal Law* (Cambridge, 1957)

—— 'Restoration Political Theory', *Cambridge Historical Journal*, X, No. 2 (1951)

Shaw, W. A., *A History of the English Church, 1640–60* (London, 1900)

Soden, G. I., *Godfrey Goodman, Bishop of Gloucester, 1583–1656* (London, 1953)

Stearns, R. P., *The Strenuous Puritan: Hugh Peter, 1598–1660* (Urbana, 1954)

Stuart, D. M., 'Milton and Prynne. Some New Light on the Secret History of the Commonwealth', *New Statesman and Nation*, 28 February 1931

Trevor-Roper, H. R., *Archbishop Laud, 1573–1645* (London, 1940)

Troeltsch, E., *The Social Preaching of the Christian Churches* (London, 1931)

Warner, R., *The History of Bath* (Bath, 1801)

Wedgwood, C. V., *The King's War, 1641–1647* (London, 1958)

Whiting, C. E., *Studies in English Puritanism from the Restoration to the Revolution, 1660–1688* (London, 1931)

Wolf, L., *Manesseh Ben Israel's Mission to Oliver Cromwell* (London, 1901)

Wolfe, D. M., 'Unsigned Pamphlets of Richard Overton: 1641–1649', *Huntington Library Quarterly*, XXI, No. 2 (February, 1958)

Woodhouse, A. S. P., *Puritanism and Liberty* (London, 1950)

Woolrych, A. H., 'The Good Old Cause and the Fall of the Protectorate', *Cambridge Historical Journal*, XIII, 2 (1957)

Wordsworth, C., *The Manner of the Coronation of King Charles the First . . .* (London, 1892)

Wormald, B. H. G., *Clarendon: Politics, History and Religion, 1640–60* (Cambridge, 1951)

Yates, F. A., 'Queen Elizabeth as Astraea', Journal of the Warburg and Courtauld Institute, X, (1947)

Yule, G., *The Independents in the English Civil War* (Cambridge, 1958)

# INDEX

Abbott, George, 3, 74, 75, 111, 213, 216
Allestree, Richard, 213, 214
Ames, William, 86
Andrewes, Lancelot, 3, 141
Arminianism, 14, 21, 123, 126, 127
Arundel of Wardour, Lord, 144

Bacon, Robert, 166
Bagshaw, Edward, the elder, 20, 84
Baillie, Robert, 49, 50, 53, 55, 58, 64, 149, 150, 151, 152, 154, 156, 166, 173, 174, 215
Baker, Sir Richard, 6, 12
Bale, John, 70
Ball, John, 41, 61, 91
Bancroft, Richard, 3, 19, 21, 69, 74, 82, 141
Barlow, Thomas, 56, 147, 148, 213
Barlow, William, 19, 51
Barnes, Robert, 71, 76
Baro, Peter, 14
Basire, Isaac, 143
Bastwick, John, 11, 12, 20, 33, 35–8, 40, 45, 47, 48, 50, 108, 123, 220
Baxter, Richard, 5, 12, 44, 58, 138, 150, 151, 166, 173, 196, 197, 198, 202, 203, 212, 230
Baynes, Paul, 19, 20
Beard, Thomas, 31, 111, 112, 117, 201
Becket, Thomas, 54, 78, 81
Bedloe, William, 145
Beverley, John, 160
Beza, Theodore, 156, 173
Bilson, Thomas, 3, 19, 21, 94, 114, 116, 118, 213
Birch, Colonel John, 196, 206, 207, 218
Birkenhead, Sir John, 226
Bodin, John, 91, 100, 104, 105
Bolton, Robert, 19, 20
Bonner, Edmund, 54, 78
Book of Discipline, 36
Book of Sports, 123
Booth, Sir George, 196

Boswell, Sir William, 124, 137
Boughen, Edward, 17, 18, 95
Bradshaw, William, 19, 189
Bramston, Sir John, 38
Bridges, Sir Thomas, 116, 208
Brightman, Thomas, 59–64, 66, 84, 177
Browne, John, 120, 125–7, 129, 134
Bucer, Martin, 196
Burges, Cornelius, 51, 58, 151, 153, 170
Burnet, Thomas, 218
Burton, Henry, 11, 12, 20, 27, 31, 33–8, 40–2, 45, 47–50, 57, 108, 122, 131
Butler, Samuel, 6

Calamy, Edmund, 154, 155
Calley, Sir William, 45
Calvin, John, 2, 92, 164, 172, 196
Camden, William, 43,
Campanella, Thomas, 141, 142, 144
Canne, John, 61
Carleton, George, 18, 21, 200–2
Cartwright, Christopher, 166
Cartwright, Thomas, 2, 19, 36, 44, 45, 61, 73, 82
Case, Thomas, 51, 52, 61, 62, 155, 167
Charles I, 2, 18, 23, 25, 26, 31, 55, 74, 93, 96, 98, 108–12, 118, 126, 129, 138, 139, 145, 146, 148, 163, 184, 185, 187–9, 194, 215, 221, 222, 228
Charles II, 2, 163, 189, 193–5, 206, 215, 222, 229
Charlton, Stephen, 228
Chilmead, Edmund, 142
Clark, Samuel, 213
Coke, Sir Edward, 93, 94, 100, 117, 177–80, 219–22
Coke, Thomas, 188
Coleman, Thomas, 51, 145, 150, 166–8, 172, 173
Collings, John, 160, 199
Con, George, 124, 140
Constantine, Emperor, 2, 16, 17, 26, 30, 31, 45, 52, 60, 62, 67, 68, 112, 161, 188

247

# INDEX

Cooper, Anthony Ashley, first Earl of Shaftesbury, 224
Coronation Oath, 103, 222
Cosin, John, 17, 18, 21, 22, 27, 34, 44, 77, 131
Cotton, Sir Robert, 91, 166
Covenant, Solemn League and, 18, 26, 58, 91-3, 115, 149-51
Cranmer, Thomas, 2, 18, 28, 35, 54, 68, 71-3, 188
Crofton, Zachary, 215
Cromwell, Oliver, 2, 23, 24, 140, 187, 189, 190, 195, 214, 228
Cromwell, Thomas, 71
Culmer, Richard, 203
Cunningham, Alexander, 50

Davenant, John, 21, 22, 213
Davenport, Christopher, ('Sancta Clara'), 123, 126, 127, 138
Dell, William, 164
Denton, William, 144
Dering, Sir Edward, 61, 62
D'Ewes, Richard, 169
D'Ewes, Simonds, 20 169, 170, 172
Dickinson, William, 14
Digby, Sir Kenelm, 40
Digges, Dudley, 90
Dow, Christopher, 38
Downame, George, 19, 21, 45, 51, 65, 66, 81, 82, 214
Drake, Roger, 160
Du Moulin, Lewis, 53
Du Moulin, Peter, 138, 139, 148
Dunster, Castle, 188
Durie, John, 42, 196

Edward II, 89, 112, 180
Edward VI, 81
Edwards, Thomas, 61, 167
Elizabeth I, 2, 13, 16, 17, 19, 27, 30, 32, 44, 45, 54, 55, 59, 60, 62, 67, 68, 82, 102, 112
Erasmus, 16
Erastianism, 51, 52, 84, 149, 150, 152, 154-7, 173, 199
Erastus, 52, 149, 155, 156, 157, 160, 162, 165, 166, 172, 173, 197

Fairfax, Sir Thomas, 62
Falkland, Lord, 52, 53, 84
Featley, Daniel, 78, 141, 167
Ferne, Henry, 87, 106, 114, 115
Ferrers, George, 221
Fiennes, Nathaniel, 54, 170, 172
Fifth Monarchy Men, 144
Filmer, Sir Robert, 177-80, 187, 195
Finch, Sir Heneage, 211, 226
Foulis, Oliver, 160

Foxe, John, 16, 17, 19-21, 26, 27, 31, 32, 35, 36, 40, 43, 47, 59, 61, 65-72, 76, 84, 94, 138, 146, 147, 162, 177, 180, 210, 213, 231
Frith, John, 71, 76
Fuller, Thomas, 46, 61, 73, 172

Garrard, George, 45
Gauden, John, 58, 84
Geree, John, 95
Gibson, Thomas, 70, 81
Gillespie, George, 44, 52, 150, 156, 157, 158, 166, 167, 173, 199
Goodman, Godfrey, 56, 75
Goodwin, John, 44, 61, 117, 162, 163, 184, 196
Gouge, William, 167
Grand Remonstrance, The, 15, 20, 103
Great Fire, The, 143, 145
Gregory, Pope, 74
Grey, Lady Jane, 54, 72
Grimston, Sir Harbottle, 206
Grindal, Edmund, 68, 73, 75
Grotius, 113, 173
Gunning, Peter, 210
Gunpowder Plot, 74, 82, 140, 141, 144, 161

Habernfeld, Andreas, 124, 134
Habernfeld Plot, 109, 124, 126, 127, 132-4, 136-8, 140, 143-8
Hacket, John, 22, 54
Hakewill, George, 111
Hall, Joseph, 21-3, 30, 32, 34, 37, 50, 51, 65, 66, 77, 78, 123, 214
Hammond, Henry, 214, 215
Hardcastle, Ephraim, 205, 208
Hartlib, Samuel, 42
Haselrig, Sir Arthur, 191
Heath, Sir Robert, 31, 32
Henderson, Alexander, 53, 152, 167
Henrietta Maria, 123, 127
Henry I, 178, 192
Henry III, 78, 97, 180, 187
Henry VI, 89
Henry VIII, 32, 67, 71, 72
Herbert, Lord, 225-7
Herle, Charles, 88, 90, 95, 98, 106, 115, 117
Heylyn, Peter, 13, 17, 18, 21, 22, 29, 34, 38, 44, 45, 50, 51, 56, 74, 120, 125, 126, 128, 129, 135, 215
Hill, Thomas, 51, 153, 154
Hoard, Samuel, 17
Hobbes, Thomas, 87, 90, 102, 155, 160, 161, 164, 168, 172, 173
Holmes, Nathaniel, 62
Hooker, Richard, 32
Hooker, Thomas, 91
Hotham, Sir John, the elder, 113

# INDEX

Howell, James, 109
Hubbard, Benjamin, 61
Hudson, Samuel, 196
Humfrey, John, 160, 210
Hunton, Philip, 78, 87, 90, 93, 98, 102, 106, 107, 113, 115
Hussey, William, 172
Hyde, Edward, Earl of Clarendon, 3, 6, 35–7, 84, 162, 183, 193, 195, 222, 223, 229

Independents, 8, 24, 35, 42, 43, 141, 144, 149, 152, 154, 157, 158, 164–6, 198, 199
Ireton, Henry, 186
Isham, Sir Justinian, 29

James I, 19, 24, 60, 69, 74, 109, 111, 216, 222
James II, 117, 230
Jenkins, David, 98
Jesuits, 1–3, 14
Jewel, John, 3, 16, 17, 19–21, 26, 31, 43, 65, 76, 118, 162, 199, 213, 219, 231
John, King, 16, 67, 78, 81, 89, 94–8, 105, 162, 180
Juxon, William, 20, 56, 208

Kennett, White, 148

Lamb, Sir John, 22
Lambert, John, 71
Lambeth, Chapel, 122
Langton, Stephen, 78, 94, 96
Latimer, Hugh, 17, 27, 54, 68, 76
Laud, William, 3, 4, 5, 8, 11, 13, 14, 18, 20–3, 25–9, 31–5, 37–42, 45–7, 49–52, 54–6, 58, 65, 74, 77, 78, 96, 111, 115, 119–38, 140, 145–7, 151, 153, 162, 163, 190, 210, 214, 215, 218–20, 228, 229
Leighton, Alexander, 36, 39, 41, 45, 46, 81–3
L'Estrange, Hamon, 135
Leveson, Sir Richard, 142
Ley, John, 154
Lightfoot, John, 170–3
Lilburne, John, 95, 160, 176, 177, 180, 187
Lilly, William, 110, 141
Lincoln's Inn, 6, 12, 13, 27, 31, 92, 191, 218, 221
Littleton, Sir Thomas, 208, 216, 217
Long Parliament, The, 28, 96, 191, 193, 207
Loyola, Ignatius, 140
Ludlow, Sir Edmund, 193, 207, 213

Magna Carta, 93–8, 180, 222, 224
Mainwaring, Roger, 14, 17, 23, 25, 26, 34, 190

Manton, Thomas, 151, 197
Marprelate, Martin, 4
Marshall, Anthony, 37
Marshall, Stephen, 18, 51, 64
Mary I, 26, 54, 66, 75, 123, 147
Masham, Sir John, 211, 212
Massey, Major General Edward, 193
Matthew, Sir Toby, 124
Mayne, Jasper, 172
Mede, Joseph, 29
Militia Ordinance, 90, 103
Milton, John, 6, 26, 43, 66–8, 73
Milward, John, 217, 218
Monk, George, 194
Mordaunt, John, Viscount, 193, 222
Morice, Sir William, 138, 194, 203, 210, 216
Morley, George, 53
Morton, Thomas, 21–3, 45, 77, 78, 81, 115
Mountague, Richard, 22, 23, 26, 34, 50, 78, 126, 200, 201

Nalson, John, 177, 183
Nalton, John, 154
Neale, Richard, 20, 115
Needham, Marchamont, 7
Nero, Emperor, 31, 32, 112
Newport, Andrew, 142, 215
Nicholas, Sir Edward, 50, 126, 208
North, Sir Harry, 206
Norwood, Richard, 172
Noy, William, 32
Nye, Philip, 167

Oates, Titus, 143–5, 147
Oath of Allegiance, 211
Osborne, John, 143
Overton, Richard, 176
Owen, John, 134

Page, William, 160
Pagitt, Ephraim, 29, 32
Palmer, Herbert, 51, 63, 64, 153, 154
Pareus, 113, 196
Paris, Matthew, 94, 98
Parker, Henry, 15, 25, 26, 48, 86, 90, 95, 98, 107, 108, 113, 117, 135, 136, 137, 140, 146, 170–2, 177
Parker, Matthew, 72, 73
Parsons, Robert, 140, 141, 144
Partridge, Sir Edward, 195
Pendennis Castle, 183, 188
Pepys, Samuel, 11, 143, 194, 211
Perkins, William, 12
Peter, Hugh, 42, 43, 190, 196
Petition of Right, 24, 96, 103, 210, 221
Pocklington, John, 17, 61, 77
Pole, Reginald, 73
Ponet, John, 32

249

## DATE DUE